Craig Storti is founder and co-director of Communicating Across Cultures, an intercultural communication training and consulting firm based in Washington, DC. He is the author of ten books, most recently *Why Travel Matters*, and has written for the *Washington Post*, *Los Angeles Times* and *Chicago Tribune*. Having lived in Nepal for several years and trekked extensively in the Himalayas, he now lives in Maryland.

Praise for *The Hunt for Mount Everest*

'Tense and detailed . . . A lively and useful addition to the shelves of Everestiana' John Keay, author of *India: A History*

'A rich and fascinating book that tells the story of Everest in glimpses from unexpected angles, revealing one face then another, discovering surprising new routes through well-trodden terrain. Getting to the top isn't the point – the point is the mountain itself' Nick Hunt, author of *Where the Wild Winds Are*

'Storti does an admirable job of guiding us up the slopes and is an enjoyable companion' *Literary Review*

'An entertaining and enlightening account of how the British identified the highest mountain, ensured that it was their preserve, and made the first attempt to climb it' Peter Gillman, co-author of *The Wildest Dream: The Biography of George Mallory*

'A very readable and entertaining account of the earliest days of Everest, with a cast of great characters and driving narrative which reaches a terrific climax in 1921' Mike Conefrey, author of *Everest, 1953*

D1387017

'A compelling account of the essential back story to the epic twentieth-century attempt by British mountaineering expeditions to ascend the world's highest mountain . . . This is great mountaineering history' Maurice Isserman, co-author of *Fallen Giants*

'To climb the world's highest mountain was one thing; to find it quite another. In this compelling new contribution to the cultural history of mountaineering, Storti composes the definitive back story of Mount Everest' Stewart Weaver, co-author of *Fallen Giants*

'Storti has given us the Everest book that we've needed all along . . . *The Hunt for Mount Everest* is the necessary, and admirably written, historical prelude to the great age of Himalayan mountaineering' Scott Ellsworth, author of *The World Beneath Their Feet*

'Even if you think you know the history of the world's tallest mountain well, you can pick up this book and become mesmerised by the peculiar personalities, political limitations and animal appearances that played their part in bringing climbers to Everest' *How It Works*

The Hunt for Mount Everest

Also by Craig Storti

The Art of Crossing Cultures
The Art of Coming Home
Cross-Cultural Dialogues
Figuring Foreigners Out
Old World/New World
Americans at Work
Speaking of India
Understanding the World's Cultures
The Art of Doing Business Across Cultures
Why Travel Matters

The Hunt for Mount Everest

CRAIG STORTI

First published in Great Britain in 2021 by John Murray (Publishers)
First published in the United States of America in 2021
By Nicholas Brealey Publishing
Imprints of John Murray Press
An Hachette UK Company

This paperback edition published in 2022

1

Copyright © Craig Storti 2021

The right of Craig Storti to be identified
as the Author of the Work has been asserted by him in accordance
with the Copyright, Designs and Patents Act 1988.

Maps drawn by Rodney Paull

All rights reserved. No part of this publication may be reproduced, stored
in a retrieval system, or transmitted, in any form or by any means without the
prior written permission of the publisher, nor be otherwise circulated in any form
of binding or cover other than that in which it is published and without a
similar condition being imposed on the subsequent purchaser.

A CIP catalogue record for this title is available from the British Library

Paperback ISBN 978-1-529-33155-4
UK Ebook ISBN 978-1-529-33156-1
US Ebook ISBN 978-1-529-36629-7

Typeset in Bembo by Palimpsest Book Production Limited, Falkirk, Stirlingshire

Printed and bound in Great Britain by Clays Ltd, Elcograf S.p.A.

John Murray Press policy is to use papers that are natural, renewable and
recyclable products and made from wood grown in sustainable forests.
The logging and manufacturing processes are expected to conform
to the environmental regulations of the country of origin.

John Murray (Publishers)   Nicholas Brealey Publishing
Carmelite House   Hachette Book Group
50 Victoria Embankment   Market Place Centre, 53 State Street
London EC4Y 0DZ   Boston, MA 02109, USA

www.johnmurraypress.co.uk
www.nbuspublishing.com
www.craigstorti.com

For Charlotte

Contents

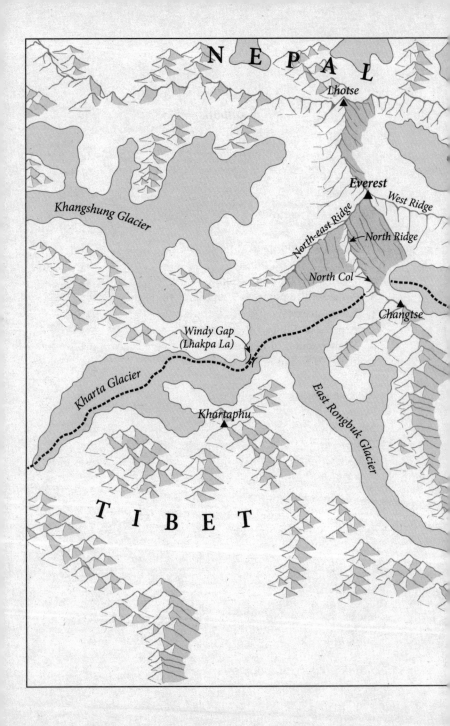

Western Cwm

Lho La

▲ Lingtren

West Rongbuk Glacier

Rongbuk Glacier

Base Camp ■

S
E ⊕ W
N

0 miles 3

0 km 3

The Reconnaissance

·············· 1921 route

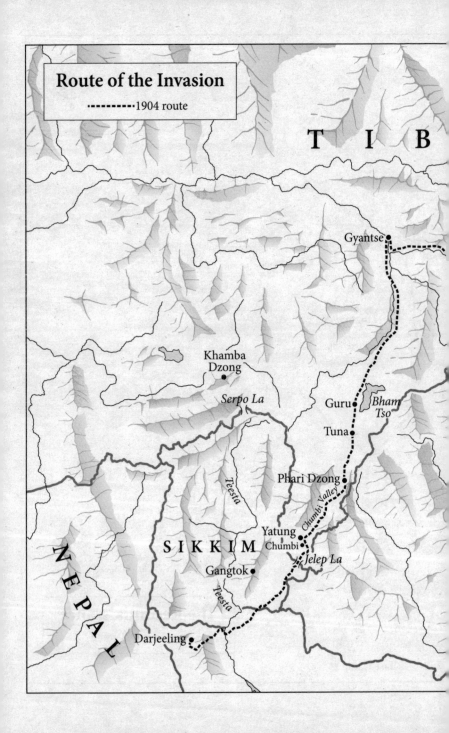

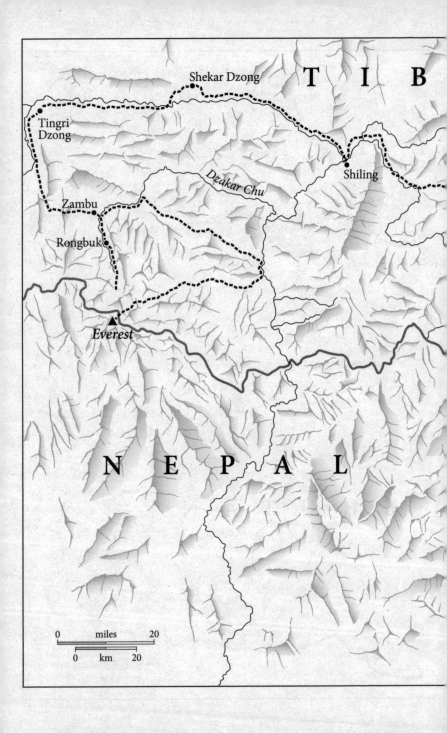

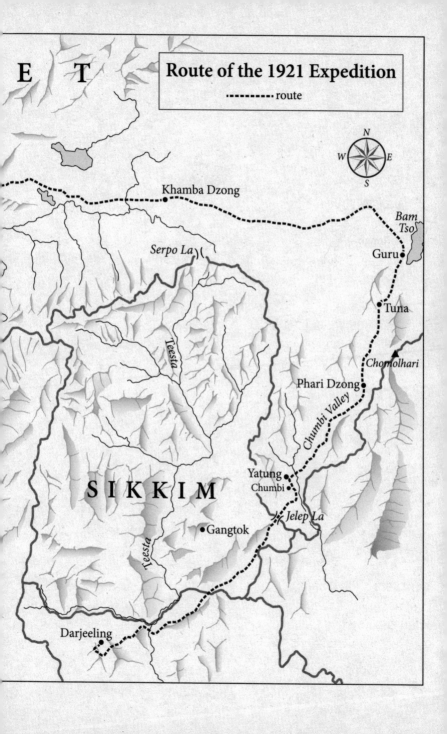

It would be necessary in the first place to find the mountain.

George Mallory

Prologue

'I could stand it no longer'

The atmosphere became electric. The faces of all were set. One of the generals left the room; trumpets outside were sounded, and attendants closed round behind us.

Francis Younghusband

O N THE MORNING of 13 January 1904, while he was staying at the hamlet of Tuna on the Tibetan plateau, Colonel Francis Younghusband, in an act of 'staggering foolhardiness', took the greatest gamble of his career, one, it should be noted, already rich in gambles.[1] He was restless all night long on the 12th, he recalled, until the next morning when

> [a]t last I could stand it no longer and taking only Captain O'Connor and Captain Sawyer with me, I rode over without any escort and without giving them warning, straight into the Tibetan camp about [ten] miles away. I had awakened in the night with the strong conviction that this was what I ought to do and I . . . proceeded to carry my conviction into effect.[2]

The Tibetan camp at a place called Guru contained more than fifteen hundred soldiers, the flower of the Tibetan army, who had assembled for the express purpose of blocking Younghusband's advance to Gyantse on the road to Lhasa. By entering the camp unarmed, unannounced and unescorted, Younghusband was placing his entire 1,100-man mission to Tibet in serious jeopardy and running the very real risk of being kidnapped or at least detained. He later received a severe rebuke for his carelessness from Lord Curzon the Viceroy of India.

Younghusband, General Macdonald, and their troops were part of what was officially known as the Tibet Frontier Commission, a body authorised by His Majesty's Government, at the repeated urging of the viceroy, to enter Tibet and negotiate certain outstanding trade and border issues. Curzon believed it was absurd at best – and quite possibly dangerous – that Great Britain, and especially the British government in India (known as the Raj), had no relations of any kind with a country with whom it shared a 1,000-mile border. Moreover, Curzon believed the Tibetans were flirting with the Russians – and probably worse – and was convinced, as he assumed every thinking person must be, that the Russians were determined to undermine British influence in Central Asia and quite possibly threaten British control of India.

Curzon had twice written to the Dalai Lama to request permission to send a delegation to Lhasa to discuss establishing formal ties, but both letters had been returned unopened. While this was not unusual behaviour for the notoriously xenophobic Tibetans, the proud Lord Curzon, not used to being ignored, was 'greatly affronted by seeing his imperial authority thus flouted by a political nonentity'.[3] He chose to interpret the Dalai Lama's action as a personal insult and then prevailed upon the British government in the summer of 1903 to allow him to dispatch a commission to the Tibetan village of Khamba Dzong to open negotiations.

Younghusband, who had also led that earlier, much smaller mission, had waited in vain for Tibetan officials to come to the negotiating table and was eventually recalled to India in late 1903. Thus, by the following January, when he 'could stand it no longer' and embarked on his reckless gamble, Younghusband had been trying for the better part of six months to find some Tibetans he could talk to. The difference was that in January 1904 Younghusband was now back in Tibet at the head of an 1,100-man invading army whose mission was to compel the Tibetans to negotiate. For their part, the Tibetans had maintained a consistent position on the border matter from the beginning, one that was the soul of reason and logically unassailable: What good could possibly come from negotiating with a frontier commission that was itself in open and flagrant violation of your frontier?

Younghusband was certainly no stranger to risk, but in the past he had only taken risks either when he had had no choice, or, if he had had a choice, then only when he thought the results were worth the gamble. But nothing about the present circumstances forced Younghusband's hand; he could easily have requested a meeting, to begin with, and even if his request was turned down, he could still have at least announced his intention to visit Guru; he could certainly have ridden over with a small escort without arousing any alarm; and as a colonel in the British army, there was no reason he should be riding about unarmed. Moreover, Younghusband knew better: 'Ordinarily, I do not think a British Commissioner should take personal risks,' he wrote. '[I]t endangers the position of the whole mission and doubles the difficulties of his Government.' Younghusband understood that the proper thing for someone in his position was to 'send one of his junior officers. I went only as a last resort. Fighting was almost inevitable now. I wanted to make one last bid to achieve my end without resorting to force.'[4]

Admirable, perhaps, but not convincing. There were no reasons for Younghusband to suppose that the results of his gamble were worth the risk, the foremost of which, after all, was the possibility of being detained *at best*. Moreover, the Tibetans had not requested a meeting – they had, in fact, repeatedly asked the British to return to Sikkim – and Younghusband had no way of knowing who might meet him in Guru. But based on his experience in Khamba Dzong the previous summer, he knew better than anyone that all important decisions were made in Lhasa and that whoever he might sit down with in Guru would not be in a position to decide anything of consequence. But he went anyway: 'I was heartily tired of this fencing about at a distance.'[5]

In the early hours he summoned Captain Frederick O'Connor, his Tibetan translator – 'I was horrified when he suggested [this],' O'Connor wrote to a friend – and Lieutenant Sawyer, another Tibetan-speaking officer, and the three men made ready to depart.[6] It might be said in Younghusband's defence that he sincerely believed that if he could just sit down with his Tibetan counterpart man to man, drink tea, and have a civil conversation about their differences, there was no need for armies to clash and for blood to be spilled. 'I wanted to get the *feel* of the Tibetans . . . If I could once meet them face to face I should be able to size them up, get the hang of them, and know how they should be handled.'[7]

The ride to Guru took ninety minutes. All along the way the three men encountered Tibetans out collecting yak dung, the sole source of fuel on the Tibetan plateau; O'Connor noted that they were 'not met with any scowls, [the Tibetans were] laughing to each other as if we were excellent entertainment'.[8] As they entered the village, they asked to see the man they called the 'Lhasa General' and were directed to a large, two-storey stone house where the grinning general greeted them cordially at the top of the stairs. In the room they entered there were several other generals, all smiles, and three utterly sullen Tibetan lamas. '[The lamas] made no attempt to rise and only made a barely civil salutation from their cushions. One object of my visit had already been attained: I could from this in itself see how the land lay and where the real obstruction came from.'[9]

The men were given sheepskins to sit on, served tea, and the Lhasa General enquired politely after Younghusband's health. He then made the standard observation that Tibet was closed to foreigners – to protect and preserve the Tibetan religion – and respectfully requested the mission move back to Yatung where the necessary negotiations could proceed. Younghusband replied with the standard refusal and then, dropping all pretence, he waded with abandon into the geopolitical swamp by asking the general why the Tibetans dealt regularly with the Russians but refused even to open the viceroy's letters. The query jolted the lamas out of their seats; they rose en masse to loudly denounce the allegation, denying any contact with the Russians whatsoever, and assuring Younghusband, a tad undiplomatically, that they loathed the Russians every bit as much as they loathed the British.

When the initial outburst had subsided, Younghusband tried to reason with the Tibetans, asking them if they had ever heard of the British interfering with anyone's religion, and they had to admit they had not. But the conversation went in circles for nearly two hours, after which Younghusband stood up and announced he had to leave. 'The monks, looking black as devils,' he wrote,

> shouted out: 'No, you won't; you'll stop here.' One of the generals said, quite politely, that we had broken the rules of the road in coming into their country, and we were nothing but thieves and brigands in occupying Phari Fort. The monks, using forms of speech which Captain O'Connor told me were only used for addressing

inferiors, loudly clamoured for us to name a date when we would retire from Tuna before they would let me leave the room. The atmosphere became electric. The faces of all were set. One of the generals left the room; trumpets outside were sounded, and attendants closed round behind us.

'A real crisis was upon us', Younghusband observed, 'when any false step might be fatal.'[10]

The highest point on earth was once at the bottom of the Tethys Sea. The fossils of invertebrate sea creatures found near the summit of Everest have established that the mountain is composed of sediment that originally formed at the bottom of that vast ocean over 450 million years ago. More recently, some 120 million years ago, a piece of the giant super-continent Gondwana broke off and began drifting north, pushing part of the floor of the Tethys Sea with it, until this mass, now the Indian subcontinent, collided with Asia, and the seabed was slowly pushed up, creating the 1,500-mile long Karakoram-Himalayan range – the fabled roof of the world – whose mountains continue to rise at the rate of approximately six centimetres a year.

The Himalayas comprise seventy-five peaks over 24,000 feet (7,300m) and eighteen over 26,000 feet (7,920m), the highest of which is Everest at 29,029 feet (8,848m).* Everest is not only the highest mountain in the world, it is higher than its closest rival, K2 in the Karakorams, by almost 800 feet (243m). By way of comparison, Mont Blanc, the highest peak in the Alps, is 15,774 feet (4,808m) or just over half the height of Everest, and there are over 130 peaks in the Himalayas that are higher than the tallest peak in the western hemisphere, Aconcagua at 22,837 feet (6,960m). Before the Himalayas were known in the west, it was widely believed that the earth's upper limit was just over 26,000 feet (7,924m), and long after the

---

* For years China and Nepal have claimed a different figure for the height of Everest, with Nepal's slightly higher figure (29,029 feet/8,848m) widely used in the west. In December 2020, after remeasurements by both countries, an agreement was reached to settle on 29,032 feet (8,848.86m), adding 2.8 feet (0.86m) to the elevation – a figure that will probably become standard in years to come.

mountains were known, it was commonly held that human beings would pass out and die above 22,000 feet (6,705m).

The first westerners to encounter the Himalayas were probably the Greek soldiers in Alexander the Great's army which invaded India in 326 BC. Marco Polo is thought to have passed just north of the Karakorams on his way to China in 1272, and beginning in 1590 a succession of Spanish, Portuguese and Italian Jesuits visited Asia, including Tibet, one of whom, Father Antonio Monserrate, a missionary to the court of the Moghul emperor Akbar, is considered the first westerner known for certain to have seen the Himalayas and the first to depict them on a map. As they penetrated 'the apparently inextricable labyrinth of snowy peaks' these early missionaries 'were simply appalled at the horrid aspect of the mountains and at the eternal winter'.[11]

As for Everest itself, its human history is thought to have begun around 925 when a monastery was built at the head of the Rongbuk Valley a few miles north of where the Rongbuk Glacier coming off the north face of Everest stops. The first westerners to look upon Everest were probably the Austrian Jesuit Johann Grueber and his Belgian companion Albert d'Orville, travelling from Beijing to Agra by way of Lhasa and Kathmandu in 1661. The first time Everest appeared on a map was in 1719, the result of explorations carried out by Jesuit missionaries from Beijing at the request of the Chinese emperor Kangshi. A copy of the map, first printed in the Han language, was sent to the French king Louis XV and to the French mapmaker J. B. B. d'Anville who brought out the *Carte générale du Tibet ou Bout-tan* in 1733. On this map in the position of the mountain is the name *Tchoumour Lancma*, the French rendering of Chomolungma, the Tibetan name for Everest still in use today.

Beginning in the first decade of the 1600s, the story of the Himalayas, and especially of Himalayan exploration, roughly parallels the history of the British in India. In 1612 the British East India Company opened for business in Surat, up the Tapti river from present-day Mumbai, just as Moghul power in India was beginning to wane. As the Company's commercial ventures continued to expand, so did its political and military might. In 1757 Robert Clive, at the head of the Company's army, defeated an Indian army at the battle of Plassey, and from then on the East India Company – and later the British government itself – gradually amassed more and more power and territory until India officially became part of the British Empire in 1857.

Knowledge of the largely unknown and unmapped Himalayas became a political and military priority as the Raj's territorial reach slowly grew, eventually spanning the entire length of the nearly 1,500-mile Himalayan border separating India/present-day Pakistan from Tibet, Afghanistan and other parts of Central Asia. This knowledge gap was filled by numerous teams of surveyors, whose efforts were eventually consolidated under the Survey of India in the first decade of the nineteenth century. In due course the survey turned its sights – its theodolites, to be precise – on the Himalayas, and it was only a matter of time before surveyors in Darjeeling took a closer look at a smudge on the horizon some 120 miles to the north-west and carefully recorded a series of measurements. The smudge turned out to be the highest mountain on earth, and its 'discovery' in 1850 touched off a seventy-one-year hunt to find the peak at the top of the world.

The existence of Mount Everest may have been confirmed in 1850, but the closest any westerner had got to the mountain at the time of the invasion of Tibet in 1904 was a hundred miles. By this time, Everest had become one of the three last great, unclaimed prizes in the history of modern exploration. The other two, the North Pole and the South Pole, would fall in 1909 and 1911, respectively, leaving only Everest – which soon came to be known as the Third Pole – unconquered and apparently unreachable. It sat squarely on the Tibetan–Nepalese border, and both countries had been completely closed to foreigners for over a hundred years.

By coincidence the sport of mountaineering had begun to mature in Europe in the 1850s, climaxing in the golden age of Alpine climbing which began in 1854, soon after Everest's discovery, and ended in 1865 with the first ascent of the Matterhorn. During these eleven years there were forty-three first ascents, including nearly all the most important peaks in the Alps. As peak after peak fell, climbers inevitably began turning their attention towards the east, first to the Caucasus, the highest mountains in Europe, and ultimately to the Himalayas and Everest.

And so it was that during the latter half of the nineteenth century and the early years of the twentieth, the world's climbing community – to say nothing of its geographers, cartographers and explorers, both armchair and professional – grew ever more obsessed with Everest. But in spite of the mounting interest and fascination, it would be almost three-quarters of a century from when the discovery of the mountain was first announced until the moment in June 1921 when two Englishmen, George Mallory and Guy Bullock, became the first people ever to stand at the foot of Mount Everest. And Francis Younghusband's mission to Tibet in 1903–4 would turn out to be the key that unlocked the door to that elusive land – and ultimately to the highest mountain of all. This is the story of the hunt for Mount Everest.

It is a tale of high drama, of larger-than-life characters – George Everest, Francis Younghusband, Lords Curzon and Kitchener, George Mallory – and a few quiet heroes: Radanath Sickdhar, Alexander Kellas, the 13th Dalai Lama, Sir Charles Bell. It is a tale of spies, intrigue and beheadings; of war (two wars, in fact) and massacre; of breath-taking political, diplomatic and military bungling; of derring-do, hair-raising escapes and genuine bravery. The wind is a powerful presence, as are the rain and the mud, along with rhodo-dendrons and orchids, leeches and butterflies, mosquitoes, gnats and sandflies. Hundreds of bullocks, yaks and mules are featured, as are thousands of camels, numerous elephants and at least two zebrules (they were not a success). And its setting is some of the most spec-tacular geography on earth.

For seventy-one years the true nature of Everest remained oddly unsettled and unresolved; it was as much myth as reality, part symbol and part substance, and above all a metaphor, a stand-in for that which is supreme yet unattainable. This is a tale of how a metaphor became a mountain.

Back in Guru, surrounded by 1,500 shouting Tibetans, Francis Younghusband's gamble was going terribly wrong, having reached the point where 'any false step might be fatal'. The angry senior lamas had demanded the colonel set a date for when he and his troops would leave Tibet or he would not be allowed to leave the camp. 'I told Captain O'Connor, though there was really no necessity to give such a warning to anyone so imperturbable, to keep his voice studiously calm and to smile as much as he possibly could.'[12] Younghusband then defused the situation somewhat by declaring that it was not his place to choose a date, but that he would gladly ask the viceroy, and then added that if the viceroy ordered him back to India, he would be 'only too thankful, for [Tibet] was a cold, barren and inhospitable country, and I had a wife and child at Darjeeling whom I was anxious to see as soon as I could'.[13]

While the senior Tibetan general, who had already become a favourite of Younghusband and his officers, found this solution reasonable enough, the bellicose monks were not appeased and insisted the colonel name a date. The impasse was finally resolved when the general suggested 'that a messenger should return with me to Tuna to receive there the answer from the Viceroy'. Everyone was smiling again now save for the monks 'who remained seated and as surly and evil-looking as men well could look'.[14]

In the end the colonel's gamble yielded no results, except for the strong reprimand from Curzon, although the daring move is said to have greatly impressed the troops and added considerably to Younghusband's growing legend. Writing of the incident later, the translator O'Connor (who went by the name of Frank) remarked that 'it was quite interesting & not devoid of excitement. No one but [Younghusband] would have thought of or done it . . . His perfect coolness and sangfroid saved the situation & we got away all right.'[15] They may have saved the situation, but the colonel's coolness and sangfroid did nothing to prevent the coming clash with the Tibetan army, a clash which would elevate the invasion of Tibet into one of the most shameful episodes in British imperial history.

And prise open the door to Mount Everest.

I am now in possession of the final values of the peak designated XV in the list of the office of the Surveyor General. We have for some years known that this mountain is higher than any hitherto measured in India and most probably it is the highest in the whole world.

Andrew Waugh, Surveyor General
Survey of India

O N A SERIES of clear mornings between November 1849 and January 1850, James Nicholson, on orders from his superior Andrew Waugh, led a team of porters to the top of six different peaks in the vicinity of the British hill station at Darjeeling, India. As Nicholson unpacked and set up his surveying equipment, including a large theodolite it took twelve porters to carry, the massive bulk of Kangchenjunga, 35 miles due north, sat just off his right shoulder. At 28,169 feet (8,586m), it was the highest mountain in the world. It was Andrew Waugh himself who had 'discovered' Kangchenjunga two years earlier, but although he had determined it was an astonishing 2,526 feet (770m) higher than Nanda Devi, the then-contender for world's highest peak, he had been reluctant to announce this finding due to suspicions he and others harboured about a blot on the horizon some 120 miles to the north-west of Darjeeling on the Tibetan–Nepalese border.

It was towards this distant shape that Nicholson and company trained their theodolite from the six hills around Darjeeling in an attempt to prove whether or not it was the highest mountain in the world. It had previously been called 'peak b' then 'gamma' and now it was known simply as 'peak XV', and Waugh had already spent a year trying unsuccessfully to measure it. The only reason Waugh and Nicholson could be at all confident in the accuracy of the measurements they were now making was thanks to the achievements of the enterprise the two men worked for: the Great Trigonometrical Survey of India. Waugh was its chief and Nicholson one of his subordinates.

In its fiftieth year when Nicholson took to the hills outside Darjeeling, the survey had only recently reached the mountains, making it possible for the first time to measure the remote Himalayan peaks, if only by triangulation, by establishing an all-important baseline. The peaks could not be measured from any closer as they lay either in Nepal or Tibet, and both countries were closed to foreigners. But the existence of the baseline meant that Nicholson and his team could know with considerable accuracy the height of each of the six hills on which they stood and from which Nicholson took his measurements. Only if that number were known would it be possible (by trigonometry) to calculate the elevation of the distant peak on which Nicholson had trained his theodolite. As it happened, Nicholson not unexpectedly obtained different readings from all six of the observation points, ranging from a high of 29,998 (9,143m) at the observation station at Ladnia to a low of 28,991 (8,836m) at Jirol.

But he was not unduly concerned. Nicholson was merely the collector of data; all the measurements of the survey were submitted to the number crunchers at the computational and administrative headquarters of the survey in Calcutta. These men were known as 'computors' for their skills in mathematical computation, and their head – the chief computor – was one Radanath Sickdhar, the first Indian to ever rise to that rank in the survey. What happened over the next several months in Calcutta, as Sickdhar and his team attacked the data from Nicholson and others, set in motion a story that would captivate the world.

William Lambton was in the wrong place at the wrong time. The place was Yorktown in the American colony of Virginia, and the time was mid-October 1781. Lambton was a soldier in the British infantry, 33rd Regiment of Foot, which fought in the decisive final campaign of the Revolutionary War, culminating in the British defeat at Yorktown and the surrender of the British under Lord Cornwallis on the morning of 19 October. Lambton was one of approximately 8,000 British prisoners taken at the time, most of whom were subsequently repatriated. Lambton was ordered to British New Brunswick in Canada.

Before the war, Lambton, an accomplished surveyor, had worked in the colonies as a civilian member of the 33rd, measuring parcels of land that were being granted to new settlers. After the war he was part of the group of surveyors who established the boundary between British Canada and the United States. Posted later to British Columbia, Lambton taught himself geodesy, the study of the shape of the earth, encountering in his studies the great grapefruit vs egg controversy.

Scholars knew the earth was a spheroid, but was it round or more of an oval? Was it a grapefruit or an egg? By the time Lambton took up geodesy, the French had answered the question, thanks to two expeditions they sponsored in the 1730s to measure the curvature of the earth, one to the equator in what is now Ecuador (but was then Peru) and one to Lapland in the Arctic. In Ecuador the Frenchmen Charles Marie de La Condamine and Pierre Bouguer measured an arc 180 miles in length. Initially the Peruvians were highly suspicious, assuming the foreigners were looking for gold. 'Who would cross the ocean and climb the Andes merely to measure the Earth's shape?' Bouguer asked, reporting that he and his team 'encountered difficulties not to be imagined'.[1]

In his 1871 memoir Clements Markham, the English geographer and long-serving president of the Royal Geographical Society, laments the embarrassing absence of any British participation in this noble effort. Indeed, at the time the two Frenchmen were measuring their arc, the British navy was busy bombarding ports and harassing foreign ships off the South American coast. 'It is to be regretted', Markham writes, 'that while France and Spain were thus combining in the interests of science, England was less nobly engaged in burning churches and cutting off supplies from the Peruvian coast.' Not long after, the British started to catch up when General Watson conceived the Trigonometrical Survey of Great Britain, and 'finally', Markham continues, 'the countrymen of [Sir Isaac] Newton took up the work at which they should have been foremost'.[2]

They might have been slow to start, but the British made up for their geodesic tardiness in spectacular fashion some years later when they established the Great Trigonometrical Survey of India in 1802. Heralded in due course as 'one of the most stupendous works in the whole history of science', the survey was founded and subsequently headed by none other than William Lambton, posted to India from Canada after officers who worked in civil jobs (such as surveying) were removed from the rolls of their regiments.[3] Lambton could either become a civil servant or join the regular army; he chose the army and sailed for Calcutta in 1796.

Lambton arrived just in time to take part in the Fourth Anglo-Mysore War, a contest between the British-governed territory in Madras and the notorious Tipoo Sultan of the neighbouring kingdom of Mysore. Tipoo was known as the Tiger of Mysore, largely because of a working model he commissioned of a tiger devouring a British soldier, complete with sound effects of the tiger's growl and the soldier's screams. (The model now sits in the Victoria and Albert Museum in London.) But in the end it was Tipoo who was swallowed up, dying when his capital was attacked by the forces of the East India Company.

Lambton distinguished himself at least twice in the campaign; the first time was when, thanks to his expertise in celestial navigation, he informed General Baird that the general was not in fact marching his troops north to safety, as he supposed, but straight south towards Tipoo's camp. The other notable occasion was during the storming of Tipoo's stronghold at Seringapatam, the turning point of the war, when Lambton assumed command of the assault after his senior officers had all fallen. One of the commentators on that engagement observed that Lambton 'set a rather better example of derring-do' than his commander, high praise indeed since the commander in question was a young and ambitious Arthur Wellesley, the future Duke of Wellington and victor at Waterloo.[4]

Among other things, the conquest of Mysore meant that a large new swathe of the peninsula of southern India, stretching west to the Malabar coast and south almost to the tip of India, had now been brought under British 'protection'. As his regiment and others travelled through this area during the campaign, 'subduing a recalcitrant chief here and plundering a fortress there', it occurred to Lambton, always happier as a surveyor than as a soldier, that someone would have to map this vast new acquisition.[5] A geodesist at heart, Lambton naturally thought big, and the notion of surveying Mysore soon metamorphosed into a proposal to the Madras government to measure, in the interests of science, the entire breadth and later the entire length of the massive Indian subcontinent. And thus was born the idea that became the Great Trigonometrical Survey.

when he first went out to India and forty-five when he took over the survey. He never married but had three children by his Indian mistress Kummerboo and two more by another paramour known only as Frances. His son and namesake, William junior, joined the survey as 'third sub-assistant' in 1815 at the age of eleven.

When using triangulation the accuracy of the measurements depended largely on the quality of the instruments used, especially the theodolite, a powerful telescope mounted on a tripod that can be fixed on any distant point or object and which registers the angle of the object from the horizontal, thus allowing the user, via trigonometry, to use two other known angles to determine the height of the target point. At the time Lambton was measuring his first baseline, near Madras in the spring of 1802, there were only two or three theodolites in the world capable of the precision that a survey of the scale of the GTS would require. Lambton located one in England and had it shipped out, but the vessel that carried it was captured by the French and forced to put into Port Louis in Mauritius, where the theodolite was uncrated. When the French realised what they had seized, they were happy to repack the instrument and forward it on to the governor of Madras with their compliments. Thus the survey could at last get under way, in September 1802, as Lambton carefully established his first baseline.

Lambton's first task was to measure the width of the southern part of India, sometimes known as peninsular India, and specifically that portion between Madras in the east and Mangalore in the west, including all of the land just acquired in the recent war with Tipoo Sultan. In the end, this great four-year effort, advancing triangle by triangle, constituted the earliest and one of the greatest triumphs of the survey, establishing conclusively that that part of peninsular India was not in fact 400 miles wide, as most maps depicted it, but only 360. In one stroke, 'thanks to Lambton, British India [had] sustained its greatest ever territorial loss'.[9]

The 'loss' of territory notwithstanding, the measurement of peninsular India was a triumph for Lambton, establishing beyond any doubt the 'absolute necessity for a Trigonometrical Survey, owing to the hopeless inaccuracy of other methods'.[10] And there had been many doubters, those who thought the whole enterprise was redundant, owing to other, lesser surveys being conducted at the same time in other parts of India, and those who just didn't see the point. Among the latter was a member of the finance committee of the East India Company who famously scoffed that if 'a traveller wished to proceed to Seringapatam, he need only say [so] to his head bearer and be vouchsafed that he would find his way to that place without any recourse to Colonel Lambton's map'.[11]

After his triumph in the south, Lambton turned his attention in 1806 to what became known as the Great Indian Arc, measuring the length of the subcontinent, all 1,800 miles from Cape Comorin in the south to the foothills of the Himalayas. Lambton spent the rest of his life, seventeen more years, on the north–south survey, and even then it was only half-finished when he died in 1823. The measurements themselves were time-consuming – Lambton was a stickler for precision, regularly checking and rechecking his calculations – and there were always unavoidable complications, whether it was suspicious, unfriendly locals or meddling bureaucrats.

One of the biggest setbacks Lambton faced was an accident that almost destroyed his theodolite. The instrument was being hauled by means of ropes and pulleys to the top of a temple near Tanjore when one of the ropes snapped and the theodolite crashed into the walls of the pagoda. 'Ordinary men would have been disheartened at such a mishap', Markham wrote, but not Lambton who 'was endowed with indomitable resolution and was full of resource'. He 'shut himself up in his tent, refusing admittance to all comers . . . took the instrument entirely to pieces [and in] six weeks he had brought it back nearly to its original form'.[12]

Damaged instruments were among the least of the problems the survey encountered. Dehydration and dysentery took a dreadful toll on survey parties, and then there was the sweltering heat of the tropical jungles, the blinding, choking dust of the plains, and the ever-present threats of robbers, malaria, deadly snakes, rogue elephants and tiger attacks. 'A tiger did attack the party', one account recalled, 'and carried off one of the soldiers. On another occasion, when a leopard sprang from a low bough and mauled five *sepoys*, [one of the surveyors] a slight, sinewy man, seized a bayonet and thrust it into the beast's snarling mouth.' In the circumstances, 'a

21

survey assignment in those days was often tantamount to a death sentence'.[13]

In his memoir, Markham salutes the nameless, unsung heroes who spent months in the field risking their health and often their lives making the survey happen, consisting of scores of surveyors, mostly British, and hundreds of Indians in support roles, including: the keepers of the survey's elephants (needed in the long grass) and its camels, the axemen who hacked down countless trees to create lines of sight, carpenters who built the numerous towers and scaffolding for taking long-distance measurements, the porters carrying tents and supplies, lampmen for night work, flagmen, cooks and wash-ermen, soldiers in escort, bearers who wrestled the half-ton theodolite, the size of a small tractor, up and down hills and across streams — all facing

> difficulties . . . far greater than have been encountered in the majority of Indian campaigns. Military service, plentifully rewarded by the praise of men and by prizes of all kinds, is neither so perilous nor so honourable as that of the Indian Surveyor, who devotes great talent and ability to scientific work in the midst of as deadly peril as is met with on the field of battle, and with little or no prospect of reaping the reward that he deserves. His labours, unlike those of a mere soldier, are of permanent and lasting value, but few know who obtained the results . . . [T]he average slaughter was greater than in many famous battles.[14]

Lambton led the survey for over twenty years, dying in his tent out in the field. By then recognition and honours had come his way. The French had made him a corresponding member of the French Academy of Science, and the Royal Society in London awarded him an honorary fellowship. An article in the *Edinburgh Review* compared Lambton's work favourably to that of his hero and inspiration, William Roy, noting that the two men had done 'more for the advancement of general science than had ever been performed by any other body of military men'.[15]

Lambton's successor, George Everest, brought himself to Lambton's attention through survey work he had carried out in northern India in 1816, leading to his appointment as Lambton's chief assistant in 1818, when Everest was twenty-eight. Everest had first gone out to India twelve years earlier, when he was only sixteen, after a military education at Woolwich.

Everest had his virtues, principal among which were perseverance, dedication and meticulousness, but because of his prickly personality – he was known as 'the most cantankerous *sahib* ever to have stalked the Indian stage' – he is remembered more for his faults.[16] He had an exceedingly thin skin, an exceptionally short fuse, and an uncommonly sharp tongue. He was respected and feared, but he was not liked. In places where there were no alternatives to fixing a point of triangulation or securely grounding the 1,000-pound theodolite, Everest had homes and shops knocked down, and at times he desecrated the tops of temples in using them as observation points. Small wonder the survey needed an armed escort as it made its way across India.

As soon as Everest joined the survey, stories of his temper quickly proliferated, beginning with his handling of the famous mutiny he confronted while measuring a tract of land near Hyderabad in 1819. The mutineers were part of a troop of soldiers sent as a courtesy by the Nizam of Hyderabad to offer extra protection to the survey parties. A few of these soldiers, sick of monsoon rains and jungle heat, tried to run away, but one of them was apprehended, and Everest had him publicly flogged to set an example, whereupon all forty members of the escort refused to stand duty and lay down in the shade of a nearby mango tree. But in addition to the Nizam's troops, the survey had its own in-house escort of twelve men whom Everest promptly ordered to train their muskets on the hapless mutineers; they could submit or be shot. They submitted. Everest then had three of the mutinous band flogged and thus 'was settled very early in my career a disputed point which has been a source of constant contention and annoyance'.[17]

Everest was quick to take offence, especially when he felt he was not being shown the respect his position warranted. On one occasion he was good-naturedly called a 'compass *wallah*' by a fellow officer, Colonel Young. *Wallah* denotes occupation or livelihood – a *dobi-wallah* is someone who washes clothes for a living – and 'compass *wallah*' was commonly used to refer to a surveyor. Everest, as the surveyor general at that time, felt demeaned and demanded an apology, which he received. 'I objected to a low, familiar, appellative which, though it may be in common use in the bazaar, I cannot allow to be applied to me as my official designation.'[18]

Some years later, in another fit of pique, Everest reacted poorly when the arrangements for his and the survey's reception in Gwalior State were not what he thought they should be, and he halted at the border and sent a letter of complaint to the British Resident. The Resident mentioned the complaint in a letter he subsequently wrote to the local maharajah wherein he described Everest in a phrase Everest found deeply offensive, prompting him to fire off a letter to the Resident's superior demanding an apology.

> It is totally impossible for me to proceed under the [treatment shown] towards me by that functionary . . . Forms of courtesy which are deemed essential at native courts have been entirely violated. I am spoken of in his communication with the [maharajah] as 'one major Everest engaged in measuring' and my assistants in the same unceremonious style.

But the government chose to reprimand Everest instead for wasting time and for insulting one of His Majesty's senior officials. '[T]here is a dictatorial tone pervading your letter,' Everest was told by the Resident's superior, 'which I cannot think that the Surveyor General of India is justified in using towards the Resident at Gwalior.'[19] Everest was unrepentant.

Everest, who was a perfectionist, could be scathing towards his subordinates when they let him down. 'You have detained my party 3 days here looking in vain for your heliotrope [mirror],' he wrote to one of his assistants, 'and I intend to hand you up [report you] to Government . . . as your shameful negligence and misconduct deserve.'[20] To another he fumed:

> You are mismanaging sadly; when directed to turn your heliotrope towards Bahin, you turned it to Pahera, and kept it there. When instructed to turn the heliotrope to Pahera, you will not do so, and I have been straining my eyes to pieces . . . I suppose you are still directing it to Bahin, but you might as well turn it to the moon.[21]

Yet another hapless colleague was told:

> You are certainly most irregular. Who but a half-crazy person would
> have chosen a time when it was blowing great guns to burn his blue
> lights in utter defiance of my orders . . . The *khalasie* tells me you
> began at 4AM, when I was obliged to hold on with both hands to
> save myself from being blown off the scaffolding.[22]

It does not excuse his vitriol, but it should be said in Everest's
defence that he held himself to the same exacting standards as any
of his men, worked as long or longer hours, and also handed out
praise where it was deserved. Summing up the differences between
Everest and his predecessor, a prominent survey historian wrote of
the two men's subordinates that 'Lambton they worshipped, but for
Everest they simply worked'.[23]

Everest clashed regularly with – and complained regularly to – the
government of India, who paid for the survey, questioned every
unusual expense, and otherwise second-guessed Everest at every
turn. 'Government was all for speed and economy, Everest for the
highest accuracy, having to justify one change of programme after
another.' Everest was also aggrieved when the government would
not approve hiring more deputies who could relieve him of some
of the onerous burdens he bore. Referring to a project near Mussoorie
in 1833, he remarked that 'it was unquestionably the most harassing
duty I ever had to perform, and I had to bear nearly the whole
burden of the arduous task myself, for there was at that time no
person at my disposal to whom I could depute any portion of the
work.' For that reason, he continued, '[d]ay and night, at all hours,
from the 13th of December . . . til the 4th May . . . I was perpetu-
ally in a state of excitement and anxiety'.[24]

Despite Everest's many faults, his numerous strengths included an
unwavering devotion to the survey, his technical expertise and his
tireless work ethic – twice he had to take leave, once for six months
to Cape Town and once for five years to England, after exhausting
himself in the first instance and contracting malaria in the second.
In his 1871 memoir of the survey, RGS secretary Clements Markham
gives Everest his due, calling him 'a creative genius' who 'had
completed one of the most stupendous works in the whole history

of science. No scientific man ever had a greater monument to his memory' than the survey.[25] Everest the man may have been widely disliked, but the work was justly celebrated.

When Everest took over from Lambton in 1823, the survey was twenty-one years old but had not quite yet covered half of its projected 1,800 miles, which would take another two decades, the entirety of Everest's term as Surveyor General. Everest made good use of his five-year convalescence back in England, researching the latest advances in surveying and geodesy, corresponding with eminent scientists, and befriending important patrons. He also oversaw the construction in England of two of the most accurate theodolites ever made, bringing them back with him to India when he returned in 1835. The theodolites weighed half a ton and were carried by twelve porters, three at each end of two poles. Everest also brought back a set of compensation bars to replace the 100-foot-long steel chains used until now for measuring baselines. Thanks to their vastly superior quality, these state-of-the-art instruments occasioned a great deal of re-measuring, especially of certain critical distances initially established by the chains, slowing down the survey, to be sure, but also adding immeasurably to its reputation for unparalleled accuracy.

While he was away in England, the government in India in its wisdom, and without consulting Everest, took it upon itself to appoint Thomas Jervis as 'Provisional Surveyor General'. Everest, who had nothing but contempt for Jervis and 'the pretty maps' he produced, was so appalled that he stopped making any references to his poor health in his correspondence with India and repeatedly insisted on complete control of the survey while he was away. The unfortunate Jervis happened to pass through England while Everest was still there and gave a speech to the British Association in London, a speech which Everest 'tore . . . to shreds' when he read it. It has been suggested that Everest delayed his own retirement until after Jervis left the survey to ensure that Andrew Waugh, not Jervis, would be his successor. 'His crowning satisfaction was that he left a man after his own heart to continue the good work.'[26]

Under Lambton and then Everest, the survey crept slowly up the centre of India throughout the first four decades of the nineteenth century, arriving in sight of the mountains by 1840. During those same years, interest in the Himalayas mounted steadily, as speculation grew that this range of peaks could be the loftiest in the world. And if they were, then somewhere among them must lie the highest mountain on earth. When the survey, with its reputation for precision, arrived in the mountains, it would be possible for the first time to take accurate readings of these towering giants and determine once and for all their elevation.

Rumours about the great height of the Himalayas began circulating as far back as 1760, forty years before the survey, when James Rennell peered out over the Himalayas from a ridge in Bhutan and pronounced them, on no evidence whatsoever, the highest in 'the old hemisphere'.[27] His qualifier was due to the fact that the scientific consensus at the time held that the Andes, in the new hemisphere, were the highest mountains of all, and that Chimborazo, at 20,549 feet (6,263m), as measured by the French team of Condamine and Bouguer, was the world's tallest peak.

The candidates for world's highest mountain came and went. As early as 1808 William Webb, assistant to the Surveyor General for the province of Bengal, took four measurements of a distant peak from the Nepal border and calculated its elevation as 26,862 feet (8,187m). When these findings were announced, the European scientific community scoffed, used as it was by now 'to absurd claims from the land of rope-tricks and reincarnation', and the announcement was likewise disparaged in an article in the prestigious *Edinburgh Review*.[28] At the time most European scholars were convinced that a vertical distance of five miles (26,400 feet/8,046m) was earth's upper limit. Some years later when the height of Webb's peak, Dhaulagiri (the white mountain), was officially determined to be 26,749 feet (8,153m), the *Review* published a tortured retraction. In the meantime, while Dhaulagiri's height was still in dispute, Webb and John Hodgson discovered a new candidate, Nanda Devi in Garhwal, which at the time came in at 25,749 feet (7,848m) and thus was, as Hodgson wrote, 'so far as our knowledge extends, the highest mountain in the world'.[29] This was in 1822, and Nanda Devi would wear the crown for another twenty-five years.

Twenty-one years later, in 1843, the Great Trigonometrical Survey had reached its northern terminus, just short of Nepal, and Everest's health had begun to deteriorate. 'I was confined to my bed from May to October,' he wrote of one especially unpleasant bout of illness, 'with little intermission, during which I was once bled to fainting [and] had upwards of 1,000 leeches [and] 30–40 cupping glasses . . . besides daily doses of nauseous medicine, all of which produced such a degree of debility as to make it of small apparent moment whether I lived or died.'[30] He was now being regularly lowered into and raised out of his surveyor's chair by two assistants, and he decided to declare his mission accomplished. 'Here closes my long and laborious undertaking,' he wrote to the directors of the survey, 'in which, though from first to last, I have necessarily gone through much hardship and privation, yet these have not been without many [moments] of gratification and amusement.'[31] He retired that year, aged fifty-three, and returned to England where he was knighted by Queen Victoria, after turning down a lesser honour he deemed insufficient to his achievements, and was made a fellow of the Royal Geographical Society. Two years after his retirement, Everest married Emma Wing and fathered three children.

The survey, meanwhile, had already spawned several offshoots, including the North-East Longitudinal Series, which would extend the effort along the front of the Himalayas from central India east to Calcutta. One of Everest's assistants, Andrew Waugh, who had succeeded him, took a particular interest in this series, and led the effort in the field which finally dethroned Nanda Devi, in 1847, by establishing the height of Kangchenjunga at 28,176 feet (8,588m).

But Kangchenjunga had a very short run. By the time Waugh announced its height, in 1849, there were already suspicions about another peak measured by John Armstrong two years earlier from Muzaffarpur in Bihar, a mountain he called simply peak 'b'. In that same month, November 1847, Waugh himself had made observations from Darjeeling of a distant peak then known as 'gamma' and he concluded that 'b' and 'gamma' were one and the same and that it was quite possibly higher than Kangchenjunga.

The meticulous Waugh ordered one of his assistants, John Peyton, to make additional measurements during the 1848–9 surveying season. 'I particularly wish you to verify Mr. Armstrong's peak "b",' Waugh wrote. But the mountain was only visible for one or two hours every morning during November and December, and by the time Peyton had unpacked and positioned his theodolite, clouds had invariably moved in. A year later, during the 1849–50 season, by which time the mountains had been assigned Roman numerals, Waugh asked another surveyor, James Nicholson, to try again, whereupon Nicholson measured the elusive peak XV from six different hills around Darjeeling and then turned his data over to Babu Radanath Sickdhar and his number crunchers in Calcutta. The 'discovery' of Mount Everest had begun.

On 3 July 1840, George Everest sent a note to the father of Radanath Sickdhar. 'My dear sir,' he began:

> Your son Radhanath Sikdar has applied to me to proceed to Meerut to meet you, and I have consented, though in truth he can be but ill-spared at the present moment, as he is one of the persons whose aid is most important. I wish I could have persuaded you to come to Dehra Dun . . . for not only would it have given me the greatest pleasure to [show] you personally how much I honour you for having such a son as Radhanath, but you would yourself have, I am sure, been infinitely gratified at witnessing the high esteem in which he is held by his superiors and equals.[32]

High praise indeed from the normally acerbic Everest. But who was this apparent paragon – he has been called the first scientist of modern India – who inspired such uncharacteristic sentiments in the famously cantankerous sahib?

Radanath Sickdhar, the eldest of two sons, was born to Bengali parents in October 1813 in the Jorasanko district of Calcutta. He and his brother both earned scholarships to a village school, but while Srinath used most of his funds to help support the family, the scholarly Radanath used his to buy books. In 1824, when he was eleven, Radanath was admitted to Hindu College in Calcutta (now Presidency University, Kolkata) where he began studying mathematics, including Euclidian geometry, under the renowned Professor John Tytler. It is said that during his seven years at the college, Sickdhar was one of the first of two Indians ever to read all the way through Sir Isaac Newton's *Principia Mathematica*.

Before he was twenty, Sickdhar had made a modest name for himself by devising a new method for connecting common tangents to two circles, his paper on which was published in the prestigious *Gleanings of Science*. 'A good deal having appeared in the public prints lately respecting the Hindoo College,' the journal's editor wrote, introducing the paper, 'it may not be uninteresting to publish the accompanying solution of a geometrical problem by one of the pupils there, Radhanath Sickdhar. The solution is altogether his own discovery, and I have not altered a word in his composition.'[33]

Sickdhar left the college in 1831, the same year Everest wrote to Professor Tytler asking for the names of outstanding pupils, and upon being recommended, Sickdhar – 'the star of the students' – was hired by the survey in December and sent to work on the Barrackpore Trunk Road linking Calcutta to its suburbs.[34] Three years later Sickdhar was working alongside Everest himself as the survey was establishing a baseline near Dehradun, and Everest liked what he saw of the young Bengali. 'Of the qualifications of the young man,' he wrote, 'I cannot speak too highly . . . [I]n his mathematical attainments there are few in India, whether European or native, who can at all compete with him, and even in Europe his attainments would rank very high.'[35]

Sometime later, when Everest learned that Sickdhar was planning to leave the survey to become a deputy tax collector, a post that was better paid, he intervened to stop the transfer, which was his right as Sickdhar's supervisor. He explained that the young Indian's

> qualifications, so eminently valuable to my Department, would be thrown away upon that to which he now seeks to be transferred. [H]e has become . . . my right arm in all matters connected with computation and registry of data, and the loss of his services at this critical moment would be one of the most severe privations that could be inflicted upon me.[36]

Later Sickdhar did manage to secure Everest's permission to transfer from the surveying department, with its headquarters in the field at Dehradun, to become a 'computor' in the calculating department in Calcutta, where he distinguished himself and eventually became the first Indian ever appointed by the survey to the position of 'sub-assistant'. Andrew Waugh, Everest's successor and Sickdhar's subsequent superior, likewise thought highly of him: 'Radanath Sikdar and Ramdial were both appointed sub-assistants; the former achieved brilliant success but the latter failed.'[37]

A report on the survey's progress submitted to the British Parliament at the time specifically singled out the contributions of Indian sub-assistants – 'a more loyal, zealous and energetic body of men is no-where to be found' – and of one in particular: 'Among them may be mentioned as most conspicuous for ability, Babu Radhanath Sikdar, a native of India of Brahminical extraction whose mathematical attainments are of the highest order.'[38] Sickdhar was later appointed 'chief computor', the head of the survey's entire calculating and computing department.

His reputation quickly grew. In 1851, Sickdhar was asked to contribute to the prestigious Indian *Manual of Surveying*, the bible of the surveying field, eventually writing several chapters and submitting a set of auxiliary tables. His significant contributions were acknowledged at some length in the introduction to the first and second editions of the manual, but all mention of Sickdhar had disappeared by the third edition, in 1875, after his demise. The uproar caused by this omission speaks to the high regard in which Sickdhar was still held by the survey six years after his death. The omission was widely reported in the press and publicly criticised in several Indian newspapers. One Colonel Macdonald, deputy superintendent of the survey at the time, even went so far as to criticise his superior, the superintendent, over the omission in two articles in the *Daily Friend of India*. For his sins, Macdonald was suspended for three months and then demoted to deputy second class.

At some point during the spring of 1851, Sickdhar and his team of computors turned their attention to peak XV and began to work through the data they had received from Waugh, Armstrong, Nicholson and others – a variety of readings and observations taken at different times by different people from different locations, with different results. There were also the unusual technical and mathematical challenges to be faced in calculating the elevation of a mountain as high and as distant as Everest, requiring 'a knowledge of advance theory of refraction, plumb-line deflection, gravity, geoids, datums of reference', technical details so complicated, one geodesist has observed, that 'even geographers find them difficult'.[39] Not surprisingly, the work of the computors took nearly two years, so it was not until late 1852 that the results were made known to Waugh.

Just *how* the results were communicated to Waugh is one of the best-known stories in all the lore of Mount Everest, diminished somewhat by the fact that it's almost certainly not true.

The story – one of the first to tell it was Francis Younghusband – is that Radanath Sickdhar ran breathless into Andrew Waugh's office one day and announced, 'Sir, I have discovered the highest mountain in the world.' Younghusband was not there, of course, so he must have heard the story from someone else. But whatever its origins, it was picked up and repeated over the years by a number of reputable Everest historians and has survived down to the present. And it's easy to see why: it's perfect – a lone individual making the dramatic discovery of the world's highest mountain. Clearly this is how Everest *should* have been announced to the world, but it is too good to be true.

To begin with, there is the problem that Sickdhar worked in the offices of the computation department in Calcutta, and Andrew Waugh worked 1,000 miles away in the survey headquarters in Dehradun, although this does not preclude the possibility that Sickdhar travelled out to Dehradun to deliver the momentous news to Waugh in person. Another weakness of the anecdote is that whenever it is told, it is told in exactly the same ten words – Sir, I have discovered the highest mountain in the world – and completely devoid of details. Surely if this were a well-known, much-discussed incident, there would be numerous versions with colourful commentary. Moreover, the famous quotation is not consistent with Sickdhar's personality; he was genuinely solicitous of his staff and would never have presumed to take personal credit for the work of an entire team.

And finally there is the problem of one John Hennessey, who is credited with discovering Everest in some versions of the story but not others. Hennessey worked closely alongside Waugh in the survey field headquarters in Dehradun where calculations were also carried out in addition to those produced in Calcutta, where Sickdhar worked. Waugh even thanks Hennessey for his calculations by name in his famous letter announcing the discovery of Everest.

Who did discover Everest? Was it Radanath Sickdhar or John Hennessey? When all the conflicting accounts are set side by side and compared, the following scenario hews closest to the facts as they are known. The measurements of peak XV by Waugh and Nicholson were indeed turned over to Sickdhar and friends in Calcutta; they did spend two years poring over the figures, producing the initial numbers; and their results were presented to Waugh in 1852 (although probably not by Sickdhar in person). The record then shows clearly that four more years elapsed while the ever-cautious Waugh and others checked and rechecked the data – adjusting and correcting for such factors as light refraction, barometric pressure, temperature, gravity, and new tidal observations that had to be obtained from Karachi.

Only then, in March 1856, was Waugh confident enough in the calculations to write a letter to his deputy in Calcutta announcing the discovery, with its famous two opening sentences: 'I am now in possession of the final values of the peak designated XV in the list of the office of the Surveyor General. We have for some years known that this mountain is higher than any hitherto measured in India and most probably it is the highest in the whole world.'[40]

The next sentence of this document is often omitted, but it is key to answering the question of who discovered Everest: 'In justice to my able assistant J. Hennessey,' Waugh continues, 'it is proper that I acknowledge that I am greatly indebted to him for his cordial cooperation in *revising these computations*' (italics added).[41] When set alongside the rest of the record, a fair reading of this passage supports the conclusion that the computors in Calcutta did the original computations, and in the following four years their work was reviewed and in some cases revised by their colleagues in Dehradun. Indeed, survey records show that calculations were regularly passed back and forth between the two locations.

The discovery controversy lasted for nearly a hundred and fifty years, regularly revisited and reargued throughout the rest of the nineteenth century and well into the twentieth. One of the most careful and thorough examinations of the varying accounts was undertaken in the early 1980s by the prominent earth scientist Parke Dickey who published his conclusions in the October 1985 issue of *EOS* magazine, throwing his lot in with Sickdhar, although he is scientist enough to know that findings such as these are seldom the work of a single individual. His concluding sentence in the *EOS* article is to date the last word on the controversy: 'Actually the discovery was made not by one person but by a group of highly skilled and dedicated scientists, trained by George Everest and working according to a plan that he devised.'[42] In the usual sense of the word, then, it cannot truly be said that Everest was 'discovered', and certainly not by a single person. Nor did Radanath Sickdhar ever make such a claim. That said, Sickdhar and Hennessey, along with their boss Andrew Waugh, surely deserve any and all acclaim that accrues to them.

An amusing coda to the measurement saga involves the often-told story of the first published height of 29,003 feet (8,840m). The calculations of Sickdhar et al. apparently established that the mountain stood at an even 29,000 feet, but fearing no one would believe such a round number, the computors added three feet to their total. Today the official height is given as 29,029 (8,848m).

All that remained now was to assign a name to peak XV, a task – he called it a privilege – that fell to Andrew Waugh. Choosing a name for what would immediately become the most famous mountain in the world was never going to be an easy matter. Virtually any name Waugh decided on under the circumstances was bound to be controversial. And so it proved. In point of fact, however, it should have been entirely straightforward, thanks to a more than sixty-year precedent established by the survey – and religiously observed by Everest himself – that mountains and other significant geographic features should always be given the name used by locals. All Waugh had to do, in theory, was determine the local name for peak XV and use it.

Instead, Waugh proposed Everest's name, igniting a controversy that lasted for more than fifty years. 'Here is a mountain, most probably the highest in the world,' he writes in his letter of 1856,

without any local name that we can discover, whose native appellation, if it has any, will not very likely be ascertained before we are
allowed to penetrate into Nepal and to approach close to this stupendous snowy mass.

In the meantime the privilege as well as the duty devolves on me
to assign to this lofty pinnacle of our globe a name whereby it may
be known among geographers and become a household word among
civilized nations.

In virtue of this privilege, in testimony to my affectionate respect
for a revered chief, in conformity with what I believe to be the wish
of all the members of the scientific department over which I have
the honour to preside, and to perpetuate the memory of that illus-
trious master of accurate geographical research, I have determined
to name this noble peak of the Himalayas Mont [sic] Everest.[43]

We are told that among the 'members of the scientific department'
that Waugh consulted was Radanath Sickdhar, who readily gave his
approval.

Waugh's defence of departing from the precedent rests on the
sketchy argument that as Nepal was closed to outsiders, it was not
possible to enter the country and ask the locals what they called
the noble peak. This is disingenuous at best, for Waugh certainly
knew that outsiders had been going in and out of Nepal for years.
Moreover, for some years now the British had been allowed by
the king of Nepal to post an official British representative (called
a political officer) in Kathmandu, and this individual could easily
have made enquiries. From the beginning, there was a strong
suspicion in many quarters that Waugh simply did not want to
know of any local names so he could indulge his wish to honour
his predecessor.

Challenges to the name came thick and fast and almost immediately. The first – mere weeks after Waugh's announcement – was
from Brian Hodgson, who had served as political officer in
Kathmandu for some years and from where he claimed to have
observed Everest and heard it referred to quite regularly by its local
name Deodanga. In letters to the Royal Geographical Society and
the Royal Asiatic Society, Hodgson politely suggested that Colonel

Waugh was mistaken that there was no local name, and much to Waugh's dismay the Asiatic Society agreed with Hodgson.

An equally serious challenge and one that gained considerable traction came from the German explorer Hermann Schlagintweit. Sponsored by the king of Prussia, Hermann and his two brothers undertook a three-year scientific expedition to India and Central Asia, entering Nepal in 1855, measuring the same peak Hodgson mistakenly thought was Everest (the one he said locals called Deodanga), only claiming it was called Gauri Sankar. The Schlagintweits published a map in Berlin in 1862 using that name for the mountain, and the Royal Geographical Society, which had originally sided with Waugh, changed its mind and supported the Germans rather than the Raj's own survey. While the RGS changed its mind again in 1865, officially adopting the name of Everest, most maps of the Himalayas printed in Europe were using the name Gauri Sankar as late as 1904. Writing of the great Everest–Gauri Sankar naming controversy many years later, the celebrated Himalayan mountaineer Bill Tilman remarked on how the 'identification of very distant peaks is a harmless and fascinating amusement so long as the results are not taken seriously'.[44]

At the time, however, Andrew Waugh did take the results very seriously, and he immediately embarked on an aggressive campaign to defend his decision. To begin with, he made it clear in a letter of 5 August 1857 to the surveyor general that he was quite aware of the policy to use local names. 'I was taught by my respected chief and predecessor, Colonel George Everest, to assign every geological object its true local or native appellation, and I have always adhered scrupulously to this rule, as I have in fact to all other principles laid down by that eminent geodist.'[45] In other words, Waugh would never have named the mountain after Everest if he knew of any local name.

Waugh then launched into a diatribe against Hodgson, charging that his arguments were 'so palpably conjectural . . . that it [was] needless to refute them'. And as for the Germans, their support for and use of the name Gauri Sankar on German maps 'proves nothing more than that German geographers are rash enough to lay down anything upon hearsay'. If the English do not use the name Gauri

Sankar on their maps, he continued, that's because 'the rigorous notions which prevail among English scientific men' prevent them from giving 'the position of a point on the earth's surface' on the basis of rumour.[46]

Waugh then convened a committee consisting of five members of the survey to review the controversy. The committee found, among other things, that 'Mr Hodgson has advanced no evidence whatever to prove his' claim,[47] that it is based on 'data which . . . are purely conjectural' and 'upon the vague information of untrained travellers',[48] and that 'no person who has had any surveying experience can doubt [certain reports Hodgson cited as] being absolutely useless as evidence . . .'[49] Another member of the committee opined that 'it would be most inadvisable . . . to abandon this definite name, which will soon be familiar to every English or European child, [in favour of] one of the, to Europeans, unpronounceable names given by Mr Hodgson.'[50] In the end the committee declared that Gauri Sankar/Deodanga was 'indefinite and unacceptable'.[51]

Not everyone was happy with the survey and the RGS's ultimate decision in favour of Everest, including none other than Douglas Freshfield, the well-known Himalayan explorer, secretary and later president of the RGS and also of the Alpine Club, who observed in the *Alpine Journal*, with reference to the conclusion of Waugh's hand-picked five-man committee, that '[n]one of the officers appears to have been at Kathmandu, and the weight of their remarks seems to me to be further diminished by the fact that they were summoned not as impartial jurymen but as subordinates to support their chief.'[52] Freshfield actually continued to use Gauri Sankar even while serving as RGS president. 'With every respect for . . . the Indian Survey, it is impossible to acquiesce in the attempt permanently to attach to the highest mountain in the world a personal and inappropriate name in place of its own.'[53]

Meanwhile the great man himself had been invited to weigh in on the controversy. At a meeting called by the RGS in 1857 to discuss the matter, Everest pronounced himself 'gratified' by the proposed honour and then added, according to committee minutes, that 'he must confess there were objections to his name being given to this mountain which did not strike everybody. One was that his name was not pronounceable by the native of India . . . [and] it could not be written in Persian or Hindi.'[54]

Everest and Gauri Sankar battled it out for forty years until Lord Curzon, Viceroy of India, sent Captain Henry Wood to Nepal in 1903 to decide the question once and for all. Captain Wood took numerous measurements and observations and determined beyond any doubt that there was indeed a mountain by the local name of Gauri Sankar, but that it was in fact another mountain altogether, some 36 miles east of Everest. S. G. Burrard, a prominent historian of the survey, was greatly relieved. 'After fifty years of controversy,' he wrote in 1907, 'no true native name has been produced for Mount Everest; each of those suggested has in time been shown to be inapplicable, and the evidence that no such name exists is over-whelming.'[55]

Only it wasn't. As it happens, there was a second candidate and a second controversy. While the Nepalis had no local name for Everest, the Tibetans did – they called it Chomolungma – and that name, with a different spelling, had actually appeared on a French map as far back as 1733, the one brought out by the respected firm of D'Anville of Paris with the mountain correctly situated and clearly marked 'Tchoumour-Lancma'. Defenders of Waugh maintained that while he and the survey must surely have known of this map, the word Chomolungma, meaning 'mother goddess of the world', was more often than not applied to an entire massif, not a single mountain. There was some support for this theory, but it fell away completely when members of the first Everest expedition entered Tibet in 1921 and heard the name Chomolungma applied consistently and invariably to the single peak they knew as Everest. Needless to say, that embarrassing holdout Douglas Freshfield, even though he had been using Gauri Sankar, was overjoyed to have an authentic local name confirmed: 'The expedition to the Himalaya of 1921 has accomplished one remarkable feat which as yet has hardly attained the recognition it deserves. It has succeeded where the Survey of India during the past sixty-six years has singularly failed.'[56]

But by 1921 the western world had known the peak as Everest for nearly sixty years, and the hard-to-pronounce (for westerners) Chomolungma could not compete. Francis Younghusband spoke for many in a letter he wrote to the *Morning Post* in 1920 as talk of the first-ever expedition was heating up. 'It would be a great misfortune', he wrote, 'if the beautiful and suitable name of Mt Everest was ever changed . . . Even if this proposed expedition finds its real name written clearly upon the mountain, I hope it will take no notice.'[57]

And now it was done. The mountain had been observed, it had been measured, and it had been named. All that remained was to find it.

It has always seemed to me a reproach that with the second highest mountain in the world for the most part in British territory and with the highest in a neighbouring and friendly state, we, the mountaineers and pioneers par excellence of the universe, make no sustained and scientific attempt to climb to the top of either of them.

Lord Curzon to Douglas Freshfield

'ONE . . . HAD THE body of a snake and the head of a cat. Another had four short legs and a coxcomb. A third was a snake equipped with bat's wings.' Thus begins Professor Johann Scheuzer's celebrated catalogue of the many kinds of dragons that can be found in the Alps. 'Some had crests,' he continued, but 'the best specimen of all had the head of a ginger tom, a snake's tongue, scaly legs, and a hairy two-pronged tail.'[1] Dr Scheuzer was a distinguished lecturer in physics at Zurich University whose dragon catalogue appeared in his account of a journey he took through the Alps in 1723. While Scheuzer believed in these particular creatures, he was still a scientist, after all, and dismissed tales he heard of even more fantastic creatures. In the end he concluded that the Alps were 'so mountainous and so well provided with caves that it would be odd not to find dragons there'.[2] Small wonder that well into the 1700s travellers crossing the Alps were blindfolded lest they be overcome by the frightful creatures they might otherwise be forced to look upon.

Those who weren't afraid of mountains found them untamed, unsightly, even ugly – 'nature's rough productions', as one writer called them.[3] Another explained how '[t]he politer inhabitants of the seventeenth century referred to mountains disapprovingly as "deserts"; they were also castigated as "boils" on the earth's complexion, "warts", "wens" [and] "excrescences"'.[4] They spoiled the earth's otherwise perfect sphere. Even Wolfgang von Goethe, the father of German Romanticism, subscribed to this dim view of mountains. 'When travellers take a delight in climbing mountains,' he writes in his account of his first trip to Italy, 'I regard the mania as profane and barbaric . . . These zig-zags and irritating silhouettes and shapeless piles of granite, making the fairest portion of the earth a polar region, cannot be liked by any kindly man.'[5]

If Mount Everest had been discovered seventy-five or even fifty years earlier, almost no one would have noticed. Indeed, apart from the protection they offered as natural barriers, there was nothing about mountains that recommended them to mankind for most of human history – and much that did not. For the most part, they inspired fear and were widely regarded as full of dangers, some of which were natural – avalanches, rock slides, violent storms, dangerous precipices, deep crevasses, fierce animals – and some that were decidedly unnatural: dragons, demons, trolls, witches, banshees, and all manner of half- and proto-human abominations of nature. No one ventured into the mountains who didn't have to, and the notion of climbing a mountain was preposterous.

Then in 1741, only eighteen years after Scheuzer published his list of dragons, a certain William Windham, an expatriate Englishman living in Switzerland, escorted the English curate Richard Pococke and a few friends from Geneva into the valley of the Haute-Savoie as far as the village of Chamonix at the foot of Mont Blanc, with the object of venturing out onto the *mer de glace* or glacier just outside the town. When the group arrived in Chamonix, Swiss locals tried to frighten the Englishmen with dire warnings about what they might encounter. Windham copied into his diary 'many strange Stories of Witches etc who came to play their Pranks upon the Glaciers and dance to the Sound of Instruments'.[6] But the glacier looked harmless enough to the visitors, so they engaged a few local peasants to guide them out onto the great sea of ice. Amateurish in the extreme, Windham's excursion is still considered the first instance of 'climbing' in the Alps.

Windham and Pococke's fabled 1741 romp prefigured a change of attitude towards mountains, which began to take hold as early as 1757 when Edmund Burke published a book on what he called the Sublime, the notion that natural landscapes could produce the deepest emotions 'the mind is capable of feeling'.[7] Landscapes, especially dramatic ones, became associated with profound emotional and aesthetic experiences that could be acquired in no other way. Once the Sublime became associated with landscape, mountains acquired cachet, and once mountains became respectable, a visit to the Alps, home of some of the highest and most picturesque peaks in Europe, became highly desirable.

Once mountains became safe, scenic and inspiring, it was only a matter of time before some people wanted to climb them. Windham and Pococke paved the way, but they were tourists, not climbers. Historians agree that the climbing history of the Alps, hence the birth of mountaineering, begins in earnest in 1760, and they also agree on the two names that bookend the narrative: the Genevan Horace Bénédict de Saussure and the Englishman Edward Whymper; and on the two mountains that dominate the tale: Mont Blanc, the highest peak in the Alps, and the Matterhorn, the most difficult to climb.

There are many better climbers than Bénédict de Saussure in the history of Alpine mountaineering, but none who are better known or more influential. At the age of twenty-two de Saussure was named professor of natural philosophy at Geneva and quickly became celebrated across Europe as a scientist and then, after publication of his four-volume *Voyages dans les Alpes*, as a climber of great distinction. In 1760, when he was only twenty and still a university student, he visited Chamonix where he had heard that the views of the Alps and of Mont Blanc were far superior to those from his native Geneva. 'I was desperately anxious', he wrote, 'to see at close quarters the great Alpine summits.' Upon entering Chamonix for the first time, de Saussure was besotted: 'These majestic glaciers, separated by great forests, and crowned by granite crags of astounding heights . . . and mixed with snow and ice, present one of the noblest and most singular spectacles it is possible to imagine.'[8]

De Saussure spent several weeks in the vicinity, and before he left he posted a famous notice in all the local churches announcing a reward – the sum has never been verified – for the first person to climb Mont Blanc. He even offered to pay the expenses of anyone who tried and failed, and de Saussure renewed the offer one year later. Naturally, he hoped he might be the first to summit the supreme Alpine giant himself, but repeated attempts were fruitless. 'It had become with me a species of disease,' he wrote. 'My eyes never rested upon Mont Blanc without my undergoing a fresh attack of melancholy.'[9]

One of de Saussure's most serious efforts took place in the summer of 1785, twenty-five years after he had posted his reward, in the company of Marc-Théodore Bourrit and Bourrit's son. When the attempt failed, Bourrit Jr wrote de Saussure a mocking letter criticising the latter for clinging to his guides as he came down off the mountain, contrasting this with his own considerably more 'agile' descent. 'Sir,' he wrote, 'do you not envy me my twenty-one years? Who will wonder if a youth of this age, who has nothing to lose, is bolder than a father of a family [and] a man of forty-six?'

Ever the gentleman, de Saussure was temperate – and scrupulously fair – in his reply. 'Monsieur: A moderate amount of boastfulness is no great crime,' he began,

especially at your age . . . You say you descended agilely. It is true; you descended agilely enough in the easy places, but in the difficult places you were, like your father, resting on the shoulder of one guide in front and held up behind by another. I do not blame you for these precautions; they were wise, prudent, even indispensable; but in no language in the world is that manner of progress styled agile climbing.[10]

Just one year later, in August 1786, two Swiss climbers – Michel-Gabriel Paccard, a doctor, and Jacques Balmat, a local farmer, guide and crystal hunter – finally got the job done. They were an unlikely pair. The well-born Paccard was an amateur scientist and collector of Alpine flora and later the mayor of Chamonix. Balmat, in contrast, was a somewhat cruder, boastful character, although much admired for his physical strength and his skill on ice. 'In those days I really was something to look at,' Balmat wrote. 'I had a famous calf and a stomach like cast-iron,' and he bragged that he could walk for three days without eating anything, except for 'munch[ing] a little snow. Every now and then I cast a sidelong look at Mont Blanc and said to myself, "My fine fellow, whatever you may say or whatever you may do, I shall get to the top of you one day."'[11]

The surviving accounts of Paccard and Balmat's ascent fall into two versions: those where Balmat is the hero and Paccard the foil, and vice versa, prefiguring, in a way, conflicting accounts in later years of some of the most famous ascents in mountaineering history. The two men, it is agreed, set off from two different locations at 5 p.m. on 7 August, meeting up and spending the night on a glacier above the village of La Côte. Balmat describes here how he tucked Paccard in for the night: 'I carried a rug and used it to muffle the Doctor up like a baby. Thanks to this precaution, he passed a tolerable night.' The two climbers woke at 2 a.m. on 8 August to a cloudless sky and set off across the Glacier de Taconnaz. 'The Doctor's first steps were halting and uncertain,' Balmat observed, 'but the sight of my alertness gave him confidence, and we went on safe and sound.'[12]

From this point the two accounts diverge. Partisans of Balmat claim that early that morning Paccard lost his hat, became demoralised, and continued for some distance on all fours. After some time Paccard sat down with his back to the wind, whereupon Balmat said that he would carry on – the summit was not far now – and then come back for Paccard. Balmat then pushed on and a short time later became the first man on the summit of the highest mountain in the Alps. 'Behold I was at the end of my journey. I had come alone with no help but my own will and my own strength. Everything around belonged to me. I was the Monarch of Mont Blanc!' Balmat then 'remembered Paccard', hurried back to fetch him, and pushed him to the summit.[13]

Supporters of Paccard describe how Balmat wanted to turn around when the going got rough upon encountering a fresh snowfall below the Rochers Rouges, and Balmat's eyes started burning. His wife had just given birth to their daughter, he explained to Paccard, both were unwell, and Balmat wanted to go back down and look after them. Paccard was immediately suspicious and wouldn't hear of it, 'realising it for the excuse it was', but he did offer to carry some of Balmat's load, which was much heavier than Paccard's. The two men pushed on, alternating as trail breakers in the heavy snow, but once they were above the Rochers Paccard 'made straight for the top' while Balmat, with his heavier load, 'took an easier slope and had to put on a spurt to catch up with his companion'.[14] In this version the two men arrived on top together at 6.23 p.m. and waved to the cheering crowd below watching through spyglasses from Chamonix.

From this point, the duelling accounts converge, both agreeing that the two men left their descent dangerously late, with only two more hours of daylight remaining. Luckily, there was a full moon that night, and they managed, after five hours, to reach their camp above La Côte where they slept until dawn. By now Paccard was almost completely snow-blind and had to be led into Chamonix by Balmat. The two men fell out almost immediately, soon after Balmat returned from Geneva where he had rushed off to claim his part of de Saussure's reward, and they nearly came to blows at a local inn in Chamonix. One year later, de Saussure himself reached the summit of Mont Blanc.

Looking back, the first ascent of Mont Blanc was a major milestone in the history of Alpine climbing. At the time, however, in 1786, there was virtually no climbing history to speak of. The sport (though it was not yet called that) was only twenty-five years old; there was no equipment, save for rudimentary crampons and simple alpenstocks; no special clothing other than ordinary street-wear, albeit generously layered on; no established techniques; no knowledge yet of frostbite, snow-blindness or the effects of altitude. Indeed, Paccard and Balmat, courageous though they were, made a number of what would now be considered highly amateur mistakes in their famous ascent: Paccard lost his hat (though it was tied on by strings); Paccard's gloves were inadequate and he had to borrow one of Balmat's (who said that while he might lend one glove to a climbing companion, he would never lend two, not even to his brother); both men suffered from snow-blindness; once or twice they almost fell into a crevasse; Paccard suffered from frostbite; and the pair of them reached the summit so late they had to descend after dark. If there had not been a full moon and almost no wind that night, their story could have had a very different ending. The first successful ascent of Mont Blanc, in short, was not so much a triumph of the sport of mountaineering as it was a happy accident. Indeed, the term mountaineering would not be invented for another seventy-five years.

If it was not altogether a triumph, the first ascent of Mont Blanc was nevertheless deeply inspiring. After 1800 the pace of Alpine climbing picked up. In the fifty years before 1800, there were only thirteen ascents of major Alpine peaks; in the next fifty years, there were ninety-seven. In 1823 the authorities in Chamonix caused the Compagnie des Guides to be founded in response to the ever-increasing demand for experienced mountain guides, who soon became more numerous in the village than working farmers, although many were one and the same. The Golden Age of Alpine climbing, which began in 1854, was bracketed by two climbs, both by Englishmen: the barrister Alfred Wills* with his ascent of the Wetterhorn in 1854 – while on his honeymoon – and the wood engraver Edward Whymper who brought down the curtain on this period with the first ascent of the Matterhorn in 1865. Both men also belonged to the British Alpine Club, the first of its kind, founded in 1857, whose members were described 'as gentlemen who also climbed'. In the last two years of the Golden Age, 1864–5, there were forty-three first ascents in the Alps; all but five were by Englishmen, and they were all members of the Alpine Club.

At first glance, British dominance in mountaineering, initially in the Alps and later in the Himalayas, is something of a puzzle. By the standards of most European countries, British 'mountains' are little more than good-sized rocky outcrops; the highest spot in Great Britain, Ben Nevis in Scotland, is 4,413 feet (1,345m), one third of the elevation of a modest Alp, and the Himalayas have 185 peaks over 20,000 feet (6,096m). 'Everything was to the disadvantage of the Englishman,' C. F. Mathews, an early president of the Alpine Club wrote. 'He sees no sun-smitten Alps as he rises from his bed in the morning. How was it that the English were generally the first to carry off the honours that lay far from their own doors while the dwellers at the very feet of the mountains seemed hardly to know their position, or their names?' It transpires that Britain's modest rock mounds are a large part of the answer, for British mountaineers, confined to their rocky venues, quickly came to excel at rock climbing, as opposed to climbing on snow and ice at which their continental colleagues were much more expert. In the Alps and especially in the Himalayas, much of the hardest, most dangerous

---

* Wills was not, however, the first person to ascend the Wetterhorn.

climbing was on rock formations, most notably the famous 'steps' on Everest, which gave the English a distinct advantage. And surely the other part of the answer is the thrill of the hunt: 'It is pursuit', Mathews concludes, 'and not possession, as the philosophers say, that gives happiness to mankind.'[15]

Except for George Mallory and Mount Everest, no man is more closely associated with a mountain than Edward Whymper and the Matterhorn. When he first saw the mountain in 1860 from Zermatt, aged twenty, he vowed to climb it, and not just to climb it but to be the first to do so. Accordingly, he spent five very anxious climbing seasons, the summers of 1861–5, either trying unsuccessfully to climb the Matterhorn himself or, when his two most serious rivals – John Tyndall and Jean-Antoine Carrel – were known to be out on the mountain, pacing back and forth down in Breuil where he nervously awaited news of their success or failure.

Whymper became a wood engraver, joining the family business, although his dream was to be an Arctic explorer. He found out, however, that he could happily settle for second best, Alpine exploration, when he was sent to Switzerland in the summer of 1860 to make preliminary drawings of the mountains for a series of woodcuts to illustrate a book on the Alps. From then on he returned to the Alps every summer for more than twenty years and later climbed in Greenland and the Andes and even planned a trip to the Himalayas. It was Whymper who coined the phrase the Third Pole to refer to Everest.

Whymper was a handsome, fair-haired youth, with penetrating eyes, a sour expression and an even more sour disposition. Nothing pleased him or met his expectations, least of all the various Swiss guides he was forced to hire and whom he once described as nothing more than 'pointers out of paths and large consumers of meat and drink'.[16] He complained about the hotels ('stinking'), the chalets ('wretched'), the villages ('miserable and squalid') and, again, the guides ('abominable'). Even the mountains disappointed him; there was nothing especially beautiful about them, nothing that stirred his soul or called forth any poetry or sense of awe. 'I do not believe in the pretty views in which Switzerland is represented,' he wrote on one occasion. On another he observed that 'the rant about the awful grandeur and sublimity . . . is absurd'.[17] Not even the Matterhorn escaped Whymper's preternatural instinct for disappointment; he said it looked like 'a sugar loaf set up on a table, the sugar loaf [with] its head knocked on one side. Grand it is, but beautiful I think it is not.'[18]

Indeed, one has to wonder what it was that drew Whymper back to the mountains season after season. Most likely it was the challenge, the chance to conquer and subdue, to impose his will on these wild landscapes, trample them underfoot, and tame them. He was furious in 1861, for example, when his first attempt on the Matterhorn failed, 'taunting him with its inaccessibility', and he vowed on the spot to keep coming back until 'one or the other [of us] is vanquished'.[19]

At 14,692 feet (4,478m), the Matterhorn sits on the Swiss–Italian border. There are several higher peaks in the Alps, but none that is as hard to climb. Indeed, for more than half a century, the Matterhorn was considered unclimbable, especially from Zermatt on the Swiss side where it does not resemble a mountain as much as it does a towering rock spire. From the Italian side the mountain spreads out more, offering brief interludes of the horizontal – shoulders and plateaus – between sheer rock cliffs. For years it had been assumed that if the Matterhorn ever was to be climbed, it would have to be from the Italian side.

Whymper tried numerous times between 1861 and 1865. On his second attempt in 1862, he met and befriended Jean-Antoine Carrel, who had more experience on the Matterhorn than any other climber at that time. Carrel was an Italian – an extremely proud Italian – and a strong patriot who was determined that the first ascent of the Matterhorn must be by Italians. Whymper was initially unaware of Carrel's chauvinist sentiments and was delighted when the famous climber agreed to be his guide. The men reached 12,550 feet (3,825m) on their second day, just below a prominent chimney on the Italian side. The next day dawned cloudless, but the other guide became ill, and first he and then Carrel refused to continue.

Frustrated, disappointed and somewhat suspicious, Whymper descended to Breuil, marched around the mountain to Zermatt, and tried to interest the Swiss in having a go, but there were no takers. Whereupon he returned to Breuil and decided to climb the mountain by himself. This time he took one of his own inventions with him, a grapnel, a metal claw attached to a rope that could either be thrown up to secure purchase on overhanging rock or fixed to the end of an alpenstock. Using the grapnel, Whymper climbed the chimney where the party had turned back earlier and went on to within 1,400 feet of the summit, the highest anyone had yet climbed on the Matterhorn. On the way down the ebullient Whymper slipped and fell 72 feet (22m), finally stopping himself ten feet short of an 800-foot (243m) drop to the Glacier du Lion.

The inaptly named Whymper brushed off his near-death experience – his bleeding cuts and numerous bruises elicited screams from several fellow patrons at his inn in Breuil – and six days later, on 23 July, he once again persuaded Carrel to accompany him, his fourth try that season. They got as far as 12,992 feet (3,959m) when the weather turned, it began to snow, and Carrel refused to go any further. Two days later Whymper tried again, this time without Carrel, and actually passed his previous highest point, but the summit remained elusive. By this time Whymper had made seven attempts on the mountain.

The stage was now set for the climax of the Whymper–Carrel saga and the single most dramatic day in the history of Alpine climbing, a day that began with an honest misunderstanding – or a betrayal, if you believe Whymper – led to a triumph, and ended in tragedy. After several near misses on earlier attempts, when Whymper returned to Breuil in the summer of 1865, he was now sure the mountain could be climbed and that he could climb it. And since the same was true for Carrel, the only question that July was whether the two men would climb together or possibly lead separate expeditions. To Whymper's immense relief and delight, Carrel agreed once again to climb with him, and Whymper then dismissed the two guides he had earlier engaged as his second choice.

The story of the 1865 attempt has many moving parts, but just two dates anchor the narrative: 9 July and 11 July. Carrel told Whymper that he was free to climb with him on the 9th but unbeknown to Whymper, Carrel had been selected as the leader of an official Italian climbing party scheduled to begin a summit attempt on the 11th. And not just any attempt; this expedition was sponsored by the Italian government to celebrate the founding of the Italian Alpine Club by the first-ever ascent of the Matterhorn – from the Italian side, naturally, by an all-Italian team, of course, and led by the greatest Italian climber of them all, the great patriot Jean-Antoine Carrel.

When Whymper arrives in Breuil on the 8th, he is told of a fellow English climber who has fallen ill, and Whymper delays his climb by one day (to 10 July) while he spends the 9th on a 30-mile round trip to Chatillon in search of medicine for his sick compatriot. He tracks Carrel down early on the 9th, explains what has happened, and asks Carrel if they can postpone their climb to the following day. Carrel responds that that won't be possible because he has contracted to lead what he calls a 'family of distinction' on a tour of the Aosta valley starting on the 11th, and he will need to make preparations on the 10th. Whymper will have to find someone else to climb with him. The family of distinction was in fact the Italian government expedition.

All the evidence confirms that at least from this point on, if not before, Carrel is knowingly taking part in an elaborate deception. Indeed, Felice Giordano, one of the men in Carrel's climbing party, had already arrived in Breuil, and either with or without Carrel's knowledge, set out to do whatever he could to thwart Whymper's attempt and give the Italians the chance to summit first. 'Please send me . . . some advice,' Giordano writes to the team's patron, the Italian minister of finance, on the 8th, 'I am head over ears in difficulty here, what with the weather, the expense, and Whymper.' Giordano explains that he has tried to avoid running into Whymper lest he become suspicious 'but that fellow, whose life seems to depend on the Matterhorn, is here . . . prying into everything. I have taken all the competent men away from him.'[20]

Even if it is assumed Carrel was acting in good faith up to 8 July, guilty only of scheduling Whymper's and the official Italian attempts too close to each other, the family of distinction story was deliberately misleading. Indeed, on the evening of the 9th, after returning from

Chatillon, Whymper invited Carrel and his cousin Cesar to his inn and 'we sat up til midnight, recounting our old adventures', but the two Italians made no mention of their real plans for the 11th.[21]

The 10th dawns stormy so Whymper stays in his inn all day, waiting for the weather to improve before heading out to look for new climbing partners. On the morning of the 11th the ailing Englishman for whom Whymper had secured medicine wakes Whymper and asks him if he has heard the news. 'No; what news?' 'Why, a large party of guides swept off this morning to try the Matterhorn.' Whymper snatches a telescope and picks out the group of Italians on the lower slopes of the mountain. 'I saw in a moment that I had been bamboozled and humbugged.'[22]

Anyone else would have admitted defeat at this point, but not Edward Whymper. Observing the large size of the Italian party, he did a quick calculation and concluded that from the Italian side it would take the group three days of climbing to reach a point from which they could make a summit bid. Whymper then calculated that he could be in Zermatt in one day, round up a team and start up the mountain the next day, and be on the summit on the third day. The Italians did not know it, but the first ascent of the Matterhorn had just become a race.

The shock of the betrayal and the time pressure Whymper was under weighed heavily on him as he hastily assembled his team in Zermatt late on the afternoon of the 11th, a total of seven climbers. Five of the seven were experienced Alpinists and belonged on the mountain: Whymper, Charles Hudson, and the three professional guides Michel Croz, old Peter Taugwalder and young Peter Taugwalder. The other two, an English lord, the eighteen-year-old Francis Douglas, and a young friend of Hudson's, the nineteen-year-old Douglas Hadow, were dubious choices. Whymper did apparently enquire about Hadow's experience but was reassured by Hudson that Hadow 'had climbed Mont Blanc in less time than most men'. What Hudson did not say was that that was the entire extent of Hadow's climbing experience. The great climber and historian of climbing Walt Unsworth wrote that Whymper's team, with 'its mixture of experience and inexperience was horrifying for such a venture'.[23]

Climbing on the opposite side from the Italian team and unsure of its progress, Whymper's party made good time and stopped at midday to establish their camp and prepare for the summit bid on the 14th, the same day Whymper calculated that the Italians would be making their attempt. Croz and young Taugwalder went ahead to survey the route for the 14th and they returned 'cock-a-hoop, shouting that the going was easy, and the summit was assured'.[24] In his account, Whymper recalls that that evening 'the sun went down giving as it departed a glorious promise for the morrow . . . Long after dusk the cliffs above echoed with our laughter and the songs of the guides, for we were happy that night in camp, and feared no evil.'[25]

The weather was perfect on the 14th and while the climbing took longer than usual, slowed by Hadow's inexperience, the summit was in view by 1 p.m., a few hundred feet of easy climbing. But where was Carrel? The top of the Matterhorn is a level platform 330 feet (100m) across; the Swiss summit is on the northern end of the ridge, and the Italian summit is at the southern end. If Whymper and company found footsteps in the snow on the platform, they would know they had been beaten. 'You must now carry your thoughts back to the seven Italians who started from Breuil on the 11th of July,' Whymper writes:

[Three] days had passed since their departure, and we were tormented with anxiety lest they should arrive on the top before us. All the way up we had talked of them, and many false alarms of 'men on the summit' had been raised. The higher we rose the more intense became the excitement. What if we should be beaten at the last moment. The slope eased off and at length we could be detached [from their rope], and Croz and I, dashing away, ran a neck and neck race which ended in a dead heat. At 1.40 p.m. the world was at our feet and the Matterhorn was conquered. Hurrah! Not a footstep could be seen . . . I hastened to the southern end, scanning the snow right and left eagerly . . . I peered over the cliff, half doubting, half expecting, and saw [the Italians] immediately, mere dots on the ridge, at an immense distance below . . . The Italians turned and fled.[26]

All seven climbers spent an hour on the summit, where even Whymper admired the view: 'the most rugged forms and the most graceful outlines – bold, perpendicular cliffs and gentle, undulating slopes; rocky mountains and snowy mountains. There was every combination that the world can give, and every contrast the heart could desire.'[27]

Edward Whymper was twenty-five.

The summiters began their descent around 2.30 p.m. The seven men were all roped together: Croz was in the lead, followed by the novice Hadow, then Hudson, Douglas, then old Peter Taugwalder, Whymper, and young Peter. At one point Croz lay down his ice axe, turned around, and reached up to take hold of Hadow's legs to lower him down through a difficult patch. Hadow lost his balance, fell onto Croz, and knocked him off the mountain. The weight of Croz on the rope pulled Hadow after him, and the combined weight of Croz and Hadow dislodged Hudson and Douglas. 'All this was the work of a moment,' Whymper recalled.

> Immediately we heard Croz's exclamation, old Peter and I planted ourselves as firmly as the rocks would permit; the rope was taut between us and the jerk came on us both as one man. We held; but the rope broke midway between Taugwalder and Lord Francis Douglas. For a few seconds we saw our four unfortunate companions sliding downwards on their backs and spreading out their hands endeavouring to save themselves. They passed from our sight uninjured, disappeared one by one, and fell from precipice to precipice on the Matterhorn glacier below, a distance of nearly 4,000 feet in height. From the moment the rope broke, it was impossible to help them.[28]

Whymper and the two Taugwalders froze and could not move for half an hour. 'The two men, paralysed by terror, cried like infants', Whymper wrote, 'and trembled in such a manner as to threaten us with the fate of the others . . . I thought that every moment would be my last, for the Taugwalders, utterly unnerved, were not only incapable of giving assistance but were in such a state that a slip might have been expected from one or the other at any moment.' Eventually Whymper, in his version of events, persuaded young Peter to move his feet and descend a few steps, managed to get old Peter moving, and then led father and son off the mountain and safely back to Zermatt.[29] Years later, young Peter, in his only written account of the incident, begged to differ: 'At last we tried to move on, but Whymper was trembling so violently that he could hardly manage a safe step forward. My father climbed on in front, continually turning back to place Whymper's legs on the broken ledges of rock . . . Without us he too would have perished.'[30] On a rescue mission the next day, three badly battered bodies were found but all that was ever found of Lord Douglas was a pair of gloves, a belt, a boot and a coat sleeve. 'We left them where they fell,' Whymper concludes in his account of the incident, 'buried in snow at the base of the grandest cliff of the most majestic mountain of the Alps.'[31]

For a time the disaster nearly overshadowed the news of the first ascent of the Matterhorn, but in due course Whymper's triumph was justly celebrated for the watershed it was in the history of mountaineering. Eventually he received a Patron's medal from the Royal Geographical Society and for a time he was said to be the most talked about man in Europe. But the tragedy haunted him: 'Every night, do you understand, I see my comrades of the Matterhorn slipping on their backs, their arms outstretched, one after the other, in perfect order at equal distances – Croz the guide, first, then Hadow, then Hudson, and lastly Douglas. Yes, I shall always see them.'[32]

On 16 July, just two days after the tragedy, Jean-Antoine Carrel, along with an Italian priest and two others, summited the Matterhorn from the Italian side, 'for the honour and vengeance of our country'. Whymper never took offence at Carrel's deception, dismissing it as all part of a friendly rivalry, and the two men continued to climb together for many years, in the Andes and elsewhere. They even arranged to meet up again in 1874 to climb the Matterhorn together for old times' sake. In 1891 Carrel died of exhaustion while guiding on the Matterhorn after making sure the party he was leading got safely off the mountain when a storm blew up.

In his book *Scrambles in the Alps* Whymper recalled how he felt on that July day back in 1865 as he peered down from the summit of the Matterhorn and watched as his great rival and the rest of the disconsolate Italian team retreated off the mountain. 'Still I would that the leader of that party could have stood with us at that moment,' he wrote, 'for our victorious shouts conveyed to him the disappointment of the ambition of a lifetime. He was *the* man, of all those who attempted the ascent of the Matterhorn, who most deserved to be the first upon its summit.'[33]

There were still virgin peaks in the Alps in 1865 and many untried routes on other mountains, but the conquest of the Matterhorn is widely regarded as the end of the Golden Age of Alpine climbing. Just eleven years later Meije, the last great unclimbed peak in the Alps, fell to Emmanuel Boileau de Castelnova, and men – climbers were nearly all men at the time – sought new heights to conquer. Some intrepid souls went west, to the Andes, where Whymper climbed Chimborazo and several other South American peaks during 1879–80, but most looked east to the Caucasus. Douglas Freshfield went there in 1868 and reached within a few hundred feet of the summit of Elbrus – 2,736 feet (834m) higher than Mont Blanc and the tallest mountain in Europe.

Even as European climbers were conquering the tallest Alps in the late 1850s and early 1860s, Radanath Sickdhar and the other computors in Calcutta and Dehradun were busy calculating the height of Everest, officially declaring it the highest mountain on earth in 1856, one year before the Alpine Club was founded. And it was in 1865, the year of Whymper's triumph on the Matterhorn, that the Royal Geographical Society, hence the climbing community, officially recognised the name of Mount Everest.

As important as these developments would soon be to the climbing fraternity, they paled beside the appalling drama that erupted in British India during those same years. It was variously known as the Sepoy Rebellion, the Great Mutiny, or as many Indians came to call it, the First War of Indian Independence, but by whatever name it was far and away the darkest hour of Britain's more than three-hundred-year history in the subcontinent: twelve long months of unimaginable violence, unspeakable atrocities on both sides, and great heroism – also on both sides. The numerous causes of the Mutiny of 1857 lay ultimately in the long overdue Indian reaction to years of increasing military, financial, economic and political oppression on the part of the East India Company, greatly encouraged and abetted by its enablers back in London. The Mutiny was confined largely to the central and northern provinces, spearheaded by Indian elements in the Company's army, and opposed and brutally repressed by the Company's British soldiers along with Indian regiments who remained loyal to the British. Reliable death tolls are not available on the Indian side, though as many as 100,000 Indians are said to have died in the province of Oudh alone. Close to 2,700 British soldiers perished, but the death toll among European civilians was much higher, close to 6,000 by one estimate.

At the end of the Mutiny in 1858, the East India Company was abolished and India became the largest, most lucrative and most important possession in the empire – the Jewel in the Crown, as it came to be known. In the years after the Mutiny, the Raj (as the government of India was called) embarked on a new round of exploring, surveying and mapping of its prized possession, especially along its northern borders, preparing the ground, or so it seemed, for the Alpine veterans and others who began arriving twenty years later in search of new mountains to climb.

Alpine climbing made climbing in the Himalayas possible. In the nearly eighty years between the first ascent of Mont Blanc and of the Matterhorn, a number of key climbing techniques and pieces of equipment were either invented or greatly improved. The use of ropes to secure climbers to each other in case someone slipped, eschewed by most Swiss guides in the early years, was widespread by the 1840s, and the quality of ropes also improved over the years. The technique of cutting steps in steep ice-covered slopes was perfected. Better, ten-point crampons came into use; ice axes, pitons, short ladders and Whymper's grapnel were gradually added to the mix; the continentals also began using karabiner clips, but the British resisted, insisting that 'the thing is un-English in name and nature'. Light-weight, silken Mummery tents (also called Whymper tents) made overnight bivouacs much safer, and windproof clothing provided increased protection and comfort. Much had been learned about snow-blindness and the effects of altitude. By the 1860s guiding had become much more of a profession rather than just a farmer's or shepherd's sideline. A few Swiss guides were taken out to the Himalayas by some of the earliest climbers and used to train local porters. 'In many respects', one chronicler wrote, Himalayan climbing 'began not in trans-Himalayan Kashmir but in those Alpine border-lands of France, Italy and Switzerland.'[34]

As one by one the giants began to fall across Europe, attention inevitably shifted to the Himalayas, and an obsession with Everest began to take hold. But while it might have been on everyone's mind, Everest was still a pipe dream. It stood squarely on the border between Nepal and Tibet, and both countries were completely closed to westerners. They could all dream of Everest, perhaps, these soon-to-be-legendary climbers, but for the time being none of them could get anywhere near it.

Climbing in the Himalayas started in the early 1880s, when it could take as long as four weeks to cover the nearly 8,000 nautical miles (12,821 km) from London to Calcutta, with stops at Gibraltar, Malta, Alexandria, Aden, Colombo and Madras. There had been plenty of activity in the mountains before then – surveying, mapping, botanising, ethnologising, geologising, and a great deal of exploring – but no climbing as such. It was 'the period of passes rather than peaks'. The distinction of the first climber falls to an accomplished Alpine veteran, the English barrister William Graham (also accom-panied by Swiss guides), who climbed in the region around Kangchenjunga in 1883 and later further west in Garhwal. While there is no doubt Graham deserves his pioneer status, his accounts of some of his climbs are rather confused and on occasion inaccurate, so that his achievements have at times been minimised, most notably by members of the Survey of India, and especially when they are set down next to those of the man who followed him, Martin Conway, who led the first-ever full-scale expedition to the Himalayas in 1892.

Conway's expedition to K2 established a number of precedents and created the template for nearly all the Himalayan expeditions that followed for the next seventy years. And a template was sorely needed, for while Alpine climbing may have made Himalayan climbing possible, especially advances in equipment and technique, the Alps were nothing like the Himalayas. Between the Alps and

the Himalayas 'lay differences of degree and kind and for a generation at least after Whymper, the great Alpinists of the day, one after
another, would flail and falter before them'.[35] One of these Alpinists
was the great Albert Mummery who declared after his first season
in the Himalayas: 'Of mountaineering as we know it in the Alps,
there is little or none [in the Himalayas].'[36] Alpine climbing, in short,
was a necessary prelude to Himalayan climbing, but it was hardly a
preparation.

The differences in scale were enormous, starting with elevation.
Just the Tibetan plateau, leaving aside the mountains for the moment,
sits at an average altitude of 13,000 feet (3,960m) – higher than all
but the very tallest of the Alps – and over 150 passes exceed 16,000
feet (4,875m), higher than Mont Blanc. A modest Himalayan peak
was higher than anything in Europe by at least 3,000 feet (915m);
any one of the vast majority of Alpine peaks could be placed on
top of the Matterhorn and it would still not be a mountain as high
as Everest or the eight other highest Himalayan peaks. Whatever
Alpinists had learned about the effects of altitude on climbers would
have to be relearned in the Himalayas. Indeed, it was widely believed
at the end of the nineteenth century that human beings could not
survive above 24,000 feet (7,315m). No less a figure than T. W.
Hinchcliff, then president of the Alpine Club, wrote in 1876 that
'21,500 feet [6,550m] is near the limit at which man ceases to be
capable of the slightest further exertion'.[37] As Mallory and Irvine
would demonstrate on Everest (in 1924), T. W.'s estimate was off by
more than 6,000 feet (1,828m).

Along with elevation, the sheer size of the Himalayan giants
changed the climbing calculus completely. While one man and his
guide could easily climb most of the Alps in a day – Whymper,
climbing alone, reached within 1,400 feet (426m) of the summit of
the Matterhorn – the higher Himalayas take a team of climbers
(along with numerous porters) more than a week to summit, and
only then after they have allowed several days for adjusting to the
altitude and have established and provisioned successive camps at
ever-higher elevations.

The Himalayas are also extremely remote compared with the Alps.
There are no villages nestled at the bottom of Everest, Nanga Parbat

or Annapurna, with cheering locals following the progress of their favourite climbers through spyglasses. Most of the tallest Himalayan peaks are even today at least a week's trek from the closest villages, and they were even further away at the turn of the last century. Supplying a major expedition – westerners could not be self-sufficient here – could take more than a hundred porters and any number of pack animals, a supply line that might stretch for as much as a mile behind the team of climbers.

Martin Conway was an art historian, professor and Alpine veteran – he 'once did the Matterhorn from Zermatt and was back for afternoon tea' – with a lot of time on his hands in London in 1891 after quitting his job as a lecturer at Liverpool University. That year Conway decided he wanted to make a name for himself in the Himalayas, and specifically he wanted to climb in the Karakorams, with a possible attempt on K2 itself, the highest mountain in the region and second highest in the world.

Conway was aware of the many novel challenges his expedition would face in the Himalayas, and he made careful and elaborate preparations, beginning with his choice of guides. He was fortunate to secure the services of Matthias Zurbriggen, a Swiss climber who would subsequently be the first man to climb Mount Aconcagua, the highest mountain in the western hemisphere – by himself. In many ways Conway's most consequential choice was one Charles Granville Bruce, a young subaltern with the 5th Gurkha Rifles stationed on the Indian North-West Frontier. Bruce had intimate knowledge of the region the expedition was planning to explore, had considerable experience with local Gurkha soldiers – he was convinced they could do as well or better than the Swiss guides just then showing up in the Himalayas – and persuaded Conway to accept four Gurkhas as part of the team. Bruce would later play a key role in all three of the British expeditions to climb Everest and was the leader of two of them.

Conway and friends set sail for India in February 1892. The expedition took its time getting to the Karakorams, but it finally arrived at the top of the Baltoro Glacier in early August, a caravan of 80 men and 103 loads. At this spot, named Concordia by Conway, two glaciers coming off the highest of the Karakorams merge to form the Baltoro, creating what has been called 'the most magnificent mountain amphitheatre in the world'.[38] And with good reason: it offers a 360-degree panorama that includes seven of the world's highest peaks, with the spectacular pyramid of K2, 12,000 feet (3,660m) from base to summit, towering at the head of the valley. When the Swiss guide Matthias Zurbriggen saw it, he famously exclaimed: 'Name of a brigand; they don't know what mountains are in Switzerland.'[39]

In the end, Conway did not climb or come close to climbing K2 – Zurbriggen claimed it 'frightened him' even to look at the mountain – nor did anyone else for another sixty-two years until 1954 when K2 was finally summited, one year after the first ascent of Everest. But Conway was satisfied with his achievement, which 'marked a definitive moment in European comprehension of the scale of the Himalaya'.[40] Conway had also answered one of the two most pressing questions in mountaineering at the time: was it possible for a team of climbers to penetrate into extremely remote parts of the Himalayas and still be provisioned with adequate supplies over an extended period? The other question had to do with altitude and was in effect a series of related questions: was there an elevation beyond which man could no longer breathe well enough to keep climbing? If not, how long could a climber stay at extreme altitude without having to descend? Could climbers bivouac overnight at extreme altitude? Two nights? The latter questions were being asked as it became clear that climbing some of the higher peaks could take several days and involve staying overnight at extremely high camps. These questions, it turned out, would not be answered for another seventeen years, during the expedition of Prince Luigi Amedeo, Duke of the Abruzzi to the Karakorams in 1909.

When Conway returned he lectured all over the British Isles, including at the Alpine Club and the Royal Geographical Society, and was planning to take his lecture tour to the United States, but his American father-in-law dissuaded him. 'I do not overlook the climbing,' he wrote to Conway, 'the immense glaciers, the tip-top mark, but nobody here has heard anything but Mt Everest [and] not of your K2.'[41] The first serious expedition to the Himalayas was just a few weeks old and already all the talk was of Everest.

And the talk intensified later that same year when Clinton Dent, the English surgeon and later head of the Alpine Club, cautiously proposed in an 1892 article in the magazine *Nineteenth Century* that an attempt on Everest should be considered. 'I do not for a moment say that it would be wise to ascend Mount Everest,' Dent wrote, 'but I believe most firmly that it is humanly possible to do so.'[42] It was the first time the idea of climbing Everest ever appeared in print.

One year later two of the best-known names in Everest history, Francis Younghusband and Charles Bruce, while strolling across the polo grounds in Chitral on the North-West Frontier cooked up a scheme to steal into Tibet, explore the foothills around Everest, and even attempt to climb it. This discussion led to a formal written proposal that got as far as Mortimer Durand, the Foreign Secretary of the Indian government, who approved it, but it was later turned down for political reasons. Others had expressed an interest in climbing the mountain – Conway and Whymper, among them – but the Bruce–Younghusband plan is widely regarded as the first specific proposal to climb Mount Everest ever made.

In the end, all the plans to climb Everest foundered on the same rock: there was no way to get to the mountain. Everest straddles the Tibet-Nepal border, and the Tibetans had closed their border back in 1792 at the conclusion of a war the Chinese had fought on Tibet's behalf after an invasion from Nepal. Even before this incursion from beyond their borders, the Tibetans were fanatically anti-foreigner, especially anti-westerner, and anti-British most of all. They watched with alarm as the British snapped up more and more territories in India and were afraid – correctly – that even the mighty Himalayas would not be enough to keep the British out of Tibet.

In Nepal the situation was quite different. Its borders were closed to foreigners, too, but it was a decision reached and subsequently implemented with the full support of the British government. The British had designs on Nepal, of course, as they did on most of the kingdoms along the southern slopes of the Himalayas, and they fought a three-year war (1814–16) to make their point, appropriating in the process two provinces, Garhwal and Kumaon, recently annexed by Nepal. During the war, however, the British were so impressed with the bravery and ferocity of the Gurkha soldiers who comprised the Nepali army that in the treaty ending the war they agreed to respect Nepal's complete independence in return for the right to recruit Gurkhas into British regiments in India and to station a British Resident in Kathmandu. Nepal promptly closed its borders at the war's end – they were only opened again 134 years later in 1950 – and the British next door in India scrupulously observed and strictly enforced the closed-door policy during that entire period. Nepal may have lost the Gurkha War, but since the British were specifically required by the terms of the treaty to keep their hands off the kingdom, the Nepalis must have wondered just how winning the war could have improved upon losing it.

The arrival in India of the new viceroy, George Nathaniel Curzon, in 1899 marked a turning point in the story of Everest. Curzon was a deeply committed imperialist and expansionist, a strong advocate of the 'forward school' of British diplomacy, and the epitome of what the Victorians called a 'thruster'. An explorer himself – he received the gold medal from the Royal Geographical Society for exploring the source of the Oxus – Curzon was keenly interested in Everest. In July 1899, just six months after his appointment, he learned that Douglas Freshfield, former head of the Alpine Club and future president of the Royal Geographical Society, was planning to enter Tibet surreptitiously and circumnavigate Kanchenjunga. Curzon wrote to Freshfield suggesting, in effect, that he might consider transgressing even further on Tibetan sovereignty and extending his range to explore the region around Everest. 'I have always regarded it as rather a reproach,' Curzon wrote, 'that having the tallest . . . mountains in the world on the borders of British . . . territory, we have for the last twenty years equipped no scientific expedition and done practically nothing to explore them. I should like to see a thoroughly competent party sent out to ascend or attempt the ascent of Kangchenjunga *or Mt Everest*.'[43] Freshfield was enthusiastic and raised the idea of Everest with the Royal Geographical Society and the Royal Society, but they were both fixated at the time on polar exploration.

Curzon may have been keenly interested in Everest, but he was

As a student of Russian aspirations and methods for fifteen years, I assert with confidence . . . that her ultimate ambition is the dominion of Asia . . . [I]f Russia is entitled to these ambitions, still more is Britain entitled, nay compelled, to defend that which she has won.

George Curzon, Viceroy of India

The stronger Russia is in Central Asia, the weaker England is in India.

General Mikhail Skobelev

The Englishmen are dangerous to you. [They] . . . collect countries.

Captain Nikoforov to the Khan of Khiva

H<small>E WENT BY</small> many names. His Polish birth name was Jan Prosper Witkiewicz. His Russian name was Ivan Viktorovich Vitkievich. In the domains of Allah he adopted Persian dress and went by his Muslim name Omar Beg. To many he was known simply as Captain Beekavitch. By whatever name he went, he was the scourge of the Raj and the worst nightmare of Lord Ellenborough, Governor General of India. Except for the assorted British mandarins involved, Vitkievich would play a greater role than almost anyone else in igniting one of the greatest follies of British imperial history.

Lieutenant Henry Rawlinson had lost his way late one night on his 800-mile, six-day dash from Tehran (in Persia) to Herat (on the Afghan border) in late October 1837 when, just as dawn broke over the Aladagh mountains of far-eastern Persia, a party of horsemen swept past him and disappeared into a gorge a few miles further ahead. The riders were Cossacks, and Rawlinson, who was well aware of the Russian presence in Persia, was nevertheless surprised to see Russians this far east, especially so close to the Persian–Afghan frontier. Rawlinson caught up with the Russians as they were having breakfast beside a secluded stream and tried to engage them, but their leader – Rawlinson referred to him as 'the Russian gentleman' – did not seem to know French, Persian or English. 'All I could find out was that he was a *bona fide* Russian officer carrying presents from the [Russian] emperor to the [Persian] ruler Mohamed Shah.'[1]

Rawlinson was also on his way to confer with Mohamed Shah, just then moving with his army towards Herat on the Afghan border where he planned to conquer the city and restore it to Persian sovereignty. Rawlinson's surprise turned to genuine alarm when he caught up with the Persian ruler and mentioned to him that he had run into a party of Russians, and Mohamed Shah replied that he was expecting the party and then added, referring to their leader: 'He is sent direct from the Russian emperor to Dost Mohamed in Kabul, and I am merely asked to help him on his journey.'[2]

Rawlinson realised that he had stumbled onto evidence of a truly ominous development: the Russians were angling for influence and an alliance with the leader of the Afghans. Even though he was exhausted from his journey, Rawlinson set out the next day to return to Tehran where the news he brought set off alarm bells in the British mission, sent shock waves through the highest circles of the British Raj, and electrified the implacable Russophobes in London. That the Russians were in Persia was troubling enough – Rawlinson himself was there as part of the British attempt to counteract growing Russian influence – but that the Russians might soon be in Afghanistan was unthinkable. Before Rawlinson left for Tehran, the Russians had arrived in the Persian camp and their leader had introduced himself: the Russian gentleman was Captain Ivan Viktorovich Vitkievich.

The meeting between the two men would turn out to be one of the most consequential encounters of what became known as the Great Game, the rivalry between Russia and Great Britain for influence and control in Central Asia. Ironically, the first-known appearance of that phrase, popularised much later in Rudyard Kipling's novel *Kim*, appeared in a letter Rawlinson received from his friend Lieutenant Arthur Conolly of the 6th Bengal Native Light Cavalry who had just completed a spying mission (he called it 'reconnoitring') in the vast no-man's-land between the Caucasus and the Hindu Kush where he had been sent by the Raj to find out what the Russians were up to in Central Asia. In the letter sent just after Rawlinson had taken up the post of political agent in Kandahar, Conolly wrote: 'You've a great game, a noble one, before you.'[3]

By 1837 the Great Game was in full swing, and the disastrous invasion of Tibet some sixty years later would be its last major act. Like many of the most serious moves of the Game, the invasion would be motivated by intense Russophobia, sparked by rumour and exaggeration, bolstered by manipulated intelligence, designed by officials with limited or no first-hand knowledge of the region or its people, second-guessed by politicians in London, and typically accomplished next to nothing or made matters even worse.

The Great Game, or the 'Tournament of Shadows' as the Russians styled it, had its origins in 1801, more than thirty years before the fateful Rawlinson–Vitkievich meeting, with a mad scheme hatched by Tsar Paul I, the son of Catherine the Great, to march 35,000 Cossacks across Turkestan, recruiting fierce Turcoman tribesmen along the way, meet up somewhere in Persia with 40,000 French troops to be supplied by Napoleon, invade India, and drive the British into the sea. When Napoleon declined to participate, although he later briefly considered an invasion plan of his own in cahoots with the Shah of Persia, the Tsar decided to proceed without the French, issuing orders to the Don Cossacks on 24 January 1801 to muster an army and begin the long march south. 'You are to offer peace to all who are against the British', he told the commanding officer, promising that 'all the wealth of the Indies shall be your reward'.[4]

At the time, no one – not the French, not the Russians, and not even the British – had any idea of the distances or the formidable geographies involved, hence the complete absurdity of the plan. But the directors of the East India Company, who controlled and operated all British commercial interests in India, were duly alarmed and prevailed upon the British government to send emissaries to Persia and Afghanistan to warn them of the consequences of conspiring with the Russians and the benefits of remaining in Britain's good graces.

The hapless Tsar Paul was assassinated in March, and the Cossacks turned back a mere 400 miles into their journey. While the Tsar's scheme came to nothing, it did succeed in planting a deep suspicion of the Russians in the British national psyche, especially with regard to India, and launched nearly a century of Russophobia. After the Indian Mutiny of 1857, the British government assumed control of British affairs in the subcontinent and kept an increasingly close watch on Russia's every move within a thousand miles of India.

As India became by far the most important and most lucrative of all British possessions, the security of the Raj became an overriding imperial priority. For the British, any threat to India was tantamount to an act of aggression against England itself, a view British envoys in St Petersburg regularly made plain to a succession of Tsars and their generals, who were known to have drawn up elaborate plans for invading India as far back as 1791 at the instigation of Catherine the Great.

Russia was very far from India, of course, and so long as the Russians stayed on their side of the Caucasus, they would never be a threat. But the Russians had their own dreams of empire, and while they included the Caucasus, which Russia had absorbed by the late 1700s, they did not end there. Russia's expansionist ambitions were not driven primarily by economic opportunity, as was the case with the Raj, but by fear, specifically fear of invasion from the Far East, such as it had experienced for more than three centuries at the hands of the Mongols. The trauma resulting from the slaughter and devastation wrought by Genghis Khan and his successors was so deep that it lingered in the Russian national psyche long after the Mongols were finally defeated in 1553 by Ivan the Terrible, a victory that left 'the way open for the greatest colonial enterprise in history – Russia's expansion eastwards'.[5]

Russia's eastward expansion would last for four centuries, as she relentlessly extended her influence and control beyond the Caucasus and deeper into Central Asia, expanding her empire by fifty-five square miles a day, 20,000 every year, first all the way to Siberia and as far east as the Pacific and then south towards the Caspian Sea. Lord Ellenborough, then a Member of Parliament, succinctly summarised the growing fears of Russophobes when he wrote in his diary in 1829: 'I feel confident that we shall have to fight the Russians on the Indus.'[6]

As the British and Russian empires grew – the British expanding north and west from India, the Russians south and east from the Caucasus – they were initially separated by 2,000 miles, but by the end of the nineteenth century by just a few hundred, and by only twenty miles in one place on the northern Afghan border. Sooner or later, they were destined to meet, most likely somewhere in that vast no-man's-land where four of the world's greatest mountain ranges – the Hindu Kush, the Tien Shan, the Pamirs and the

Himalayas – all come together. The Russians were determined that the meeting place, wherever it might be, should be as far as possible from the motherland, while for the British it had to be one or preferably two buffer states away from India.

But before the Game could be played properly, the two sides needed a rough idea of the size and shape of the board. Hence, the first few decades of the rivalry became a time of dazzling feats of exploration, of the first crossing (by westerners) of numerous 20,000-foot-high (6,100m) mountain passes, and of brazen spy missions, a few ending in beheadings. Year after year these intrepid explorer-spies began filling in the map of Central Asia, thus enabling the politicians on both sides to assess for the first time just how bold a move their rivals in the Game were making and whether it called for a countermove.

At times the early years of the Game took on an air of good-natured competition, as men from the two sides vied with each other to be the first westerner to reach Samarkand, or Khiva or Bokhara. At other times the Game became a genuine power struggle, as the British lion and the Russian bear competed for control of various client states. And at still other times the Game turned deadly. While British and Russian troops never met on the battlefield during the period, each side fought fierce proxy battles against the armies of the khanates, local tribes, and others in the territories they annexed as part of their inexorable expansion; campaigns and engagements inevitably triggered by moves or rumours of moves by their rival.

The flashpoint for the most serious of these encounters was almost always the same – Afghanistan – and almost always for the same reason: access to and control of the Khyber Pass, which connected southeastern Afghanistan with the North-West Frontier (now in modern-day Pakistan). Everyone agreed that if India was going to be invaded from the north, the only feasible route was through the Khyber Pass, although its neighbour to the south, the Bolan Pass, was another possibility. If the Russians were coming, in short, they would come through the Khyber, partly because of its close proximity to India but also because of its topography; it was especially broad, gently sloping, with a very modest elevation. An army could march through the Khyber and have every chance of defending itself in the process, which was not true for many of the more narrow passes and gorges leading out of the mountains.

Both sides in the Game courted the allegiance of the Afghans, the British to secure the border with India, the Russians to gain access to the Khyber. For the most part the Afghans sided with Britain – British India was much closer than Russia – but the Afghans were especially adept at playing the two rivals off against each other. The British usually tolerated the games the Afghans played, confident that Britain would prevail in the end, but in one case the Afghans went too far, prompting the British to occupy the country and setting the stage for one of the two or three greatest military debacles in British imperial history. '[N]o disaster was more complete, more astonishing, and, one may fairly add, more warranted, than the British defeat in the First Afghan War.'[7] Many historians consider that war to be the opening gambit of the Great Game, but even those who think the game began earlier agree that it certainly signalled the start of a more serious phase of Anglo-Russian tension.

For the most part, the details of the First Anglo-Afghan War are beyond the scope of the Everest story, except as they preview what would happen later in Tibet. The trouble began when Lieutenant Rawlinson informed his superiors in Tehran that Captain Vitkievich was en route to Afghanistan bearing gifts and a letter from Tsar Nicholas, and that the Russian captain had effectively been authorised 'to offer the Afghans the moon in order to displace the British in Kabul'.[8] The British were not amused; Lord Palmerston, the Foreign Secretary, notified the British ambassador in St Petersburg that the Governor General of India, Lord Auckland, 'has been told to take Afghanistan in hand and make it a British dependency . . . We have long declined to meddle with the Afghans, but if the Russians try to make them Russian, we must take care that they become British.'[9]

Lord Auckland, who was shockingly ignorant of regional politics and Afghan sensitivities and who had developed a strong dislike for the Afghan ruler, Dost Mohamed, was persuaded by his advisers to fire off an ultimatum to Dost in which he explained that if the king 'were to enter into any alliance with the Russians, or any other power, which was considered detrimental to British interests, then he would be forcibly removed from his throne'.[10] When Auckland followed up this intemperate outburst with subsequent, equally high-handed ultimatums, Vitkievich was received most cordially by Dost in his palace. 'We hope that the magnanimity and unparalleled bounties showered on the Persian court', Dost told Vitkievich, 'will also rain down on the Afghan government and on our dynasty which, with the beneficent gaze of your imperial greatness' will be restored to its former glory.[11] When Auckland got this news, he was incensed; as long as Dost Mohamed was on the throne, he declared, there was 'no reason to expect that the interests of our Indian empire would be preserved inviolate'.[12]

In fact Dost Mohamed much preferred to be allied with the British than with the Russians, if only the British would show more interest and offer more inducements. Lord Auckland had repeatedly been warned by Alexander Burnes, a political officer and seasoned Afghan expert stationed in Kabul, that if his lordship would simply evince more friendliness and sympathy towards Dost – and issue fewer threats – Dost would be more than happy to do his lordship's bidding. It was later discovered that Burnes's reports to Auckland were edited by two of Auckland's rabidly anti-Dost advisers, paving the way for the unnecessary war to remove Dost that followed. 'Twenty thousand men', Burnes wrote to a friend when he learned the British were sending an army, 'are now under orders to do what a word would have done earlier.'[13]

In the spring of 1839, a total of 16,000 British and Indian troops, some 38,000 camp followers and 30,000 camels set out through the Bolan Pass – another, smaller force was proceeding via the Khyber Pass – on their way to Afghanistan. One British brigadier alone needed sixty camels for his camp gear, and the officers of one regiment appropriated two camels just for their cigars. Even as the nearly 60,000-strong force entered southern Afghanistan, the entire rationale for the invasion abruptly collapsed as the Russians, alarmed by British resolve, withdrew their offer of support to Dost Mohamed, Vitkievich was recalled in some disgrace to Moscow, and Russian presence in Persia was scaled back. But it was too late; if the point of the invasion could no longer be the defence of India, then let it be an object lesson to any of India's neighbours foolish enough to flirt with the Russian bear. The invasion force met no resistance at Kandahar, the first major city on their line of march, but they encountered fierce opposition at the next, the well-defended fortress of Ghazni, which eventually fell to the invaders. By the time the British force reached Kabul, one hundred miles to the east, news of the fall of Ghazni, widely considered impregnable, so demoralised Dost Mohamed's army that they dispersed without firing a shot, prompting the king to flee – and Kabul fell without any fighting.

If the invasion of Afghanistan was a modest success, the brief occupation was a fiasco, and the subsequent retreat was a catastrophe. The proud and fiercely independent Afghans were outraged by the presence of an occupying force of foreign infidels and by the behaviour of many of the occupying soldiers, especially the drinking and womanising, which fuelled growing anger and resentment in the deeply conservative Muslim population. The widespread unpopularity of the British puppet king who had replaced Dost, Shah Shujah – 'a tubby little man as inoffensive as he was ineffectual' – and soaring food prices in the bazaar, as several thousand British and Indian soldiers spent their wages in the local economy, added to the growing tensions.[14] The British were not unaware of the local reaction, but William Macnaghten, one of the editors of Burnes's memos and the most senior adviser at the mission in Kabul, did not want to hear about unhappy Afghans, and he especially did not want news of that kind to reach London or Calcutta (the seat of the Raj), lest he lose the post of governor general of Bombay he had been promised by Lord Auckland if the occupation of Afghanistan was a success.

Kabul exploded in mob violence on 2 November 1841, and one of the first infidels to die was Alexander Burnes, cut down along with his Indian bodyguards and their families. In the weeks that followed, Macnaghten tried several times to negotiate a settlement of the hostilities with Akhbar Khan, the son of Dost Mohamed, offering him the post of vizier. The last negotiation took place on 23 December when Macnaghten and three political officers agreed to meet Akhbar Khan to discuss a new proposal from the Afghans. Major General William Elphinstone, the military commander in Kabul, warned Macnaghten of a possible trap, but Macnaghten was not afraid. 'Leave it all to me,' he told Elphinstone. 'I understand these things better than you.'[15] But he did not: Macnaghten and the three officers were cut down, and Macnaghten's body was later displayed in the bazaar, minus its head and limbs.

Two months later, in January 1842, Elphinstone completed his own negotiations with the treacherous Akhbar Khan, who agreed to allow safe passage of all 4,500 British and Indian troops and their dependants still in Kabul and the remaining 12,000 camp followers, a total of 16,500 souls, out of Kabul and through a number of gorges to Jalalabad, the entrance to the Khyber Pass and India. The withdrawal began on 6 January and was to have ended one week later, on the 13th. On that day, a single soldier, Dr William Brydon of the 44th Regiment of Foot, stumbled into Jalalabad with the astonishing news that he was the sole survivor of the retreat from Kabul. While Brydon was not in fact the only survivor, the numbers were appalling; only 750 out of 4,500 soldiers were estimated to have survived, and less than 3,000 out of the 12,000 camp followers. The rest were slain in the gorges by the Afghans, died of starvation or froze to death. Over 500 survivors, who lost limbs due to frostbite, made their way back to Kabul where they became beggars. Elphinstone himself was wounded in the retreat and died three months later. While the British military, stationed in scores of possessions across three continents, was bound to make mistakes and suffer setbacks now and then, the epic scale of its losses in the First Anglo-Afghan War went unmatched until the First World War.

What Afghanistan was to the British, the central Asian khanates were to the Russians: kingdoms on the periphery of their sphere of influence which could serve as a buffer between the homeland, in Russia's case the Caucasus, and expansion-minded rivals. These khanates stretched west to east, from Khiva, the westernmost and closest to Russia, to Bokhara, Khokand, Kashgar and finally Yarkand, the easternmost, just north of the Karakorams, hence due north of British India. Beginning in 1873 the Russians began annexing these kingdoms, starting with Khiva and then moving on to Khokand in 1875, in the end acquiring new territory half the size of the United States. For the most part these states were too far from India for the British to care what the Russians did there, although the viceroy Lord Mayo did get nervous the closer the Russians came to Yarkand and Kashgar, hence to the northern border of Afghanistan.

In February 1884 all that changed when the Russians seized the city of Merv, and in a few short weeks the two empires were at the brink of war for the first and only time in the Great Game. The problem with Merv was that it did not lie in that west-to-east line of the other khanates, all tucked safely way (from the British perspective) behind the four most formidable mountain ranges in the world. Merv lay to the south of the Caucasus, on the direct route to Herat in western Afghanistan and, most importantly, there were no mountains between Merv and Afghanistan. Merv, in short, was a step too far. Indeed, General Sir Frederick Roberts, commander-in-chief of the Raj's armies, called the seizure of Merv 'the most important step ever made by Russia on her march towards India'.[16] And as if that wasn't worry enough for the Russophobes, the Russians were now building a railroad across Central Asia towards Merv, which would permit them to transport thousands of troops to that city – thus threatening Afghanistan – at the alarming speed of 15 miles an hour.

But the Russians were not completely oblivious to British concerns about their move on Merv, and in the autumn of 1884 they agreed to come together with their rival to form the Joint Afghan Boundary Commission, with a brief to establish once and for all the north-western boundary of Afghanistan. The gesture was well received in Calcutta and London, and the two sides agreed to meet on 13 October at the oasis of Sarakhs, south of Merv. But when Sir Peter Lumsden arrived to begin negotiations, he was told his Russian counterpart, General Zelenov, had been taken ill and could not come until the following spring. Meanwhile, Sir Peter could not help but notice the considerable Russian military presence in the area and correctly concluded that whatever the Tsar and his diplomats had in mind, the generals were intent on pushing the Russian frontier as close to Herat as possible before the commission could meet in the spring. When the Russians then seized the village of Panjdeh, between Merv and the Afghan border, and which, moreover, was claimed by Afghanistan, the die was cast. In India, General Roberts mobilised two army corps for the purpose of reinforcing Herat, the Royal Navy was put on worldwide alert to monitor all Russian warships, the War Office printed up official announcements of the outbreak of hostilities, and far off in America the first sentence of the lead story in the normally staid *New York Times*, under the headline ENGLAND AND RUSSIA TO FIGHT, was notably succinct: 'It is war'.[17]

But it was not war. In the end, cooler heads prevailed, not the least of which belonged to Abdur Rahman, the Afghan ruler, who happened to be visiting India at the time of the Panjdeh incident and was surprisingly sanguine when he heard Panjdeh had been overrun, with the loss of close to 800 lives. 'He begged me not to be troubled,' the Foreign Secretary to the Indian government wrote. 'He said that the loss of two hundred or even two thousand men was a mere nothing.' Lord Dufferin went on to praise Abdur Rahman as 'a prince of great capacity [whose] calm judgment' helped prevent what would otherwise have been 'a long and miserable war'.[18] When the Russians saw the dramatic response of the British to the seizure of Panjdeh, they realised they had overreached and withdrew to one mile west of the village to await the decisions of the Boundary Commission, which concluded its work in the summer of 1887 when both sides agreed to its recommendations.

This might have been the closing gambit of the Great Game – and it was for the westernmost parts of Central Asia – but as it happened the Game merely moved further east, thanks largely to two prominent new players: Tsar Nicholas II of Russia and the new viceroy, Lord Curzon. Nicholas II, who acceded to the throne in 1894, had expansionist impulses of his own, and they were greatly abetted by his minister of finance, Count Witte, who persuaded the Tsar that there was no reason why pieces of the crumbling Manchu Empire – especially Mongolia, Tibet and Sinkiang – could not be annexed by Russia as part of a scheme to extend the empire's influence deeper into Central Asia to the very edge of the Far East.

Enter George Nathaniel Curzon. Throughout the Great Game, two competing schools fought to dominate British foreign policy: the forward school and the school of what was called masterly inactivity.

The forward school argued that if Britain did not match Russia aggression for aggression, acquisition by acquisition, there were no limits to the Tsar's expansionist dreams. Moreover, Britain must be seen to be the Game's dominant player in the eyes of her Indian subjects and those in other client states, lest they have reason to doubt her resolve and be tempted to throw off her yoke and seek common cause with her enemies. The masterly inactivists claimed that aggression only begat more aggression, that the best way to check the Russian bear was to forge alliances with as many khans, shahs, emirs and tribal chiefs as they could win over, equip and train the armies of these key client states, and otherwise make conspicuous pledges of military support in the event of invasion: a show of force, in short, as opposed to the actual use of force. To the masterly inactivists, the forward schoolers were little more than a gang of sabre rattlers for whom a ten-pounder was the answer to every disagreement, while the forward schoolers regarded masterly inactivity as paralysis by another name.

If the forward school had not existed when George Curzon entered Parliament in 1887, he would have founded it. When he was still at Eton, aged eighteen, he already believed that 'the interests of England were opposed to those of Russia', as he wrote in a student essay, and that it might very well 'suit Russia to send out an army to watch our Indian frontier'. And he had no truck whatsoever with the do-nothing strategy, writing that he disagreed completely 'with those who decry British interference anywhere and extol the odious theory of sedentary and culpable inaction'.[19]

In 1888, aged twenty-nine, he set out to observe Russia up close as one of the first foreigners to ride the new railway Russia had built from the Caspian Sea to Samarkand, through many of its new possessions: Geok-Tepe, Ashkhabad, Merv, Bokhara, Samarkand and, when it was finished, as far as Tashkent. Everywhere Curzon went, there were military garrisons; he estimated that if Russia wanted to invade India using the new Trans-Caspian railway, she could amass as many as 100,000 troops – from the Caucasus, Central Asia and even a few from Siberia – on the border of Persia or Afghanistan in a matter of weeks. The railway, in short, had significantly changed the power dynamic in the region. 'This railway makes [the Russians] prodigiously strong,' Curzon wrote to a friend. 'And they mean business.'[20]

Curzon was not interested in merely influencing imperial policy, he was determined to make it. Though not yet thirty, he did not hide the fact that he intended to be viceroy one day, and he set out to burnish his credentials. The train journey and his first book were a good start, and they were followed by two other books, by one stint as deputy Secretary of State for India, and by a fact-finding visit in 1894 to the state of Chitral in the Hindu Kush, the centre of a minor Great Game skirmish. From Chitral Curzon went to India for briefings and concluded his trip with a flourish: an audience with the Emir of Afghanistan, preceded by Curzon entering Kabul with an escort of 200 Afghan cavalry and wearing an elaborate costume, parts of which had been purchased at a theatrical supply shop. Four years later Curzon became viceroy.

The masterly inactivists were dismayed, and several of them, including several lords, wrote to Curzon urging him not to overreach. 'Let me beg as a personal favour,' one peer wrote, 'that you will not make war on Russia in my life-time.' Another peer wrote: 'It will amuse you to hear that I am being told by the Anti-Forward Policy people that now I shall have as many wars as I want.' As one of Curzon's biographers later wrote: 'It cannot be said that these apprehensions were altogether without justification.'[21]

To be sure, Curzon came by his anti-Russian convictions and his overall geopolitical opinions honestly; no viceroy in living memory had travelled more extensively or had more in-depth, first-hand experience of the board on which the Great Game was played. If anything, he had perhaps seen too much, which, combined with a certain haughtiness and dismissive tendency, made him rigid and inflexible. 'There was no middle path for him between rigidity and collapse.'[22] Curzon knew he suffered from a surplus of self-regard, and in private he could be charmingly self-deprecating. He appreciated the advice he received from his nominal superior Lord George Hamilton, Secretary of State for India, that he should '[t]ry to suffer fools more gladly', and doubtless also agreed with his lordship's follow-on observation: 'They constitute the majority of mankind.'[23]

To give him credit, Curzon did not actively provoke the Russians, but neither did he overlook any provocations on their part. By the time Curzon arrived in India, in January 1899, the Game had moved still further east, and the focus had unexpectedly become the country of Tibet. Unexpectedly, because although Tibet bordered British India along more than 500 miles, that border consisted of the Himalayas, the highest mountains in the world. Moreover, the Russians had to date shown no interest in Tibet, which, in any case, was a semi-autonomous province of China (which oversaw Tibet's foreign policy), and above Tibet sat the province of Sinkiang, also part of China. In this part of Asia, then, there was a massive mountain range and two huge buffer states between India and any place in Russia's sphere of influence. Curzon, naturally, was disappointed, preferring 'a board which offered possibilities for a sudden, paralysing coup by his queen'.[24]

Beginning in May 1899, the board started looking more to Curzon's liking when rumours reached him of a visit by Russians to Lhasa, the Tibetan capital, the previous winter. 'There seems little doubt', he wrote to the Secretary of State for India that month, 'that Russian agents, and possibly even someone of Russian origin, have been at Lhasa, and I believe that the Tibetan government is coming to the conclusion that it will have to make friends with one or the other of the two Great Powers.'[25] This was pure Curzon; he must have known this was hyperbole, but he also knew that if he didn't exaggerate, elevating rumour into fact, he was unlikely to get the current government's attention, especially since that government was already deeply suspicious of his notoriously forward sympathies.

But in the end rumour was all Curzon or the British government ever got. Rumour and speculation, like so many moves of the Great Game, were part of every major decision of the entire Tibetan affair, both those made in India and ultimately those made in London. The notion of invading Tibet was prompted by rumours; the idea grew into a full-blown crisis thanks to rumours; and the invasion was ultimately approved and carried out based on rumours – the most compelling of which, that the Russians were arming the Tibetans, turned out to be pure fiction. In the words of one historian of the Raj, the entire Tibetan affair was 'an absurd response to a ragbag of rumours'.[26]

But how could it have been otherwise? None of the Gamers, Russian or British, knew anything about Tibet; almost no one around Curzon had ever been to Tibet; and senior officials in London knew even less. The result was an almost complete intelligence vacuum; *all* information about Tibet was rumour. Decisions, in short, either had to be postponed, awaiting good intelligence, or be made in the dark. Curzon was not inclined to wait; if rumour was all there was, it would have to suffice. 'Lack of exact knowledge had never been an impediment to Russophobe scaremongers in the past, and it did not stop Curzon . . .' Indeed, if anything rumours were preferable under the circumstances; facts could easily undermine Curzon's plans. '[Curzon] invoked that principle of the Great Game which was to act rather than to wait and see.'[27]

The rumour about Russians in Lhasa was soon followed by alarming reports of Tibetans in St Petersburg. The reports, in the *Journal de Saint-Pétersbourg* and later in the foreign press as well, were accurate; the Tsar did receive a delegation of Tibetans in June 1901 and again later that summer. The delegation delivered a letter from the Dalai Lama to the Tsar, and, according to one Russian diplomat, the leader of the delegation 'spoke with marked authority and expertise, and mightily pleased the Tsar . . .' The purpose of the visit was for the Tibetans 'to put out feelers and try to direct the attention of the Russian government to Tibet, and particularly to gain diplomatic support against China and Britain'.[28] While the Tsar does not appear to have been sympathetic to the overture, the mere presence of an official Tibetan delegation currying favour in Russia, something unprecedented in Tibetan history, was deeply troubling to Curzon, especially since the leader of the enterprise was none other than Kambo Agvan Dorjieff, a man very much on Curzon's radar.

Dorjieff, a Buryat Mongol, went to Tibet to study at a large monastery near Lhasa and eventually became a tutor and debating partner of the Dalai Lama. He first visited St Petersburg in 1898 when he met the Tsar – who gave Dorjieff a gold watch for the Dalai Lama – returning in 1900 (after a surreptitious visit to India). Then came the official visit with the delegation in 1901, which in turn was followed by yet another visit a year later, when Dorjieff was widely rumoured to be trying to conclude a secret treaty between Tibet and Russia. It was never determined exactly what Dorjieff was up to, but he was certainly a schemer and, as such, sure to arouse the suspicions of someone like Curzon, who knew the type, after all, for he was a consummate schemer himself. Indeed, while Curzon was genuinely alarmed by Dorjieff's activities, they also served his purposes, buttressing his case that something had to be done about the Russians. In the words of Younghusband's biographer, Curzon 'elevated [Dorjieff] to the position of Evil Genius at the Court of the Dalai Lama, two parts Rasputin to one part Macavity the Mystery Cat'.[29]

Dorjieff's 1902 trip coincided with a disturbing telegraph to Curzon on 2 August of that year from the British ambassador in Peking containing an extract from the China Times describing a secret agreement between Russia and China regarding Tibet. The most alarming detail was that China would 'relinquish her interest in Tibet to Russia', who would be allowed to station government officials in Tibet 'and control Tibetan affairs' in return for Russian pledges of military assistance to China in maintaining the 'integrity' of its empire. Curzon jumped on the news. 'I am myself a firm believer in the existence of a secret understanding, if not a secret treaty, between Russia and China about Tibet', he wrote to his predecessor, 'and, as I have said before, I regard it as a duty to frustrate their little game while there is yet time.'[30]

Quite apart from worrying about Russian, Chinese and Tibetan intrigues, Britain – and especially her viceroy – had her own problems with Tibet, all summarised in a lengthy dispatch to the British government in January 1903, which Curzon hoped would at long last prod London to do something about Tibet. The complaints were many: to begin with, it was simply foolish not to have any kind of official relations with a country the size of western Europe sharing a 550-mile border with India; Tibet continued to flout two treaties, one which had established the border between Tibet and Sikkim (a British possession) and the other forbidding tariffs on trade coming from India. Curzon then rehearsed what he called the considerable 'circumstantial evidence' about Russia's designs on Tibet, questioning 'the degree to which we can permit the influence of another great Power to be exercised for the first time in Tibetan affairs'; Curzon also made much of the fact that after failing to achieve satisfaction through regular channels, he had sent two letters to the Dalai Lama to request discussions on establishing diplomatic relations, both of which were returned unread. Curzon considered this a personal affront, especially after he learned that the Dalai Lama was apparently in regular correspondence with the Tsar. At the end of this dispatch, Curzon proposed that a mission should be sent to Lhasa to negotiate the border and trade matters, and that the negotiations 'should culminate in the appointment of a permanent British representative, Consular or Diplomatic, to reside at Lhasa'.[31]

When Russia firmly denied rumours that it had signed any treaties about Tibet – with China, Tibet or anyone else – and likewise denied rumours that it had agents in Tibet or was planning to send any, the viceroy was obliged to climb down from his demand for a mission to Lhasa. But both Curzon and the British government agreed that the trade and border issues should be addressed, and, accordingly, on 29 April a small mission was authorised to travel as far as Khamba Dzong and no further, just twelve miles over the border in Tibet. Curzon suspected, correctly, that the talks in Khamba Dzong would go nowhere, and with any luck authorisation for a mission to Lhasa would be sure to follow. His task now was to choose someone to head the mission, and he knew just the man.

In the autumn of 1889 Francis Younghusband took part in one of those remarkable meetings that occurred from time to time during the Great Game when the British and Russians encountered each other face-to-face somewhere in the vast Central Asian no-man's-land that was the Game's playing field. In this instance the meeting, cordial as these meetings usually were, took place in Hunza between Younghusband and Captain Grombtchevski, an ethnic Pole who was one of the Game's foremost Russian players. The two men calmly 'debated . . . in French the logistics of invading India', and then, at the end of their meeting, posed for a group photo Grombtchevski wanted to take with his new box camera.[32] Younghusband, who was a foot shorter than Grombtchevski and would be standing next to him in the photograph, found an ammunition box to stand on and then somehow manoeuvred a fallen tree into place in the foreground to completely obscure his impromptu stool. Thus could the British lion stand eye to eye in the photograph with the Russian bear.

Much to his chagrin, no doubt, Younghusband's height, 5 foot 5 inches, was usually the first thing people noticed about him, followed by his walrus moustache, and then, as one got closer, by his piercing blue eyes – some called them dark blue – and his bushy eyebrows. Younghusband was self-conscious about his diminutive stature because it belied the image of the daring adventurer he sought to project.

Francis Younghusband was a son of the Raj, born in Murree on the North-West Frontier in 1863. His father was a major general in the Royal Artillery; his uncle, Robert Shaw, was a tea planter turned explorer and the first westerner to enter Kashgar; and four of his brothers served in India, two becoming generals. He attended private school at Woolwich in Britain, where he was a champion runner, and graduated from the military academy at Sandhurst and was posted to India in 1882, at the age of nineteen.

Intrepid, unflappable, a tad reckless, always pushing himself, testing his limits, half in love with danger – Younghusband was the epitome of a thruster. He was happiest and never more alive than when he was alone, far from civilisation, pitting himself against the elements, whether a dust storm in the Gobi Desert, waist-deep snow in the Pamirs, or an impassable ice shelf on a remote pass in the Karakorams. 'It is a curious feeling,' he wrote, 'but when real difficulties seem to be closing around, your spirits rise. [D]ifficulties seem only to make you more and more cheery. Instead of depressing you, they only serve to brace up all your faculties to their highest pitch.'[33] Elsewhere Younghusband noted that 'the only drawback in such a life is the subsequent reaction when all is over and the monotonous round of ordinary existence oppresses one by its flatness and torpidity in comparison'.[34]

The men who served under Younghusband adored him, for his conspicuous courage, to be sure, but also for his even-handedness. He was 'very quiet, laconic, sturdily built', Captain O'Connor, his Tibetan translator, wrote of Younghusband. 'I never once saw him even for a moment ruffled, far less discomposed or perturbed by any circumstance or crisis we had to encounter. An imperturbable exterior covered a strong and steadfast character and most equable temperament.'[35]

Socially, Younghusband was shy, awkward, intense and private. Though he married, he considered himself unsuitable for the role of husband or even for ordinary friendship, noting in later years that he only ever opened up to his father and to his sister Emmie, with whom he had an unusually intimate bond. 'I find it very hard to face any strangers,' he wrote in his diary when he was thirty, 'and though I long not to be serious, I cannot be anything but extremely grave and feel that I am keeping others so.'[36] His shyness and reserve cost him what would have been the love of his life, one May Ewart, the daughter of friends of his parents living in the hill station of Kasauli. May and Francis became engaged in 1889, but he found himself incapable of 'show[ing] her any feeling. I stifle my ardent affection . . . and now I cannot show it and I am losing my darling May . . . all the time I am cold & stiff & formal.' One month later, she broke off the engagement. For his part, Younghusband wrote years later that in 'love I had none of the nerve I had in exploring and in dealing with wild peoples. I had very little social experience.'[37]

Younghusband met the woman he would marry, Helen Magniac, on the ship back from a stint he did as a reporter in South Africa. No one – least of all Helen herself – ever expected Miss Magniac to marry, and many of those who met the couple later wondered what Younghusband saw in her. To her credit, even Helen wondered, writing to him that his interest in her 'when there are so many charming girls about . . . alas! passes my comprehension'.[38] She was a hypochondriac, suffered from severe depression, and abhorred the thought of physical intimacy. Not even Patrick French, one of Younghusband's biographers, could explain her appeal. She may have been 'in the right place at the right time', he writes, 'but she was the wrong person'.[39] And he goes on: 'She was fatter, taller, and older than he was; had a doughy face and no interest in Asia or mountains . . . [and was] intensely snobbish.' This seems harsh, but in fact the record is not kind to Helen who appears to have had very few defenders. Of course, Younghusband was hardly perfect; he could be neglectful and impatient, insensitive and abrupt. In later years he and Helen were estranged, and he died in the arms of his mistress. Helen and Francis were married in 1897 and although she had insisted their marriage would have to be chaste – and Younghusband had acquiesced – her resolve was short-lived; within a year she became pregnant and gave birth to the couple's daughter.

Helen Magniac and marriage were far in the future when Francis Younghusband arrived in India to take up his posting in 1882, aged nineteen. Predictably, Younghusband was utterly bored with the life of a young officer in an Indian cantonment, with its endless drilling in the early mornings, long afternoons stuck in the barracks out of the stifling heat, late afternoons exercising the horses, and excruciating formal dinners where he was expected to charm his fellow officers' wives with his (non-existent) small talk. He managed to get leave and go exploring whenever he could, and then, in 1887, five years after he arrived in the subcontinent, he undertook a sensational, 4,000-mile journey that catapulted him overnight into the front ranks of British explorers and in a single stroke made him one of the foremost Great Gamers of his generation.

The magazine *Nature* called it 'one of the most remarkable [journeys] ever made' and contemporary newspapers compared the feat favourably with H. M. Stanley's discovery of the source of the Nile, noting wryly that far fewer lives were lost (none in fact).[40] While the climax of the famous journey occurred with the first crossing of the Mustagh Pass high in the Karakorams, it began 4,000 miles away in Peking when Younghusband was returning to India after a leave he had been given to explore Manchuria in response to rumours (untrue as usual) of Russian interest and possibly even a Russian presence in the Chinese province. Passing through Peking, Younghusband encountered an acquaintance, Mark Bell of the Royal Engineers, who was about to set off for India across China, and Younghusband asked if he could tag along. Bell suggested that a better use of Younghusband's time and talents would be to try a parallel, more northern route, crossing the Gobi Desert, thence over the Himalayas to Kashmir, a route never before travelled by a European, except perhaps for Marco Polo in certain sections. Younghusband got permission to extend his leave, from the viceroy himself, and began making arrangements.

The night before his departure Younghusband was invited to dinner by Sir John Walsham, the British envoy to Peking. When Lady Walsham asked him after dinner to trace his proposed route on a map, the audacity of what he was planning struck him forcefully as he began 'to appreciate the task I had before me. I had never been in a desert and here were a thousand miles or so of one to be crossed.' And then there were the Himalayas to consider, 'to cross which had previously been considered a journey in itself'. If he had had 'a companion upon whom I could rely', he wrote, 'or one good servant whom I could trust to stand by me, the task would have seemed easy in comparison. But all was utterly dark before me.'[41]

Younghusband left Peking on 4 April 1887, and was gone for nearly seven months. He entered the Gobi on 26 April and while there was water and vegetation at first, after a few weeks there was nothing but rock and sand – and sandflies. At one point he and his two companions, a Chinese servant and a Chinese cook cum groom (for the camels), travelled for over a thousand miles without seeing a single house. In the end they crossed the Gobi, 1,255 miles, in seventy days. In Yarkand, their next stop, there was a letter from Mark Bell urging the party to cross the Himalayas via the Mustagh Pass as it had never been explored before. Younghusband was about to discover why.

At 19,000 feet (5,791m), the Mustagh Pass sits in the Karakorams on the edge of K2, the second highest mountain in the world, marking the watershed between Central Asia and India. As he approached the northern side of the range, Younghusband rushed up a small rise just above a mountain lake and got his first view of the way forward. 'Before me rose tier after tier of stately mountains . . . peaks of untainted snow whose summits reach the heights of 25,000, 26,000 and in one supreme case, 28,000 feet [8,535m] above sea level . . .' Gazing upon the scene and 'realizing that this seemingly impregnable array must be pierced and overcome, seemed to put the iron into my soul and stiffen all my energies for the task before me'.[42]

Somewhere in that bewildering mass of ice and snow and stone stood Mustagh Peak, the 'ice mountain', and the pass that led over it into Kashmir and then to India. Climbing the north side to the top of the pass was 'easy enough', Younghusband noted, but when they reached the top and looked down '[t]here was nothing but a sheer precipice'. He confessed that had he been alone he 'never would have attempted the descent'. He had no climbing experience, no equipment, 'not even any proper boots', and no idea how to proceed. What saved the day, it turned out, 'was my holding my tongue. I kept quite silent as I looked over the pass, and waited to hear what the men had to say about it.' The men looked to Younghusband for guidance, and 'imagining that an Englishman never went back from an enterprise once started on, took it as a matter of course, that, as I gave no order to go back, I meant to go on.' And so they descended gingerly, 'knowing that if we slipped . . . we would roll down and over the precipice into eternity'. It did not help matters that halfway down, a Ladakhi servant and 'born hill-man thoroughly acquainted with Himalayan travel' was too afraid to continue and turned back. 'It rather upset me seeing a born hill-man so affected, but I pretended not to care a bit and laughed it off, *pour encourager les autres*, as the thing had to be done.'[43] Six hours later, the thing was done – and has only been done three other times in the more than 130 years since. When Younghusband reached the bottom of the pass and looked back, he said that 'it seemed utterly impossible that any man could have come down such a place'.[44]

The crossing of inner Manchuria, the Gobi Desert and the formidable Karakorams via Mustagh – one critic called forcing the pass 'taking lunatic risks' – was one of the great feats of exploration of the nineteenth century and would, in a few months, turn the twenty-four-year-old Francis Younghusband into a celebrity and something very close to a living legend.[45] He was invited to address the Royal Geographical Society in London, where he was elected its youngest member ever at the age of twenty-four and where he later became the youngest person ever to be awarded its prestigious Founder's Medal. He dined with the famous African explorer Henry Morton Stanley. His account of his journey, *The Heart of a Continent*, was reprinted four times in the first year of its publication and remained in print for nearly a hundred years. Curiously, although he was justly celebrated for the Mustagh crossing and later his tireless support of the Everest expeditions, Younghusband himself was not much of a climber or mountaineer. 'A scientific gentleman once asked [me]', he wrote, 'what was the chief effect of being a long time at high altitudes, and I told him the principal effect was a desire to get to a lower altitude as soon as possible.'[46]

While Younghusband's reputation continued to grow in the years after this triumph, his career in India waxed and waned. At times he was sent on thrilling Great Game missions, but at other times he was either sent back to his regiment where he endured the 'arid and meaningless life' of a cavalry officer, 'spending hour after hour looking out for microscopic atoms of dust on my men's uniforms', or appointed to minor posts where he was largely desk-bound, in one case obliged to study several volumes of the Penal Code due to a requirement that he sit for the Political Service exam.[47]

During these years Younghusband met Curzon on several occasions, the first time in London in 1892 when a young Curzon was deputy Secretary of State for India. Younghusband found him well informed about the Russians, more so than many people in India. A second, much more substantial meeting occurred two years later when Younghusband was stationed in Chitral and Curzon came through on his fact-finding tour of the subcontinent, leaving Younghusband with mixed feelings. He was 'both a pleasure and a trial', Younghusband remembered. 'We resented Curzon's cocksuredness. His manner grated on us on the frontier as all through his life it grated on the British public.' Younghusband found Curzon 'smart and clever and wonderfully clear-headed and strong, too, but there seems so little real depth and so little sympathy. He will, though, undoubtedly rise to great eminence because he has indomitable energy and industry . . .'[48]

After he became viceroy, Curzon kept in touch with Younghusband and, in a singular honour, even invited him and his wife twice to Simla, summer home of the British Raj. During these years, Younghusband came to hold Curzon in increasingly high regard, noting decades later that his father and George Curzon were the two people who had done the most for him in his life. For his part the viceroy clearly regarded Younghusband as something of a soulmate. Though Curzon was not a military man – and did not understand military matters – he too fancied himself an explorer, and Younghusband's Russophobia was, if anything, even stronger than Curzon's. Indeed, if the forward school of British diplomacy had had an advance guard, it would have been led by Francis Younghusband. When it came time to choose someone to lead the Tibet Frontier Commission, in May 1903, Curzon did not have to look far.

'[I] was leading a gilded life of perfect security and much pomposity,' Younghusband remembered, 'when in early May I received a telegram ordering me to proceed at once to Simla. And I was then told I was to lead a mission to Tibet.'[49] As the two men watched horse races, Curzon explained the mission and, as Younghusband wrote to his father, the viceroy then added that 'there was no man in India he could trust better than me to carry out his plans'.[50] Younghusband was flattered and relished the prospects and the challenge. 'Hardship and dangers I knew I should have. But men always do prefer risk to ease. Comfort only lulls and softens their capacities, whereas danger tautens every faculty.' As he wrote to his father, 'This really is a magnificent business that I have dropped in for.'[51]

While he was proud to be chosen, he was also puzzled. Curzon 'was risking much in selecting me', he wrote. 'I had never seen a Tibetan or served on the North-Eastern frontier . . . I might make a hideous mess of it with the Tibetans. I quite saw the risks that Lord Curzon was taking, and this made me all the keener to justify his choice.'[52] In one sense, it is easy to understand why Younghusband might wonder what qualified him for the position, but on the other hand, it is entirely possible – and quite in character – that Curzon did not select Younghusband so much for his strengths as he did for one of his greatest weaknesses: his impetuosity. It was no secret to those close to him that Curzon's endgame for the Tibetan affair was for British troops to march on Lhasa and wrest some kind of treaty from the Dalai Lama; nothing less would suffice. On the other hand, given geopolitical and diplomatic niceties, Curzon was not in a position to order such an action, he would have to publicly disavow it if it occurred, and if the colonel ignored orders and undertook it on his own, such a move could very well cost Younghusband his career. To get the job done properly, Curzon needed a man who was even more of a Russophobe than he was, someone he could count on to exceed his authority and get British soldiers closer to Lhasa. If this calculation did in fact play any part in Curzon's decision to select Younghusband for the mission, then he would not be disappointed.

Sometime around midday on 7 July 1903, the citizens of Khamba Dzong – a district centre twelve miles north of Sikkim on the Tibetan plateau – would have spotted a line of 200 soldiers of the 32nd Pioneers regiment filing out of the gorge just below the town's massive fort and setting up camp on the nearby plain. For nearly all of the Tibetans this would have been the first time they had ever laid eyes on a westerner (locally known as foreign devils). Captain Bethune and his largely Sikh retinue, the advance guard of the Tibet Frontier Commission, had crossed the border that morning in carefully calculated disregard of express orders from the British government.

The man doing the calculating, and especially the disregarding, was Francis Younghusband, one of the two Frontier Commissioners, who had received specific instructions not to enter Tibet until he was assured that a negotiating party had assembled at Khamba Dzong and that the members of that party were of sufficient stature to conduct negotiations. Since the Tibetans had no interest in discussing the frontier and were, in fact, adamantly opposed to allowing any foreigners into Tibet, Younghusband rightly suspected that unless he forced the issue, no Tibetan officials were ever going to come to Khamba Dzong to meet him. Or, if they did, it would not be to discuss the border but to tell him to get back behind it. Thus he chose to interpret his instructions not to proceed 'as personal to my self', he wrote to his father, 'that is to say I'm going to read the "you" in the telegram as meaning F. E. Y. only and I am going to send on the escort'.[53] The escort were told to impress upon any officials they might meet the elevated status of their leader, and that he would only cross the border to meet Tibetans of equal or greater status.

It turned out three officials were waiting for the colonel, two Tibetans and one Chinese, and Captain Bethune dispatched a runner to inform Younghusband, who decided to keep the men waiting for ten days while he collected orchids and primulas and read Tennyson. The longer he waited, he reasoned, the more serious the situation would become and the more eager the officials would be to negotiate and avoid a crisis. Finally, on 18 July 1903, Younghusband and a small armed escort of mounted soldiers descended the northern slope of the Kangra La and proceeded slowly out onto the vast Tibetan plateau. Thus did the Tibet Frontier Commission officially begin its disastrous mission to Tibet.

There was a delegation waiting for Younghusband, with whom he conducted a brief, unsatisfactory exchange. In the meeting Younghusband made a formal speech outlining the Indian govern-ment's principal grievances: that Tibet was actively restricting trade with India, that some Tibetans had moved some stones marking the boundary with Sikkim, and that the viceroy's letters to the Dalai Lama (about these and other offences) had been returned unopened. Unsure of who was the decision-maker among the group, if anyone, Younghusband provided the delegation with a written copy of the grievances in the event they needed to be passed up the chain of command. 'But they could not have got rid of a viper with greater haste than they got rid of that paper,' he wrote later.[54]

The Tibetans were completely unfazed; there could be no discus-sions on these or any other issues until the commission and its escort removed themselves from Tibetan territory and returned to Sikkim. Moreover, the officials took issue with the size of Younghusband's escort. 'I explained that it was merely the escort which was becoming to my rank,' Younghusband noted. But the Tibetans countered that they had been led to believe 'that the negotiations . . . were to be friendly, and so they themselves had brought no armed escort. I replied that the negotiations certainly were to be friendly and that if I had had any hostile intentions, I should have brought many more than 200 men.'[55]

The discussions were not off to a good start. 'These so-called delegates never came near us again at Khamba Jong [Dzong],' Younghusband wrote, 'but shut themselves up in the fort and sulked.'[56] In his frustration at the ensuing stalemate, Younghusband forgot his wedding anniversary. 'My precious darling,' he wrote to his wife one month later, 'I cannot tell you how grieved and vexed I am that I should have let our wedding day go by without noticing it.'[57]

A stalemate ensued for several weeks. Younghusband dismissed suggestions that he temporarily pull his forces back to Sikkim where the weather was warmer, saying that would only 'elate the Tibetans'.[58] Things looked up briefly in late August when a group of Tibetans from the Tashilhunpo monastery, representing the Panchen Lama, the second highest spiritual leader in the country, arrived for talks, but it was soon apparent that the head abbot only wanted to talk science, *Tibetan* science, as it turned out. The abbot himself was 'a charming old gentleman', Younghusband wrote, but his 'intellectual capacity' was limited. 'He corrected me when I inadvertently let slip some observations implying that the earth was round, and [he] assured me that when I had lived longer in Tibet and had more time to study, I should find that it was not round, but flat, and not circular, but triangular, like the bone of a shoulder of mutton.'[59]

The situation grew more intolerable by the day. Younghusband forwarded to Curzon every rumour he could find about Russian meddling, no matter how preposterous, and otherwise tried every means he could think of to provoke his own government to authorise the use of force or, failing that, to provoke the Tibetan government into doing something foolish. He sent one of his officers, Frederick Bailey, with a troop of sepoys to a nearby village where the residents were said to be hostile. 'We want to start a row,' Bailey told his parents, 'and are going to send patrols [out] like this.'[60] One of the villagers seized the bridle of Bailey's horse to stop him from advancing, and Bailey threatened to shoot him. The man begged Bailey to turn back, saying that if he continued all the villagers would have their heads cut off. On another occasion Bailey arrested several Tibetans and brought them back to camp as prisoners. But there was no reaction from the Tibetans.

Meanwhile, Younghusband received reports that 2,600 Tibetan troops had assembled at Phari, on the road to Lhasa, and that they 'were quite prepared to go to war'. As a precaution, he strengthened his escort by another hundred men, and he sent a report back to the viceroy pointing out that he had now been in Khamba Dzong three months 'without being able even to commence negotiations' and that from the Tibetans he had met with nothing but 'pure obstruction'.[61] And then he added: 'I was informed by a trustworthy person that he was convinced the Tibetans would do nothing till they were made to and a situation had arisen.'[62]

Situations could be arranged, and in the end Younghusband got two, one arranged by himself and the other a gift from some Tibetan yak rustlers. After several frustrating weeks in Khamba Dzong, Younghusband decided he needed better intelligence about what the Tibetans were saying and doing behind the scenes. To that end he directed Frank O'Connor to recruit two Sikkimese men to act as spies for the British. O'Connor dispatched the two men and became concerned two weeks later when they had not returned. On 6 August word was received that the two spies had been captured and imprisoned, whereupon Younghusband gave the Tibetan government ten days to release the two prisoners. When there was no response, Younghusband wrote to Curzon, suggesting the government of India 'may wish to take more special notice of the case'.[63]

It was just the provocation both Curzon and Younghusband had been waiting for – one that Curzon had even privately urged Younghusband to 'manufacture' if necessary – as a way to end the impasse. Curzon eagerly passed on the news in a telegram to the Secretary of State for India, citing this 'most conspicuous proof of the hostility of the Tibetan government and of their contemptuous disregard for the usages of civilisation' in arresting two British subjects and sending them to Lhasa where 'it is credibly asserted, [they] have been tortured and killed'.[64] In fact the men had been neither tortured nor killed, were released unharmed sometime later, and reported that they had been well treated.

The incident was not perfect. Neither Younghusband nor Curzon could ever explain, for example, how the presence of two British agents spying on Tibetans constituted an affront against the *British* government. Nor could they explain how the subsequent arrest of the two men constituted Tibetan provocation, as they claimed, instead of being merely what most nations did when they discovered spies in their midst. Indeed, most countries executed spies in such circumstances. In the end the Secretary of State for India did not take the bait, citing the Cabinet's 'strong and unanimous feeling against any permanent entanglement in Tibet'.[65]

A few weeks later, however, in early November, there was a second situation, and while decidedly less robust than the first, this one proved decisive. It seems that some Tibetan troops had absconded with a handful of Nepalese yaks that had wandered across the border into Tibet. In Curzon's excited telegram to the Cabinet, this frontier spat became 'an overt act of hostility' in which 'Tibetan troops . . . attacked Nepalese yaks on the frontier and carried many of them off'.[66] The yak-rustling bombshell apparently carried the day, for the same government that a few weeks earlier had been utterly opposed to any permanent entanglement in Tibet now telegrammed Curzon that '[i]n view of the recent conduct of the Tibetans, His Majesty's Government feel that it would be impossible not to take action, and they accordingly sanction the advance of the Mission to Gyantse', halfway to Lhasa.[67] Curzon immediately recalled Younghusband to Simla for urgent consultations. The mighty British Empire, it seemed, was going to war because some Tibetan soldiers had run off with half-a-dozen Nepalese yaks that did not belong to them.

Newly arrived in Simla, Younghusband had a private meeting with the viceroy, a meeting, he wrote later, that was classic Curzon.

> On arrival I had a thoroughly characteristic interview with him. He first asked me to describe the situation. I did so. He then asked what I would propose to do now. I said that I did not believe that we should do any business unless we went to Lhasa itself; at any rate we ought to go to Gyantse, half way. He raised every objection. We might have the whole country up [in arms]. We would require a considerably increased escort. How should we get them across the Himalayas, how would we get supplies, where would we find transport? Every objection he could think of he raised . . . [But] when I attended a meeting of Council the next day I found he had precisely the same views as my own and pounced on any member who raised the objections he [himself] had [raised].[68]

The meeting the next day was effectively a council of war. Younghusband sat between Lord Kitchener, commander-in-chief of Indian armed forces on one side, and Lord Curzon on the other, with an assortment of other senior officials of the Raj all around the table. The purpose of the meeting was to plan the invasion of Tibet, although no one called it an invasion, either then or later. It was officially still the Tibet Frontier Commission, albeit a commission which, in the considered opinion of the assembled notables, apparently needed the protection of 1,100 armed soldiers (known as the 'escort'), two machine guns (firing 700 rounds per minute) and four cannons.

The mandarins in London were naturally suspicious of both Curzon and Younghusband, and their telegram approving an advance as far as Gyantse went on to state that '[HMG] are of the opinion that this step should not be allowed to lead to occupation or to permanent intervention in Tibetan affairs in any form. The advance should be made for the sole purpose of obtaining satisfaction . . .'[69] Unfortunately, just how that satisfaction was to be obtained was not spelled out, which was deeply worrying to John Brodrick, the Secretary of State for India, who immediately wrote to Curzon to emphasise just 'how little appetite there is in England at this moment for another little war *of any description*' (italics added).[70] But the damage had already been done; Younghusband was on his way to Lhasa.

On 13 December Younghusband reached the top of the Jelep La, the 14,009-foot (4,270m) pass separating Sikkim from Tibet. Spread out along the route to the Chumbi Valley, in front of and behind him, were 10,091 porters and labourers, 7,096 mules, 5,234 bullocks, 1,513 Tibetan yaks, 1,372 pack ponies, 185 riding ponies, 138 buffaloes, 6 camels and 2 zebrules (half zebra, half donkey) – nearly half the animals would die along the way – in addition to the more than 1,100 troops, mostly Sikhs and Gurkhas with a few British officers in overall command.

The first stop was the village of Yatung, which sat behind a stout wall that blocked the road from Sikkim, and soon after entering Tibetan territory the group was met by emissaries from Yatung with three requests. The first was to ask the colonel and his troops to retreat back behind the border, promising negotiations as the reward. The colonel refused. The second was to ask Younghusband to remain where he was until such time as negotiators could be sent from Lhasa, which Younghusband knew would take two to three months. The colonel refused again. The third was to ask the colonel what he would do if he found the massive gate in the Yatung wall closed to him. The colonel said he would blow it open, pointing to one of his 10-pounders. In the end, the gate to Yatung was found open, and the troops and baggage train marched on into the beautiful Chumbi Valley without incident.

The commission expected its first real resistance would occur 40 miles further into Tibet, at the imposing fortress known as Phari Dzong, which sat on a ridge overlooking the road to Gyantse and Lhasa. But when the gates of the fort opened, hundreds of smiling, unarmed Tibetans poured forth, sticking out their tongues in the traditional friendly greeting, promising not to fight. General James Macdonald, the head of the military contingent, was glad to have avoided a confrontation, but a number of his Sikh and Gurkha soldiers grumbled at the lost opportunity to show their mettle. For his part, Younghusband, head of the political delegation, was greatly encouraged that so far the mission had proceeded without violence. He was deeply annoyed, however, when Macdonald chose to occupy the fort, which while it was sound military strategy, seemed an unnecessarily provocative move for a mere frontier commission.

From Phari Dzong, the mission moved on an additional 20 miles to the godforsaken hamlet of Tuna, crossing the Tang La. For reasons no one understood, the colonel proposed to spend the winter at Tuna before advancing on Gyantse. Younghusband himself described Tuna as 'the filthiest place I have ever seen', proclaimed its immediate surroundings 'miserable in the extreme',[71] and his officers agreed, one of them calling it simply 'one of the most miserable and unin-viting spots on the face of the globe'.[72] Younghusband and his officers were offered houses in the tiny village, but the buildings were so dirty and foul-smelling, the men chose to stay in their tents instead, in spite of the biting cold wind.

General Macdonald considered Tuna spectacularly unsuitable for a winter camp; it was 30 miles from the nearest tree, three miles from the closest water, 15,000 feet (4,570m) above sea level (just short of the height of Mont Blanc), consisted of a total of three buildings, and was completely exposed out on the Tibetan plateau, where the sun seared the skin during the day, the cold caused frostbite at night (the men slept with their rifle bolts inside their sleeping bags) and the wind was strong enough to blow a man off his horse. Macdonald urged Younghusband to set up camp 60 miles to the rear, in the lower, warmer Chumbi Valley, with its scrub forests (for fuel) and pasturage for the horses and pack animals. When Younghusband refused, Macdonald reluctantly consented to leave a small defensive force behind in Tuna and, after 'a blazing row' with Younghusband, he withdrew the main body of his troops back to the valley. Writing to his wife that night, Younghusband observed that he had 'pitched into [Macdonald] harder than I have ever pitched into anybody . . . But somehow I felt with a rigid man like that I had to lay into him like I would into a donkey.'[73]

The two leaders were ill-matched. Younghusband was bold, decisive, a risk-taker; Macdonald was nervous, vacillating and cautious. Younghusband called the general a wet blanket and 'an old stick in the mud' and not-so-privately believed him to be one of the greatest obstacles to the success of the mission.[74] Behind his back Macdonald's officers referred to him as 'Retiring Mac' for his excessive caution. One Captain Prescott wrote to his wife that 'General Macdonald is losing his nerve . . . He is not quite what everyone expects. He has a weak-looking face, is absolutely run by his staff, who are a poor lot, and smokes cigarettes till he is sick.'[75] Younghusband's letters home at this time are full of harangues about Macdonald and his timidity; he acts 'as if the Tibetans were commanded by a Napoleon'.[76]

In his defence, Macdonald executed the mission with a bare minimum of British and Indian casualties, insisted on respecting the sanctity of monasteries (which many of the soldiers were keen to loot), took good care of his men, treated Tibetan prisoners with exemplary courtesy and respect, and had excellent battlefield instincts. If he had not had the misfortune to be paired with the dashing, reckless, colourful Younghusband – whose dash and brio, it must be said, were superb copy for the mission's five embedded journalists – Macdonald would doubtless have fared better in the invasion narrative.

It was after Macdonald had pulled back to Chumbi that the colonel ran out of patience and conducted his daring, abortive visit to the camp at Guru and then, after being rebuffed, settled in for three long months at Tuna. Eleven sepoys died of pneumonia that winter; one Mr Lewis of the postal department had to have both feet amputated due to frostbite and died thereafter; numerous camp followers deserted; indigestion and bronchial complaints (due to the altitude) were rife; the wind blew mercilessly; and blizzards covered the camp from time to time in several inches of snow. Every two weeks or so a deputation rode over from Guru, often led by the Lhasa General himself, to make the standard you-must-return-to-Yatung demand – and received the standard response.

By the end of March General Macdonald had moved his troops over the Jelep La and on up to Tuna, a massive logistical effort involving close to 10,000 people, an average of eight porters for every member of the expedition. One entire team of porters was tasked with carrying poles for the telegraph line the mission erected as they advanced into Tibet. It has been observed that while British labour union rules at the time stipulated that bricklayers could not carry a load over fourteen pounds, the poles the porters carried, two or three men per pole, weighed ninety pounds each. An oft-repeated story goes that one day two lamas were watching the post office engineers erecting the line, and they asked the engineer in charge, Mr Truninger, what the wire was for. He answered that the British had such poor maps of Tibet they were regularly losing their way, and as they hoped to leave Tibet as soon as possible, they would need this wire to find their way back to India. Mr Truninger's remark is credited by some as responsible for the curious fact that the Tibetans never once tried to disrupt the telegraph line.

With the arrival of the troops at Tuna, the stage was now set for the advance to Gyantse, 60 miles further into Tibet and the point beyond which the mission did not have permission to go. Six inches of snow fell on the night of 30 March, but the morning of the 31st dawned clear and sunny, and the men were ready to move out by 7.30. The soldiers were in high spirits, relieved to be on the move again after three months of waiting in Chumbi and Tuna, and they were particularly excited at the prospect of seeing action before the day was over. There were between 1,000 and 1,500 armed Tibetans waiting for them at Guru, after all, the next town along the route, and the Tibetans had orders to prevent the British from advancing any further. Even so, the men knew the prospects of a real fight were slim; the Tibetans were 'armed' with spears, broad swords, flintlocks and matchlocks (the guns required reloading after every shot), and they had twice made identical threats about stopping the mission, at Yatung and later at Phari Fort, and then simply stepped aside and let the British pass. It was also known that the Tibetans, like the British forces, had been issued orders not to fire unless fired upon. Macdonald's men were prepared to be disappointed.

The army covered the 10 miles to Guru in four hours, arriving just outside the village at 11.30. A long, low wall extended from the bottom of a ridge on the right, ran across the main road to Gyantse, and continued for several hundred feet on the left in the direction of a nearby lake. The Tibetans were massed along the wall and in some hastily assembled stone fortifications, called sangars, just behind the wall. As Younghusband and Macdonald approached, the Lhasa General rode out to meet them, and the two parties sat down to talk. The general made the customary demands and Younghusband the customary refusals, and the colonel then asked the general to move his troops so his men could advance. The general replied that his men would not move and also that they would not resist.

Younghusband gave the Tibetans fifteen minutes to move out of the way, during which time his men slowly surrounded the Tibetans on three sides and brought up their two Maxim machine guns and their cannons. After the deadline had elapsed, Macdonald twice asked Younghusband for permission to commence firing, but the colonel refused. Instead, he gave orders for the men to forcibly disarm the enemy, and the Sikhs and Gurkhas moved in to wrest their weapons, valuable family heirlooms in some cases, away from the Tibetans. Tempers flared, numerous scuffles broke out, the tension quickly mounted – and then a single shot rang out.

In the numerous subsequent accounts of what happened at Guru, both sides accused the other side of firing first and triggering the melee. The Tibetans claimed they were fired on, unprovoked, by the British and responded in self-defence. The British claimed they were fired on and attacked with swords by the Tibetans as they tried to disarm them. Several accounts, by Younghusband and by two journalists, later added the detail that it was the Lhasa General himself who started the action by grabbing his revolver and shooting off the jaw of a sepoy who was trying to restrain the general's horse. While there are disagreements about how the incident began, both sides agree that what occurred next was nothing short of a massacre.

From as close as twenty yards, sepoys fired their rifles into a large grey mass of Tibetans huddled together at the wall, their numbers swelled by soldiers routed earlier from the sangars. At the wall itself both sides fired at each other at point-blank range, but the Tibetans had to reload after every round and were lucky to get off even one shot whereas every British soldier, with his bolt-action repeating rifle, was found to have fired more than twelve rounds. While scores of Tibetans died from close-in fighting near the wall, hundreds more were mowed down by the two machine guns which between them fired just over 1,400 rounds. Remarkably, many of the Tibetans did not even try to flee but walked slowly off the battlefield, even as the Maxims were still firing, stunned at the scale of carnage wrought by modern weaponry and also stunned by the failure of the amulets they wore which, according to their lamas, would protect the soldiers from bullets. The lieutenant in charge of one of the machine guns wrote to his father that 'I got so sick of the slaughter that I ceased fire, though the General's order was to make as big a bag as possible. I hope I shall never have to shoot down men walking away again.'[77]

Those Tibetans who did try to flee did not fare much better, pursued on horseback and cut down or else felled by machine-gun fire or shrapnel from the cannons. 'The mob [at the wall] surged to the rear,' a British doctor noted, 'and, throwing away their arms, broke and ran as fast as they could . . .' As the Tibetans fled through this 'zone of fire [they] sank quietly down, riddled by the hail of our bullets and shattered by the shrapnel of the mountain batteries bursting over them, and perished almost to a man. It was all over in about ten minutes, but in that time the flower of the Lhasa army had perished.'[78]

In fact, the fighting lasted closer to five minutes than ten; one estimate even put the duration as low as two minutes, the length of time it took the Maxims to fire the 1,400 rounds whose casings were found beneath the two guns after the battle. In that time, somewhere between 600 and 700 Tibetans were killed, including the Lhasa General and several other senior officers, and another 200 were wounded, twenty of whom later died. The British suffered half-a-dozen wounded and no fatalities. 'It was nothing but pure butchery,' Younghusband wrote to his father that evening, and in a letter to Helen he wrote: 'I have had an absolutely miserable day.'[79]

Even before the machine guns stopped, a temporary dressing station had been set up on the field to tend to the wounded – the Indian soldiers initially used their own field-dressings to patch up the Tibetan casualties – and before long a field hospital was treating patients. The Tibetans fully expected to be shot – it's what they would have done to their prisoners, they cheerfully assured those attending on them – and were shocked and confused by the kindness of their captors. 'The Tibetans showed great gratitude for what we did,' Younghusband wrote later, 'though they failed to understand why we should try to take their lives one day and try to save them the next.' The British were impressed at the courage and stoicism of their prisoners, one of whom, a double amputee, joked that he guessed he would have to be a hero in the next battle because he could no longer run away.

The captured Tibetans were well looked after. 'We made the prisoners work but paid them for it,' Younghusband wrote, 'till they were so comfortable that they asked not to be set free.'[80] The British eventually released all their prisoners, save for the most senior ones, sending each man home with five rupees and a pack of cigarettes.

Although it was only the first of several pitched battles against the Tibetans, the encounter at Guru was conclusive. The sheer scale of the Tibetan defeat – the absurdly lopsided casualty figures, the fact that the battle was over in minutes – established beyond any reasonable doubt that no matter how many soldiers the Dalai Lama sent against them, the British would prevail in virtually any encounter. For all practical purposes, after Guru the British could go anywhere they pleased and do whatever they wanted in Tibet. The only real question now was what exactly did the British want?

For Younghusband, the answer was simple: he had been convinced from the outset that the only way to resolve the Tibetan problem was to march on Lhasa and negotiate an agreement with the Dalai Lama. Privately, Curzon held the same view, but officially he was obliged to execute the policy of His Majesty's Government, which in turn was obliged to consider the sensitivities of the Russians who, while their supposed rival in Tibet, were also an important ally on the European front throughout this period, having common cause with the British when it came to countering Germany's growing naval expansion and thwarting French designs on the Middle East. The British government, as its telegram had revealed, was in fact deeply conflicted about the whole Tibetan affair. While the mission had been inspired largely by rumours of Russian meddling – though this reason was never stated officially – as time went on and no Russian weapons or advisers or any other signs of Russian influence were found, the mission increasingly risked becoming an embarrassment, another example of imperial overreach, especially as it was being led by that consummate overreacher himself, Francis Younghusband, egged on, as if that were necessary, by the viceroy. After the slaughter at Guru, closely covered in the British press via regular dispatches from the five embedded journalists, much of the Cabinet in London and much of the British public became convinced that the sooner the mission could be withdrawn from Tibet the better.

On 5 April, after tending to the Tibetan wounded, the mission set out on the 60-mile march to Gyantse. They encountered resistance at Red Idol Gorge where several hundred Tibetans fired down on the column as it wound its way through the defile, but once again the invaders prevailed after sepoys stormed the heights and drove the Tibetans off. Two hundred Tibetans were killed, and three sepoys were wounded.

Three days later, on 11 April, the mission reached Gyantse where they were expecting a stiff fight to take the massive fort and adjoining monastery on top of the hill that dominated the town. But as the column arrived at the fort, the commandant hurried out to meet its two leaders and begged for their help; he informed them that he could not surrender the fort or he would have his head cut off but he also could not defend it as all the soldiers had run away. So he wondered if perhaps the British could go ahead and settle in at Gyantse and just pretend the fort wasn't there. The British could not, but after Macdonald sent a party to confirm the fort was indeed deserted, he decided not to occupy it.

Before long Gyantse, beyond which the mission did not have permission to proceed, began to feel like Khamba Dzong all over again: days filled waiting in vain for the Tibetans to show up and negotiate. After eleven such days, Younghusband had had enough, and he cabled the government of India on 22 April for permission to march on Lhasa. 'No result will be obtained', he wrote, 'until [the] power of [the] Lhasa monks is thoroughly broken.'[81] While he was waiting for a response, the colonel received disturbing reports of Tibetans massing along the route to the capital, presumably to oppose his advance, and he decided to send Colonel Brander and over 300 sepoys 40 miles beyond Gyantse to the Karo La, the next-to-last pass before Lhasa, to engage the enemy and clear the way for an advance that had not yet been authorised.

It was a supremely audacious move, even for the impetuous Younghusband who had no authority to make such a decision, a move he took moreover without consulting either Curzon or Macdonald and that could easily have ended his career. When he learned about it, Macdonald was furious and immediately wrote a note recalling Brander, but Younghusband instructed the rider delivering the message to take his time. And he added a note of his own to Brander: 'On political grounds I would have the strongest objection to your returning, unless the enemy have so increased in strength that the result of a conflict would be doubtful.'[82] The acting viceroy, Lord Ampthill (Curzon was on home leave in London), cabled the government that Younghusband was 'going off the rails' but before the wrath of Macdonald, Ampthill or the government could come down on Younghusband, the Tibetans did the colonel a great favour by choosing that moment to attack the British camp at Gyantse, now seriously undermanned after the departure of Brander's detachment.[83]

After fighting off the attackers, Younghusband turned the unprovoked assault to his advantage, seizing the moment to drive his agenda home – and to cover his backside – by again demanding, somewhat intemperately, that he be given permission to proceed to Lhasa. He asked the government to keep in mind that

I have now been ten months in Tibet, that I have been met by nothing but insults the whole time in spite of the extreme forbearance I have shown, and that I have now been deliberately attacked . . . Now that the Tibetans have thrown down the gauntlet, I trust that [the] Government will take such action as will prevent the Tibetans ever again treating [a] British representative as I have been treated.[84]

Privately, a relieved Younghusband cabled Curzon that the 'Tibetans as usual have played into our hands'.[85]

For the moment, the great bravery of the small defending force at Gyantse and the spectacular victory of Brander and company at the Karo La, at 16,522 feet (5,036m) the highest battle in military history, parts of the fighting unfolding at the foot of a massive glacier – for the moment, these heroic exploits gave Younghusband the cover he needed, and he finally got his authorisation to march on Lhasa, albeit on two conditions: he must first inform the Tibetan authorities and the Chinese Resident (China was in nominal control of Tibet's foreign affairs) of the planned advance, and these gentlemen must be given thirty days to respond.

While Younghusband did not expect this ultimatum to change anything, he was duty-bound to communicate these terms to the Amban (the official title of the Chinese Resident) and to senior Tibetan officials. During May and much of June, while the colonel waited for the deadline to expire on 25 June, the Tibetans, having reoccupied the fort at Gyantse, besieged the British camp, mostly with cannon bombardment from the fort but with some up-close fighting just outside the British lines. The deadline to negotiate was advanced into early July, to no avail, and the mission began its advance on Lhasa, some 150 miles from Gyantse, on 14 July. En route, Younghusband received a note from the Bhutanese ambassador, a sympathetic intermediary the colonel had been using, explaining that the Dalai Lama himself was finally paying attention to the crisis in his country; the ambassador reported that the god-king had written to ask him to 'request the English not [to] nibble up our country'.[86]

On 3 August the mission arrived at the gates of Lhasa and made camp just outside the city in sight of the Potala Palace, the residence of the Dalai Lama. But His Excellency was not at home, having decided three days earlier that this was an opportune moment to remove himself to Outer Mongolia, accompanied by Kambo Agvan Dorjieff, and take a three-month religious retreat during which he would be incommunicado. He left a regent to negotiate on his behalf, with guidance from the National Assembly. On the road to Lhasa Younghusband had received from the British government the final version of the terms he was to negotiate with the Tibetans. There were four main provisions:

1. The Tibetans would refrain from making treaties with foreign powers without first consulting with the British government.
2. The Tibetans would approve the opening of trade marts at Gyantse and Gartok.
3. The Tibetans would respect the terms of the Anglo-Chinese agreement of 1890 (fixing the Tibet–Sikkim border).
4. The Tibetans would pay an indemnity to the British, the amount to be determined by Younghusband, and the British would occupy the Chumbi Valley until the indemnity had been paid.

Younghusband was disappointed with these terms – they diminished the dearly won achievements of his brave Sikhs and Gurkhas – and he decided on his own to add one entirely new provision to the agreement and to considerably augment another. The new provision gave permission for the British to station an 'agent' at the trade mart in Gyantse and most importantly for that agent to have the right to 'visit Lhasa'. The other change he made to the treaty was to set the indemnity amount at 7.5 million rupees, and while fixing the amount was entirely within Younghusband's brief, the actual figure he chose meant that the Tibetans, who could only afford 100,000 rupees annually, would potentially have to suffer British occupation of the Chumbi Valley for seventy-five years as opposed to the three years desired by the British government.

These two changes were not known in London when the convention was signed, and Younghusband was well aware that what he had done could

> bring upon me the censure of Government. That, of course, is what I had to risk. I knew that I was not acting within my instructions. I was using my discretion in very difficult circumstances with what the Government of India afterwards described as 'a fearlessness of responsibility which it would be a grave mistake to discourage in any of [our] agents.' And if I really was in error, I think that those who tied their agent down . . . and bound him within such narrow lines before they were aware in what conditions he would find himself at Lhasa, cannot themselves be considered as altogether faultless.[87]

Negotiations with the Tibetans and with the Amban (the British officers called him the 'hambone') went on for more than a month, with considerable input on the British side from the government. Finally, on 7 September, the Anglo-Tibetan Convention was signed, in the Potala Palace itself at Younghusband's insistence, his reasoning being that no one in Asia would pay that much attention to the terms but they would attach great significance to the fact that the convention was signed in the Dalai Lama's fabled residence where foreigners had never before been allowed.

When news of the agreement – but not of the two changes – was officially announced, there was initially great relief that the Tibetan affair had been resolved with as much honour as possible under the circumstances, and there was likewise great praise for Younghusband from all quarters, including the government. There was even a telegram of congratulations from the king. When he returned to England in early December for his victory lap, Younghusband was awarded honorary degrees from the universities of Edinburgh, Bristol and Cambridge, was invited to address the Royal Geographical Society and the Scottish Royal Geographical Society, made an honorary member of the Alpine Club, received a knighthood, and had a private audience with the king. 'The king himself was most cordial,' Younghusband recalled later. 'I saw him quite alone. He placed me in a chair by his desk, and then in some indefinable way made it possible for me to speak to him as I would have to my own father.'[88]

Younghusband may have been a hero to his sovereign and to the British public, but when the government learned about the two unauthorised treaty provisions, they had been outraged. The fact that the agent in Gyantse would have the right 'to visit' Lhasa would be widely interpreted as his having a political portfolio instead of merely a commercial one. And the spectre of British forces occupying the Chumbi Valley for seventy-five years was an acute embarrassment. Taken together, these two provisions made it clear to anyone who was paying attention – most especially the Russians – that the government which had consistently and vehemently denied anything other than a commercial interest in Tibet, plus the desire to establish normal diplomatic relations – that that government, all denials to the contrary, obviously intended to wield considerable influence over Tibetan affairs.

Younghusband, still in Lhasa when the government learned of the two provisions, was ordered to go back to the negotiating table and repudiate them. But the colonel, who had had to wait over a year to finally sit down with the Tibetans, was having none of it. Although he received the telegram from the government the night before he left Lhasa, he sat on it for several days until he was well on his way back to Darjeeling, and then replied that it was too late to return to Lhasa if the troops were going to get over the Himalayas before winter set in. He knew very well that however displeased the government was about the two provisions, they would be even more upset if the withdrawal of the troops was delayed even slightly. As O'Connor wrote some years later, '[HMG's] chief desire, once the treaty was signed, was to get out of the country as quickly as possible and to . . . assume an appearance of never having been there at all.'[89]

In his account of this incident six years later in his book *India and Tibet*, Younghusband wrote about the moment when he received the telegram: '[I]n the midst of this dream of ease, and just the very day before I reached Darjiling, came the rude shock that the best points I had obtained at Lhasa were to be given up . . .' In an instant, 'all the pleasure of my return was dashed from me . . . and I utterly regretted ever having undertaken so delicate a task with my hands so tied'.

This is more than a little self-serving. He received the telegram before he left Lhasa, not the 'very day' before arriving in Darjeeling. Moreover, he knew these two provisions had not been authorised – 'I received instructions not to ask for permission for the Gyantse agent to proceed to Lhasa' – and would almost certainly have to be repudiated.[90] Why, then, it should have been a 'rude shock' when the government responded exactly as he had anticipated is difficult to fathom. Be that as it may, for the moment Younghusband had the upper hand, sat on the telegram, and outmanoeuvred the government.

But in the end he was too clever by half. When his two embarrassing provisions became public knowledge, prompting an official inquiry by the Russians – the government's worst fear – the government meted out the censure the colonel had predicted. Younghusband had abused his authority, defied government instructions, and jeopardised sensitive negotiations going on at the time with Russia and other European nations on certain matters concerning Egypt. 'We cannot accept the situation created for us by our representative's disobedience to orders,' the Secretary of State for India cabled the acting viceroy. The prime minister was even more critical. '[W]e are committed to a non-interventionist policy. It is melancholy to think that whatever we do now, Colonel Younghusband's indiscretions make it impossible for us fully to clear ourselves' from unfortunate and unjust accusations 'of copying the least creditable methods of Russian diplomacy . . . Colonel Younghusband . . . has inflicted upon us an injury . . .'[91]

The Secretary of State confided in Curzon, still on leave in England, that 'it seems impossible to avoid throwing over Younghusband. [The prime minister] considers the honour of the country is involved in repudiating [him].'[92] Younghusband was censured by the government, and in due course the new agent in Gyantse – it was Frank O'Connor, Younghusband's trusted translator – was ordered to renegotiate the convention, stripping it of the two offensive provisions.

Years later in the preface to his account of the invasion, Younghusband offered his last word on the whole affair in a very half-hearted mea culpa:

> I am fully conscious of having made mistakes in that part of the conduct of these affairs which fell to me to discharge. The exactly true adjustment of diplomatic with military requirements, and of the wishes of men in England with the necessities of the situation in Tibet, could only be made by a human being arrived at perfection. Not yet having arrived there, I doubtless made errors. I can only assume that if I had never made a mistake, I would never have made a success.[93]

In the end, Lord Curzon had been right: he knew the colonel would exceed his authority – indeed, he had counted on it – and now the colonel was paying the price. Henceforth, Younghusband remained *persona non grata* inside the government and his reputation never recovered. He remained a popular figure in Edwardian society, however, was much in demand as a speaker, and was eventually made president of the Royal Geographical Society. With regard to charges that he had ruffled Russian feathers, Younghusband was completely unrepentant. 'The Russians [can] protest to their heart's content. We are now . . . much at ease about our North-Eastern frontier . . .'[94]

As official government opprobrium fell on him upon his return to England in December 1904, he took great comfort in knowing that the king at least was not among his detractors. The king was well aware of the controversy Younghusband had ignited and wanted to reassure him. 'I am sorry you have had this little difference with the government . . .' was the first thing the king said to the colonel when the two men met, and then added: 'I approve of all you did.'[95]

Two nights after signing the convention in the Potala Palace, Younghusband wrote to his father from Lhasa: 'The greatest success of my life has been accomplished.'[96] He would, in fact, have at least one other great success seventeen years later when two members of an expedition sponsored mainly by the Royal Geographical Society, the honourable Francis Younghusband presiding, would be the first people ever to stand at the foot of Mount Everest.

*

In Tibet, all was quiet. After renegotiating the agreement with the Tibetans, Frank O'Connor, now the agent in Gyantse, was not especially busy. Indeed, apart from those negotiations, O'Connor is perhaps best remembered for buying a Baby Peugeot in India, having it disassembled and carted over the Himalayas, and then putting it all back together in Gyantse, where he offered short rides to delighted Tibetan friends and dignitaries. The Peugeot was always shadowed by a team of horses on these excursions due to the tendency of its carburettor to fail for lack of oxygen at such high altitude, whereupon the horses were hitched up to the Peugeot and it was dragged back to Gyantse.

From virtually any perspective – whether military, diplomatic, economic or political – the entire Tibetan affair, the last act of the Great Game, was just short of an embarrassment. For all it cost in terms of lives lost – close to 3,000 Tibetans, 4 British officers, 1 native officer and 28 sepoys – and financial outlays, almost nothing of any consequence was achieved. At the end of fourteen months of effort and several fierce battles and after the discovery of a grand total of three Russian-made rifles in Lhasa – they were 'considerably scarcer than Huntley & Palmer biscuits' – the British now had a trade mart and a commercial agent at Gyantse and another mart at Gartok.⁹⁷ Business was not brisk. But then Tibet did at least have its first Baby Peugeot.

And thus the Great Game ended, not with a bang but with a whimper.

Unless one was a mountain climber, that is, especially one from Britain, for in that case the invasion of Tibet changed everything. For one thing, it marked the beginning of the end of Tibet's isolation from the outside world, and for another the terms of the Anglo-Tibetan Convention gave the British a modest toehold in the country, just enough, it was believed, for the Tibetans in good time to be persuaded to permit the British to conduct exploration and mapmaking activities. And it was precisely this prospect that was so tantalising to climbers, for if Tibet could be explored, then sooner or later surely Mount Everest could be found.

He might be *persona non grata* to diplomats, bureaucrats and politicians, but Francis Younghusband would forever be a hero to mountaineers.

When the North and South Poles had been reached, the ambitions of explorers centred more than ever on Everest. Here was a last task, perhaps even more stupendous than the others. Here was a challenge to man's skill and courage, the alluring, fascinating challenge of Nature's last secret stronghold . . . Surrounding the great summit . . . was a blank white space on the map. The mountain stood, stupendous, seen through telescopes; its slopes untrodden by human beings . . .

John Noel, *Through Everest to Tibet*

ALEXANDER KELLAS WAS chasing a record. While not an espe-cially vain man, he was proud of his climbing achievements, and on this particular journey to the Himalayas in the summer of 1911, he knew he stood a chance of breaking Tom Longstaff's record, set four years earlier on Trisul, for the highest summit ever climbed. At the moment, however, in his camp somewhere on the lower slopes of Pauhunri, he was more concerned about two young lark chicks whose parents had apparently abandoned them. 'Quite unwit-tingly, we [had] erected our tents about three yards from a nest. From the plaintive notes heard after we had settled down, I was sure that we must be trespassing, and on looking found the nest with two young ones.' Kellas worried that the parents were hesitant to come too close and had stopped feeding the chicks. 'I was inclined to move the tents as I was afraid the [young ones] would starve.'[1]

It is typical of the man that Kellas could be absorbed in the challenge of setting a climbing record and at the same time anxious about the suffering of two young larks. He was a man of many contradictions: he was a professor and an avid climber; a scientist who heard voices; a recluse who became famous; slight of stature and yet renowned for his physical stamina. Kellas's duelling personas were a rare combination in the mountaineering fraternity, making him an unusually appealing figure, but they in no way handicapped or diminished him: he quickly became the most successful and also one of the most-beloved Himalayan climbers of his generation.

Kellas kept a vigil over the young larks for several hours and was greatly relieved when after some time 'one of the [parent] birds came to feed them and continued to do so at intervals of a few minutes during the afternoon and next morning'.[2] And what of the climbing record? Did he break it? He did manage to climb Pauhunri that summer, reaching the top on 14 June, but at 23,180 feet (7,065m) that mountain, alas, was 280 feet (85m) lower than Trisul. Or so everyone thought.

Three names dominate the Everest story during the seventeen years from 1904, when the Younghusband mission withdrew from Tibet, and 1921, the year of the first-ever attempt to reach the mountain. Cecil Rawling, John Noel and Alexander Kellas got closer to Everest during these years and unlocked more of its secrets than anyone before them. Through their explorations – and especially their photos, in the case of Noel and Kellas – these three men established for the first time that if it was somehow possible to get into Tibet, there was a very good chance of finding Mount Everest.

By the time Francis Younghusband left Lhasa in September 1904, the idea of finding Everest had been on his mind for close to twenty years. While his first glimpse of the mountain had been quite recent, fifteen months earlier in Darjeeling as he prepared to depart for Khamba Dzong, he had in fact been actively plotting to steal into Tibet, reconnoitre the area around Everest, and perhaps even climb it, since at least 1892. Those earlier schemes went nowhere, but he never lost his fascination with the mountain.

Seen from Darjeeling, Everest is just a tiny blot on the horizon, 130 miles away, but from Khamba Dzong, where Younghusband looked out at the mountain most mornings, he was 30 miles closer – closer than any European had ever come – and as the mountain caught the sun most mornings it dazzled the colonel. By the time he reached Lhasa a year later, Younghusband was for the moment the most powerful person in Tibet, and he was determined to use his position to advance the cause of finding Everest. Although in the end he himself would never get any closer to the mountain than he had been at Khamba Dzong, it is fair to say that no single individual did more than Francis Younghusband to open the way to Everest.

One of the minor terms Younghusband inserted into the Convention of 7 September, the treaty that ended the invasion of Tibet, was authorisation to send a team to explore and map the upper valley of the Brahmaputra. Before he left Lhasa, therefore,

Younghusband had received official permission for the first-ever expedition to enter and survey western Tibet, which includes the region around Everest. The official purpose of the expedition was to proceed west on horseback, tracking and mapping the Tsangpo river, known as the Brahmaputra in India, to its source and then find a way over the Himalayas back to India. A second stated object-ive was for the British to become familiar with the peoples and the geography around Gartok, the site of the second trade mart author-ised by the treaty, located in an especially remote area in far western Tibet never before visited by Europeans.

Gartok may never have been visited by the British but everyone recognised that getting to it would take an expedition very close to Everest, though exactly how far Everest stood off the route to Gartok was not known, nor even if it could be glimpsed from the proposed survey route along the Tsangpo. But there was no doubt that the members of the expedition, whether they saw the mountain or not, would come closer to Everest on this journey than any westerners had ever come before.

The leader of the Gartok expedition was Captain Cecil Rawling, an engineer-surveyor who had been assigned to the Tibet Frontier Commission to explore and survey the regions through which the Younghusband mission would pass on its way to Lhasa. The Gartok expedition represented the first time any foreigner had ever officially been allowed in Tibet – Rawling had entered unofficially a few months earlier – and, even more unprecedented, the first time any outsider had ever been allowed to carry out exploration and mapping, something normally anathema to the fiercely independent Tibetans who knew that, as far as the British were concerned, exploration was almost always the precursor to appropriation. The permit the team carried from the Dalai Lama set forth how 'the English, having come to Lhasa to settle a matter between England and Tibet, have made a Treaty of Peace' and ordered officials all along the proposed route not to 'raise any disturbance or quarrels. Each district must report to the Government the facts regarding the passage of the sahibs . . .'[3]

The thirty-four-year-old Cecil Rawling was very much in the mould of Younghusband. He relished adventure and courted danger;

he was the kind of servant of the Raj who kept the bureaucrats back in Whitehall awake at night. He could easily have been arrested or even imprisoned at any time during his earlier illegal foray into central Tibet; indeed, some earlier Indian 'spies' of the Raj had been executed by the Tibetans. Younghusband, who was well aware of Rawling's daredevil streak, cautioned him before he left Lhasa that he should under no circumstances try to climb Everest if the opportunity arose. Rawling, greatly disappointed, later said if it had not been for those instructions, he might very well have been the first man to summit Everest.

Rawling's expedition would cross 800 miles of Tibet, relying on a forty-year-old map, and would have to be completed in a matter of weeks before winter would close most Himalayan passes and strand the men on the Tibetan plateau. But the biggest concern was how the members would be treated by the people whose districts they would pass through, their permit notwithstanding. 'For the first time in the history of the country,' Rawling wrote, 'British officers with only a nominal escort were going to traverse Tibet . . . but fighting had only recently ceased and the ink was scarcely dry on the Treaty. It was impossible to tell to what extent and in what spirit the Tibetans meant to observe their obligations.'[4] Rawling, who had an escort of only five mounted Gurkhas, did not describe what he planned to do if the Tibetans chose not to observe their obligations, but he was well aware that a second expedition Younghusband had organised, to survey another part of the Tsangpo, had been deemed too dangerous by the Indian government because of hostile border tribes along its proposed route.

Rawling was fortunate in the team that assembled for his expedition. The most skilled member was the mapmaker, Captain Charles Ryder, who worked for the Survey of India – he would later become Surveyor General – and who, like Rawling, had been seconded to the Tibet mission. The most colourful member was undoubtedly Frederick 'Hatter' Bailey, so called because of his mad-as-a-hatter obsession with hunting, who had distinguished himself repeatedly during the march on Lhasa for his conspicuous bravery. Bailey had studied Tibetan and served as Rawling's translator on the trip. Later he would succeed Frank O'Connor as the agent at Gyantse and went on to become a decorated explorer and naturalist. It was Bailey who discovered the Tibetan blue poppy which now bears his name: *Meconopsis betonicifolia baileyi*. The other Englishman on the team was Captain Henry Wood, the same man Curzon had sent to Nepal in 1903 to resolve the question of whether or not there was a local Nepali name for Everest. On this expedition Wood would become the first westerner to have seen Everest from both the south and the north.

In addition to the four British members, the thirty-five-man team comprised twenty-six assorted support staff of personal servants, survey assistants, baggage handlers, mule drivers, cooks, one Sikh doctor and the five Gurkha military escorts, who, Rawling observed, 'although they did not encounter that class of difficulty which a Gurkha most loves, namely fighting, proved themselves a most valuable addition to the party'. In addition there were 43 ponies, 17 for riding and 26 for carrying baggage, and a few yaks. On the morning of 10 October the expedition marched out of Lhasa to begin its historic exploration of what Rawling called 'this weird and fascinating country'.[5]

Their first stop was at a town called Dongtse, a day's ride from Gyantse and not an especially auspicious place to begin their journey. As the visitors knew, Dongtse had been the scene twenty-five years earlier of a truly notorious incident of Tibetan anti-foreigner madness. In that year an Indian by the name of Sarat Chandra Das spent several weeks as the guest of the Dongtse abbot at his monastery. Das was actually one of the famous pundit explorers, a small, select group of Indian nationals trained in rudimentary surveying by the Survey of India and dispatched into Nepal and Tibet to carry out clandestine surveys, usually disguised as Tibetan monks. The abbot apparently did not know that Das was in effect a British spy, but whether he knew or not, he had in any event committed a crime, contact with a foreigner, for which the fanatically xenophobic senior Tibetan lamas had decreed the death penalty. When the abbot was found out, he was taken to Lhasa, tried and sentenced to death. Since the lamas' odd interpretation of Buddhism sanctioned killing but apparently not the actual spilling of blood, the abbot was sewn alive into a leather bag and thrown into the Brahmaputra. That was not enough for the lamas, however, who proceeded to track down the abbot's closest relatives and either had them killed or sold them into slavery.

Rawling and his men were treated well enough at Dongtse, and nearly everywhere else they went in Tibet. The group of thirty-five foreigners with their long baggage train winding its way across the Tibetan plateau was such a novelty that they attracted considerable interest from the curious locals, many of whom had never seen a single foreigner before. The Tibetans were interested in everything the foreign devils did, but especially their eating habits. The expedition members usually ate their breakfast out in the open as their tents were being struck, and the Tibetans would invariably gather for the show. 'This gave our wild-looking friends an opportunity of examining us at their ease,' Rawling writes, 'and a subject to discuss for weeks to come.' The natives knew the 'sahibs' ate out in the open, 'so they would collect early and spend the time until we appeared in watching the cooks prepare breakfast'. Once the foreigners were seated, the locals moved in to get 'the best points of vantage, and from there watched every mouthful disappear'. The chief attractions were the cutlery as 'such a thing as a fork or spoon is unheard of in Tibet. Chopsticks are used by the wealthier of the people, but the ordinary person only shovels the food into the chasm waiting to receive it, with the instruments Nature has provided.'[6]

On many occasions, they were invited for meals, at a local monastery, for example, or at the home of the local *dzongpen* or headman, where they often faced another eating challenge. 'Much as we wished to avail ourselves of our hosts' hospitality,' Rawling wrote, 'it was a decided trial to eat some of the dishes, and we were not yet accustomed to the horrible decoction that the Tibetans offered us as tea.' One of the most decided of these trials was known as the 'salaaming sheep', a special honour carefully prepared, Rawling tells us, in the following manner:

> The animal after being killed, skinned, and cleaned has the hind legs passed through the muscles of the fore legs and is then hung up to dry and to partly decompose. After poisoning the surrounding air for several months, the flesh is considered ripe for eating, and is in this condition ready for presentation for the guest. On being brought

in it is placed on the ground in a sitting position immediately in front of the recipient, to whom the carcass appears to bow.[7]

When not eating salaaming sheep, members of the expedition were kept well fed by the exploits of the tireless hunter 'Hatter' Bailey, who supplied the men with all manner of antelope, wild ass, gazelles, wild yak (Rawling says 'the soup made from the feet is much overrated'), hares, sand grouse, partridge and bar geese, the latter so plentiful Bailey once brought four down with a single shot.[8]

At Lhatse the team split up so that the expedition could map more of Tibet, with Wood and Bailey taking the trading route, which follows a trail far to the north of the river for 160 miles before angling south and rejoining the river further west at Ka-Sa, where the two teams agreed they would meet in fourteen days' time. Rawling and Captain Ryder were to follow the river along its banks for as long and as far as they could, mapping that largely unknown part of western Tibet.

A steadily mounting sense of anticipation must have come over Ryder and Rawling the further they got from Lhatse. They knew that their route would take them past Everest, sitting somewhere south of the range of mountains just off to their left on the other side of the river. They did not know how far away Everest stood, and they were likewise unsure if they would even catch sight of it, fearing the intervening range would block their view. But they also knew that if they did manage to see the mountain, they would be looking at it from a point closer than any westerner had ever been. In the next two or three days it was possible that the secrets of Everest, the subject of close to fifty years of intense speculation, would at long last start to be revealed.

On the night of 26 October, the two men made their camp near some shepherds' huts 2,000 feet above the river, on their way up to a high pass (the Kura La) they were planning to cross the next morning. All night a bitter cold wind blew through their campsite, prompting them to rise early and begin their ascent to the top of the pass. Before the morning was over, Rawling and Ryder would make mountaineering history.

'So unpleasant was this place', Rawling begins,

that we departed the following morning as early as possible, crossing
the Kura La [16,748 feet/5,105m] in deep snow. No sooner was the
summit [of the pass] reached than we realized that, if a conical hill
close by was climbed, we were certain to obtain a fine view of Mt
Everest, and from a direction never before seen by Europeans.

The morning was cold, crisp, and clear, so . . . we climbed steadily
until the crest of our observatory hill was reached; and well did it
repay us, for to the south, and distant about fifty miles, though to
all appearances much nearer on account of the rarefied atmosphere,
lay the wildest part of the Himalayas fully exposed to view.

Towering up thousands of feet, a glittering pinnacle of snow, rose
Everest, a giant amongst pigmies, and remarkable not only for its
height but for its perfect form. No other peaks lie near or threaten
its supremacy. From its foot a rolling mass of hills stretch away in all
directions, to the north dropping to the Dingri [Tingri] Plain, 15,000
feet [4,570m] below. To the east and west, but nowhere in the vicinity,
rise other great mountains of rock and snow, each beautiful in itself
but in no other way comparing with the famous peak in solemn
grandeur; it is difficult to give an idea of its stupendous height, its
dazzling whiteness, and overpowering size, for there is nothing in
the world to compare it with.[9]

It is one of the most famous passages in the lore of Everest, second
only, perhaps, to Mallory's own description of his first full view of
the mountain. It is also a major milestone in the history of Everest
exploration: it marked the first time Europeans saw Everest from
the north and, at a distance of only 50 miles, it was the closest any
westerner had ever come to the mountain. Moreover, it resolved a
troubling doubt about Everest 'of great interest to geographers',
Rawling explains, 'as to whether there might not be similar but
higher mountains in the neighbourhood but not visible from India.
This question we were able to settle, for the great peak has no
rival.'[10]

The next day the group reached the Tingri Plain where they
halted for a day and where Captain Ryder capped off their remarkable discovery by riding out to the far edge 'of the grassy plain we
were in and [found that] it stretched right away to the Himalayas'.[11]

Ryder studied the mountain with his binoculars and reported back to Rawling that the upper parts looked climbable if a way could be found to reach the base of the peak and negotiate its lower slopes, which he could not see from the Tingri Plain. Rawling resolved on the spot to return one day to Tibet and penetrate Everest's inner sanctum. Seventeen years later the grassy Tingri Plain would become the highway to Mount Everest.

The expedition finally reached Gartok – 'what a wretched little town' – on 8 December.[12] Winter threatened to close the passes over the Himalayas into India, so they hurried on their way, crossing by the Ayi Pass where the temperature was 24 degrees below zero, arriving in Simla on 11 January, three months and one day after setting out from Gyantse. In all they had surveyed over 40,000 square miles of Tibet, an achievement for which Ryder was awarded the Patron's Gold Medal of the Royal Geographical Society. Rawling's reward was to be made a CIE (Commander of the Indian Empire), and he too was subsequently honoured by the Royal Geographical Society for his explorations in Tibet and later in New Guinea. Younghusband congratulated the team for 'a good piece of work, magnificently executed'.[13] Reflecting on their mission on the last page of *The Great Plateau*, the normally unsentimental Rawling says how 'Tibet has an irresistible fascination' and that it was his 'last wish that someday we may [all] meet there again, as no man could desire more staunch and pleasant companions than Ryder, Wood and Bailey'.[14] But Rawling, while he still has one more part to play in the Everest saga, never saw Tibet again. On the morning of 28 October 1917, while chatting with friends outside his headquarters in Belgium where he was stationed during the Passchendaele campaign of the First World War, Brigadier General Rawling was killed by a German artillery shell.

The findings of the Gartok expedition electrified the climbing community and reignited the hunt for Everest, which until now had always been stopped at the closed borders of Nepal and Tibet. Nor did the expedition change the fact that Rawling's journey across the great plateau would be the last time any foreigners were allowed into Tibet for another seventeen years. That did not stop people from trying to get in, however, nor did it stop a few people from actually succeeding, albeit illegally. What the Gartok expedition had conclusively demonstrated – and what had the entire climbing community utterly agog – was the fact that if one could somehow get into Tibet, then it was possible to get to Everest, or at least to get very close. To be sure, the last fifty miles were still terra incognita, especially the foothills at the base of the mountain – 'foothills', it should be noted, more than 20,000 feet (6,100m) high – and could easily hold some unpleasant surprises. If Everest itself had not been found just yet, a path to it had been discovered.

No one was more excited by the findings of the Rawling expedition than Lord Curzon, who immediately proposed an Everest expedition to Douglas Freshfield, past-president of the Alpine Club, future president of the Royal Geographical Society, and himself a much-celebrated Himalayan explorer and climber. In his proposal, Curzon used almost exactly the same language he had used in a proposal to Freshfield six years earlier, explaining that 'I always thought that Kangchenjunga, being within our territory, and Everest only a little way outside it, and the English being the first mountaineering race in the world, an Englishman ought to be the first on top of Kangchenjunga and, if possible, of Everest also.'[15] But Freshfield reported that for the moment all interest at the RGS was focused on the intense, highly public international competition to reach the poles.

Freshfield then took Curzon's 1905 letter to the Alpine Club, which supported the viceroy's proposal but could only manage to come up with £100 for financing, against Curzon's estimated budget of £6,000. When A. L. Mumm, a wealthy member of the Alpine Club and himself a distinguished climber, got wind of the proposal, he agreed to finance the entire expedition on his own. Suddenly the RGS was interested; its president Sir George Goldie championed the plan, and, more importantly, so did Lord Minto, the newly appointed viceroy who was on his way out to India.

But it was not to be. Not for the last time the proposal fell foul of diplomatic and geopolitical considerations. Or, to put it another way, it fell foul of 'an austere, joyless, empty shirt of a man' by the name of John Morley, also referred to by his Cabinet colleagues by

George Everest: 'the most cantankerous *sahib* ever to have stalked the Indian stage'.

The Survey of India's 1,000-pound theodolite which needed twelve porters to carry it on expeditions from the British hill station at Darjeeling, 1849–50.

Johann Scheuzer and friend, somewhere in the Alps. Engraving from Scheuzer's account of his travels, 1723.

Edward Whymper, 1865, the year he climbed the Matterhorn.

Jean-Antoine Carrel, Whymper's Italian climbing rival. 'He was *the* man, of all those who attempted the ascent of the Matterhorn, who most deserved to be the first upon its summit.'

Two of the Great Game's greatest players, Francis Younghusband (*left*) and Captain Grombtchevski (*centre*), meet in Hunza for a friendly chat, 1889.

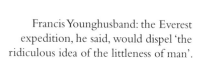

Francis Younghusband: the Everest expedition, he said, would dispel 'the ridiculous idea of the littleness of man'.

George Nathaniel Curzon, Viceroy of India, 1898–1905. 'He was both a pleasure and a trial', Younghusband said of him. 'We resented Curzon's cocksuredness.'

The fort at Khamba Dzong; the 1921 expedition camped beneath this hill.

The 1,100-man strong Tibet Frontier Commission advancing
across the Tibetan plateau to Tuna, March 1904.

Alexander Kellas: shy, self-effacing, mild-mannered – and 'one of the greatest Himalayan mountaineers of all'.

A photo of the eastern approaches to Everest which Kellas brought back in 1913.

John Noel on the 1922 expedition. Together with Alexander Kellas, he got closer to Everest than anyone had ever been before.

Charles Bell, the British government's agent in Sikkim, with the 13th Dalai Lama. 'Here is one who talks direct to our Dalai Lama, just the two together.'

The 'formidable' Arthur Hinks, secretary of the Royal Geographical Society and 'indispensable man' of the 1921 expedition.

George and Ruth Mallory. Ruth didn't want George to go to Everest, but Geoffrey Young convinced her it would make his career. In the end it made him a legend.

Mallory (*left*) and Bullock on the mules Howard-Bury obliged them to trade in for Tibetan ponies, May 1921.

The single-toothed, 137-year-old abbot of the Shekar monastery. Photo by Howard-Bury.

The members of the 1921 expedition at the camp at 17,300 feet.
(*Back row left to right*) Bullock, Morshead, Wheeler, Mallory.
(*Front row left to right*) Heron, Wollaston, Howard-Bury, Raeburn. Photo by Wollaston.

The Rongbuk Valley leading up to Everest, 'with nothing in between'.
Photo by Mallory.

'The col of our desires', with the summit of Everest on the left.
Photo by Howard-Bury.

turns as 'Aunt Priscilla' and the 'petulant spinster'.[16] Morley, the Secretary of State for India, had been strongly opposed to Curzon's Tibetan folly and was now in a position to prevent any further viceregal chest-thumping. 'I am sorry to be obliged to refuse the present request,' Morley wrote to Goldie, citing his concerns that what he called a 'furtive' expedition to Everest, one that did not involve notifying the authorities in Lhasa, was not in the British national interest.[17]

In fact there had never been any intention for the expedition to be furtive. When Freshfield read Morley's letter, he was so outraged by the insinuation that he published the letter in The Times, along with his own commentary: '[The Himalayas'] would-be conqueror has either to evade avalanches or get round Lord Morley, and I don't know which is the more awkward obstacle.'[18] Later, addressing a meeting of the Alpine Club, Freshfield was still smarting from Morley's obtuseness. Noting that he and Lord Curzon had been 'godfathers' of the scheme, he lamented that at the last moment, 'as so often happens in stories, there appears a malignant fairy who was not invited to the Christening'. He went on to state that it 'is not a little vexatious to see a Swede, Dr Sven Hedin . . . wandering at will in territory forbidden to Englishmen'.[19] The English were in fact notoriously proprietary about Everest – it was commonly referred to as 'our mountain' – believing they somehow had a prior claim on the peak, the right of first refusal, as it were, and they were regularly alarmed when other parties showed an interest, especially the Swiss and the Italians, the two most experienced climbing nationalities in all of Europe along with the British.

The year 1913 was a watershed in the history of the search for Everest; at some point in the second half of that year two men, Captain John Noel and Alexander Kellas, got closer to the mountain than anyone had ever been before. These two remarkable – and remarkably different – men not only shaved somewhere between 10 and 30 miles off the remaining gap to the foot of Everest, both of them brought back a series of photographs that would transform the search and ultimately lead to the formation of the Mount Everest Committee, the joint RGS–Alpine Club effort which sponsored the expedition that found the mountain. Noel would later become famous throughout Europe and America, while Kellas, whose contributions to the search for Everest were much greater, would languish in relative obscurity for decades to come.

John Noel might have stepped straight out of the pages of *Kim*, Rudyard Kipling's novel of the Great Game, and in particular the story of the famous pundit explorers, Indian nationals trained in basic mapping and surveying by the Survey of India and sent in disguise into Nepal and Tibet, beginning in the 1860s, to secretly map the still largely unknown and unexplored Himalayas. They were spies, in other words, for which at least two of them were executed in Tibet. Noel deeply admired the exploits of the pundits and clearly identified with them. Although he was born a few years too late, Noel himself would have made a consummate Great Gamer. He had all the traits of the most celebrated players: he was a true romantic, adventuresome, intrepid, a great raconteur, and handsome besides.

In due course Noel also became a highly successful hustler, self-promoter and a determined, infamous entrepreneur. He would just miss being on the 1921 Everest expedition and would be the official photographer for the 1922 and 1924 expeditions. In the latter capacity he was one of the last people to see George Mallory and Andrew Irvine alive, through the telescopic lens on his camera, as they disappeared into clouds just 2,000 feet (610m) short of the summit of Everest. One of the last two notes George Mallory wrote was to John Noel – it was carried down from the high camp by a Sherpa – telling Noel to look for Mallory at 8 a.m. the following morning at a spot on the mountain the two men had previously identified.

Noel's fame was more than a decade in the future when he first arrived in India in 1909 after graduating from Sandhurst. He served as captain in the Machine Gun Corps of the East Yorkshire Regiment, which was stationed in the remote town of Faizabad in northern India. During the four months of summer, Faizabad was much too hot for soldiering, making it a perfect posting for Noel whose real interests were photography and exploring. During the worst of the summer heat, Noel regularly applied for and usually received leave to explore the region around the Garhwal Himalayas.

For his most famous journey, however, Noel did not apply for leave, nor would he have got it. The journey began on the morning of 5 July 1913, when the twenty-three-year-old Noel, along with three native companions, without either the knowledge or the permission of the Lhasa government – and for that reason without informing his superiors – departed Darjeeling to go looking for Everest, a reckless excursion that would elevate Noel into the elite group of men who would come to dominate the quest for the elusive peak. Having travelled extensively in the border regions of India, Nepal and Tibet, Noel writes, 'I decided in 1913 to seek out the passes that led to Everest and if possible come to close quarters with the mountain.' The mountain was 'an alluring goal,' Noel continues, '[h]itherto unapproached by men of my race; guarded, so fantastic rumour said, by the holiest lamas dwelling in mystic contemplation of the soul of the giant peak, communing with its demons and its guardian gods'.[20]

Noel hoped he might actually find Everest, of course, but he also had a more specific and more realistic purpose: to determine whether the mountain could be approached and climbed from the east. He knew the Rawling expedition had established that approaching Everest from the north was a distinct possibility, depending on the make-up of the final 50 miles that Rawling had not had time to reconnoitre. But for some time Noel had wondered whether an approach from the east might be possible and might even be more feasible. Several sources, although not Noel himself, have suggested that Noel's excursion was actually a reconnaissance carried out in response to a request from none other than Cecil Rawling, who was putting together a formal proposal for an Everest expedition for the year 1915.

Noel had good reason to think Everest could be reached from the east, for he was in possession of and carrying with him the maps and notes that Sarat Chandra Das, one of the pundit explorers, had made on two trips, in 1887 and 1891, into the very region in south-central Tibet that Noel was now headed for. Das's maps seemed to show that there were no serious barriers to approaching Everest from the east once an expedition got beyond the village of Tashirak on the western side of the Langbu La which, according to the map, was eminently accessible. Noel was especially intrigued about a formation Das had seen from the vicinity of Tashirak that he referred to in his notes as the 'lofty Pherugh mountains'. Noel believed this was 'the Everest group' and he was determined to find it.[21]

Noel's trip was not merely inspired by his heroes, the pundit explorers, it copied their modus operandi. Just as the pundits travelled in disguise, Noel was also obliged to. 'My men were not startlingly different from the Tibetans,' he explains, 'and if I darkened my skin and my hair I could pass, not as a native – the colour and shape of my eyes would prevent that – but as a Mohammedan from India. A Moslem would be a stranger and suspect in Tibet, but not as glaringly so as a white man.'[22]

Like the famous expeditions that would follow, Noel's trip began in Calcutta where he caught the train to Siliguri. There he changed to the famous 'toy' or single-gauge train that climbs the 7,218 feet (2,200m) to Darjeeling in 55 tortuous miles, 'the crookedest and tiniest mountain railway in the world'. On at least a dozen occasions the train 'makes figures of eights and zigzags and loops, where the engine passes the tail of the train, and the driver leans out and talks to the passengers in the end coach'. At night a man sat in front of the engine holding 'a tar torch to light the track and see that no stray tigers or elephants' blocked the way.[23]

If it was a person's first time in Darjeeling, which it was for Noel, then one was expected to get up for the sunrise on Kangchenjunga. For Noel this would also be his first chance to see Everest itself, 130 miles to the west. 'At two o'clock in the morning,' Noel writes,

> the hotel porter rings a 12-inch brass bell outside your door, and he comes again every ten minutes to make certain that you do not forget that ponies and rickshaws are waiting to take you to Tiger Hill where people go to see the sun rise on Kangchenjunga . . . It is an unforgettable spectacle. Kangchenjunga commands the attention because it is so prominent, so near, and so huge. Far away to the west is a mass of huge peaks. Among them the guide points out a pyramid peeping behind the others and seeming to be smaller; that mountain is Everest.[24]

On the face of it the central premise of Noel's journey was slightly absurd: to travel extensively in Tibet without encountering any Tibetans. If it became known he was a European, he could have been arrested or jailed; at the very least he would have been escorted back to India, and his companions might have fared even worse. Nearly every major decision Noel made – from what he chose to carry with him, to the route he planned to take, to the arrangements for provisioning the party – was predicated on the necessity of avoiding contact with the locals. Thus, he planned to stay off well-travelled routes, to avoid all but the smallest villages lest he run into Tibetan officials in the major settlements, and to live off the land as much as possible. His disguise would help, of course, but not for close encounters.

Like the pundits, who hid their compasses and sextants inside their prayer wheels or in the folds of their garments, much of what Noel carried with him also had to be concealed. He had to hide his cameras – there were two – his mapping and drawing instruments, a boiling point thermometer to measure altitude, and an array of firepower, including a disassembled American rifle, a revolver, two automatic pistols for his companions, and plenty of ammunition. Most of these items had to fit into two small tin trunks he bought in the bazaar in Darjeeling. In addition the party carried blankets, bedding, medicines, two tents, and initially enough food to get them to Gangtok in Sikkim, six days out of Darjeeling.

In many ways the first few days of the journey were the most trying, not for the reasons one imagines for a Himalayan adventure – breathing the thin air at higher elevations, climbing steep moun-tain slopes, negotiating heart-stopping cliff faces, wading through waist-deep snow – but because of the sweltering heat, the drenching rains, the thick, damp air, the multitudes of swarming flies and gnats, and the masses of hungry leeches that are all part of a teeming tropical rainforest. The trail from Darjeeling, at 6,700 feet (2,042m), to the Tibetan plateau, at 13,000 feet (3,660m), first plunges more than 5,500 feet (1,524m) to the lower reaches of the Teesta river valley in Sikkim, making for a minimum of three days of very slow going, before it climbs back up the lower slopes of Kangchenjunga. Noel was not the first nor the last Everest hunter to decry the appalling conditions of those early marches along the Teesta. 'We were dropping down mile after mile,' he writes.

> The road was the hottest I had ever felt. The blazing sun boiled the thick, damp rotting jungle into a thousand oppressive smelling vapours. Swarms of insects filled the air with incessant hum and buzz. There came land leeches to attack our legs from the ground and fix themselves to our boots; others on the trees above, warned by some instinct – wonderful but horrible since they are blind – swing their bodies in the air on our approach and dropped down on us as we passed below. There is no escape from the leech. You must make up your mind that you are going to lose a lot of blood.[25]

The classic route from Darjeeling towards Everest, the one taken by all three of the British expeditions in the 1920s, is north through Sikkim, then east over the Jelep La into Tibet on the road to Lhasa, a turn to the north at Lake Bamtso, leaving the Lhasa road, and then heading straight west to Khamba Dzong, a distance of nearly 200 miles. From Khamba Dzong, the route proceeds due west to the Tingri plain, where Ryder and Rawling had their distant views of Everest. Noel followed the first part of this route, but at Lachen, still in Sikkim, he turned west and proceeded on a course roughly parallel to the Khamba Dzong to Tingri route but 50 miles further south, on a direct east–west line to Everest. He was planning to enter Tibet via the remote Choten Nyima La which he knew was no longer guarded by Tibetan authorities.

And for good reason. 'The pass looks like the work of a giant axe that has split a narrow cleft in the mountains,' he wrote. Rocks fell on the men as they climbed, and they slipped repeatedly on the loose shingle beneath their feet. 'Even the highest and loneliest Himalayan passes are crossed occasionally . . . by shepherds,' Noel noted, '[who] perform amazing feats in getting their yaks . . . across. But we were not yaks, and the men felt the burden of their loads, heavily laden as they were with our food.'[26]

As far as possible the party kept to the high ground and other steep terrain to avoid settlements or else contrived to pass by villages at night, 'to defeat observation'. Noel noted that he 'intended to avoid the . . . settled parts generally, to carry our food, and to keep to those more desolate stretches where only an occasional shepherd was to be seen'.[27] A constant danger were the ferocious Tibetan mastiffs that guarded nearly every household, picking up the scent of passing strangers as much as a mile away and then alerting entire villages with their howling. Noel and his band were often forced down to lower elevations to find firewood for cooking. They were encouraged in several places, however, by coming across landmarks described in Sarat Chandra Das's notes; if they could somehow manage to hew closely to Das's route, then there was still hope of finding those 'lofty Pherugh mountains', which just might include Everest.

After crossing over the Choten Nyima La, the party was temporarily lost, unsure of the exact whereabouts of the Langbu La that would take them to Tashirak. 'I was vague as to the way to the pass,' Noel recalled,

> so we decided boldly to turn into a certain village . . . Our approach caused the keenest excitement, the barking of dogs and the barring of doors . . . We noted peeping heads observing us from the apparently deserted houses. Keeping on our way and meeting people, we boldly insisted on being given a house to live in.

The party could not proceed without getting directions from the locals, but the decision to stop at Eunah, as the village was known, would turn out to be a costly mistake. To begin with the villagers were not helpful, 'answer[ing] "No" or "I do not know" to everything', but soon their famed Tibetan hospitality broke through, and Noel and company were offered a house to stay in, were served a meal, and eventually got the directions to the Langbu La.[28] Unbeknown to Noel, the villagers also sent a rider off to report the presence of the foreigners to the district headman in Tinki.

The next morning, the party continued on past Eunah for two miles and began to ascend the pass, hoping they would find an answer to 'the all important question: Could Everest be seen from the top of the pass? When I reached the top,' Noel continues,

> I was staggered by a magnificent view of towering snow mountains. The centre peak of the range rose as a glittering spire of rock, clothed with clinging ice and snow. Beyond rose a higher peak

twisted like a hooked tooth, a precipice on the north side and a neve [snowfield] on the south. To the left of this again was a long, ridged peak whose winding crest was fantastically corniced with overhanging ridges of ice.

What fine mountains! But they were none of them Everest; they were too near . . . Presently, while watching the panorama, the shifting of the clouds revealed other high mountain masses in the distance; and directly over the crest of Taringban appeared a sharp spire peak. This, through its magnetic bearing by my compass, proved itself to be none other than Mount Everest.[29]

This proved to be a bittersweet moment for Noel. 'Although this panorama was in itself a fitting reward for the efforts of the journey,' he wrote, 'still it was in a sense a disappointment.' He had seen Everest, albeit only the top 1,300 feet (400m) or so, but the 'towering snow mountains' in front of him were 'an impassable barrier. Tashirak was near, one had only to descend the valley to reach it; but it was plain that Tashirak offered no open road to Mount Everest. The map upon which the hopes and plans of the journey had been based was incorrect.'[30]

Noel was naturally disappointed to learn that Everest could not be approached from the east, but his other great goal for this trip was still alive: the chance of finding those elusive 'lofty Pherugh mountains'. Clearly, they were somewhere beyond Tashirak, and Tashirak was just a few miles away, down at the foot of the Langbu La. The team descended the pass and spent the night at the village of Guma Shara, where Noel's luck suddenly changed when he was visited by two lamas who 'volunteered some interesting information', namely that the coveted Pherugh region could be reached via a high yak path that led from Tashirak to the Arun Valley, 'passing a certain monastery situated on the crest of the dividing range between the two valleys. This monastery was connected with the worship of the mountain Kanchen-Lembu-Geudong, of which it commanded an open view.'[31] From the lamas' description of the mountain, Noel concluded it must be Everest, and he resolved to head for Tashirak and look for the yak trail the next day.

Tashirak is on the border with Nepal, and the Tibetan authorities on their side of the border 'were hostile and wished us to return immediately the way we had come'.[32] So the party backtracked and spent the night in a side valley three miles outside Tashirak. They were now on the south side of the mountains they had seen earlier, meaning that that range would no longer obscure a view towards Everest, if the foreigners could only get one. It was up this valley that the yak path lay to Pherugh and the monastery, as explained by the lamas of Guma Shara. 'Therefore, it would be interesting to proceed up the valley the next day.'[33] And so it would have been, but the next day brought 'an unpleasant surprise', and within thirty-six hours of that development Noel's grand Everest adventure was over, and he and his men were on their way back to India.

The surprise came in the form of a Tibetan captain and guard who had been sent 'to prevent us following the upper road to Pherugh'.[34] Noel did not know this at the time, but the rider sent from Eunah to report on Noel's party had reached Tinki and informed the district headman, who had ridden for three days to confront the foreigners and order them out of Tibet. His account of what transpired next is John Noel at his storytelling best, a saga straight out of the Great Game. How it must have amused him, disappointed though he was. 'I went down with my men,' he begins,

and, forcing the Captain to dismount, asked him what he meant by posting soldiers on us as if we were common thieves. I found that he was the Captain of the Tashirak guard, and in the background was no less a personage than the Tinki Dzongpen himself and his followers . . . We learned later that the Dzongpen, hearing of our presence, had ridden 150 miles to meet us, covering the distance in three days.

A two-hour discussion followed. 'For what reason have you come to Tibet?' the dzongpen asked.

'At the time of the War (the 1904 Mission to Lhasa) many white men and men of India came, but since that time no one has entered the country.' They repeated again and again the same sentence: 'No foreigners may come to Tibet. We do not know what you want or for what reason you come.'

I complained that I had received only discourtesy and opposition in Tibet, whereas all Tibetans coming to India were free to travel where they wished and were received as welcome visitors. This was, I protested, indeed a disgrace to Tibetan civilization and Tibetan culture.

The whole party became very excited at this juncture and all started to shout and talk together. The soldiers crowded around and unstrapped their matchlocks in a threatening manner. It was impossible to make out what they were shouting about or what plan they might be proposing. All I could make out was the Dzongpen saying: 'Go back the way you came.'

I argued but he was insistent. Then I tried the Tibetan game. I temporized, told him I would think it over and give him a reply the following day. The discussion then took another turn. He dropped his blustering, authoritative tone and became delightfully courteous. He told me he would have to get permission from Lhasa for us to pass through his province, and he begged us by no means to travel on or it would cost him his head.

I was nettled meeting this opposition when so near to my goal and at the prospect of failure after so much effort. I knew that his force of soldiers could not deter me. They were armed with an ancient variety of matchlocks, and at 3-yards range the charge of slugs they would fire would be harmless, but the Dzongpen had, in the latter part of the interview at least, been so polite that I naturally hated to do anything that would cause him to be beheaded!

Noel then took a page from the dzongpen's book and said he would think over the demand and give his answer the next day, whereupon the official galloped off with all but one of the guard who remained behind. Noel was 'on the boil' as he put it, noting that

Life at high altitudes does not conduce to placidity and evenness of temper. [A]nd the arrogance of the soldiers and their unconcealed smug satisfaction at having discovered and made us halt had distinctly got on my nerves. One of the men remained behind longer than the rest. Finally he too started, but in passing he jostled his horse against me rudely. I jumped ahead and seized his bridle. I meant to hold him and complain to the Dzongpen, but he struck me across the face with his whip and tore the bridle from my grasp. Highly enraged I ran after him. He galloped for several hundred yards with me in pursuit. Then he dismounted and swung his clumsy matchlock into action.

I was fired on by that grotesque instrument! It made enough noise for a cannon . . . I slipped behind the ruins of a Tibetan wall [and] placed a shot from my American rifle over his head, and he went off so fast and made me laugh so much that I did not think it worthwhile to follow it with another one.

Things seemed to be none the worse for this incident, save that my face smarted a bit from the blow of the whip, but my men thought otherwise. They were tremendously excited and highly perturbed. With the exchange of fire they thought the whole of Tibet would descend on us. They absolutely refused to go on.

There was nothing to be done but to turn our backs on the approaches to Everest, the mysterious lamasery, and the valley of the mountain.

Within forty miles and nearer at that time than any white man had been! I leave you to imagine my chagrin and disappointment.[35]

Chagrined and disappointed, no doubt, but Noel was also very lucky not to be arrested or even imprisoned. It's worth remembering in this context that what men like Noel, Younghusband and their Russian counterparts regarded as daring exploits and grand adventures were so many cavalier breaches of national sovereignty as far as the governments of Nepal, Tibet and other countries were concerned. While the daring and bravery of these 'explorers' cannot be denied, neither can the imperial hubris that supported their illegal forays. It's likewise worth remembering, as more than one colonial wag put it, that the reason the sun never set on the British Empire is because God didn't trust the British in the dark.

Chagrin and disappointment to be sure, but at the same time Noel surely must have taken some satisfaction from three major achievements that can be credited to his journey: he got closer to Everest – 40 miles – than any westerner to date; he established that attacking the mountain from the east was a non-starter or, at the very least, no more feasible than from the north; and he brought back pictures. In the end it was the pictures that would turn out to be by far the most important product of his journey. Indeed, six years later those pictures, plus several borrowed from Alexander Kellas, were shown to an audience at the Royal Geographical Society, transforming virtually overnight the hunt for Everest into a British national crusade. In the end, Noel's 'failure', as he called it at the time, had all the marks of a success.

Tom Longstaff needed a mountain to climb. When John Morley ('Aunt Priscilla') refused to approve the joint RGS–Alpine Club proposal for Everest back in 1906, Longstaff joined two other climbers of that disappointed team, Charles Bruce and A. L. Mumm, on an attempt some months later to climb Trisul, part of the Nanda Devi massif in the Garhwal Himalaya. By the time of the attempt on Trisul, Longstaff had become identified with the rush-to-the-summit school of climbing where small teams with minimal equipment made a dash for the top and came back down in a single sprint.

True to form, on 12 June 1907, while Bruce nursed a bad knee and Mumm fought off severe diarrhoea, Longstaff, two Alpine guides and one of Bruce's Gurkhas assaulted Trisul from their camp at 17,400 feet (5,300m), reached the top around noon, and came back down before nightfall – covering an astonishing 7,000 feet (2,130m) in a single day. The Everest veteran Edward Norton later wrote that 'Longstaff's feat in conquering Trisul . . . constitutes a *tour de force* worthy of more remark than it has received in all the quarter of a century during which he held the world's record for the highest summit conquered.'[36]

Not exactly. To be sure it remains a remarkable accomplishment by any standard – at 23,359 feet (7,119m) Trisul was the first 7,000-metre peak ever climbed – and Norton is right to underline it. But Longstaff and company did not in fact hold the record for having climbed the world's highest summit for nearly a quarter of century, from 1911 until 1930, as they and the entire Himalayan climbing fraternity believed at the time and as the climbing community continued to believe for nearly a hundred years. In fact, Longstaff held the record for just under four years, until 14 June 1911, when an obscure Scottish chemist reached the summit of a peak named Pauhunri in Sikkim which, at 23,386 feet (7,128m), is 27 feet *higher* than Trisul. At the time, however, the height of Pauhunri was given as 23,180 (7,065m) and Trisul as 23,460 (7,150m), but a number of Himalayan peaks were re-measured in the mid-1980s and their heights adjusted; Trisul was downgraded to 23,359 (7,119m), and Pauhunri was upgraded to 23,386 (7,128m). Thus it was the obscure Scot, and not Tom Longstaff, who held the record for the world's highest summit for nineteen years, although he would go to his grave unaware of his achievement. Indeed, he spent the next several years trying to beat Longstaff's record, not realising he already had. His name was Alexander Kellas.*

Obscurity suited Alexander Kellas. While many of the famous names in the Everest saga were larger than life – Francis Younghusband, George Mallory, Tom Longstaff, John Noel himself – with healthy egos, colourful personalities, reserves of bluster, a commanding presence, men who filled a room, Kellas was none of these things. If anything, he was smaller than life: modest, mild-mannered, self-effacing, of a 'retiring disposition', with a kind of absent-minded professor look.[37] He was 'untidy, stooped, thin and small, his face adorned with pebble glasses because of poor eyesight'.[38]

Kellas was naturally shy, a loner, a bachelor who lived alone in a one-room apartment, with few close friends. In his working life he was often overshadowed by more forward colleagues. He left behind only two typically modest accounts of his mountaineering exploits and no famous remarks that might immortalise him. Although shy and reclusive, he was also charming, good-natured, even-tempered and good company. He was easily the most popular of all the British members of the 1921 Everest expedition.

Kellas is usually credited with three contributions to the Everest story: his support and promotion of the Sherpas; his research into and study of the effects of altitude on human physiology; and the

---

* Neither Longstaff nor Kellas, it should be noted, held the *altitude* record during these years. That was held by the Duke of the Abruzzi who reached 24,600 feet on Chogolisa in 1906, just 557 feet short of the summit.

photos he brought back from a mysterious trip to the Himalayas in 1913, the same year Noel took his pictures. A fourth distinction, the fact that he was widely regarded as the most accomplished Himalayan climber of his generation – even by Tom Longstaff, no less, his chief rival for that honour – has been largely forgotten.

Kellas was born in Aberdeen in 1868. Like many Scottish families, Kellas's parents took him and his brother on family holidays in the Scottish highlands, especially the Cairngorms, at 4,000 feet (1,219m), the highest land massif in Britain, where he first climbed in 1883 at the age of fifteen. Kellas graduated with a degree in chemistry from University College London in 1892 and worked for a time in the lab of the Nobel Prize-winning chemist William Ramsay. Kellas got an advanced degree in chemistry from Heidelberg University in 1896 and later took a position as lecturer in chemistry at the Middlesex Hospital Medical School. He first climbed in the Alps in 1899, and six years later, in 1905, he and his brother climbed Mont Blanc.

Between 1907 and 1921, Kellas made eight trips to the Himalayas, excursions the typically modest Kellas referred to as 'hurried holiday visits', although they included a number of first summits, the most for any Himalayan climber in a single year, as well as that record for the highest summit yet climbed that would last from 1911 to 1930. Kellas was not given to false modesty – he was clearly aware of the significance of his achievements – but for him climbing was as much research as it was sport due to his keen interest in studying the effect of altitude on the body. He 'considered himself less a climber than a scientist who frequently found himself on the summits of mountains'.[39]

Kellas was not chasing notoriety; he was chasing knowledge. 'Kellas did not advertise,' John Noel wrote of his friend. 'Few people knew about him. He would emerge each year from his chemical research work at the hospital. He did not tell the newspapers when he set out to climb a mountain higher than any climber had ever tackled before. He just went unobserved.'[40] Or, as Noel might have added, he went *to* observe.

And Noel went on to point out how Kellas did not merely climb these summits, he traversed many of them. 'No peak could defy him,' Noel continues. 'He conquered great Kangchenjhau, Chomiomo, and Pauhunri. He walked up one side of this mountain, walked down the other, and then round the base back to his camp . . .' Traversing, as this is called, is something that most climbers 'attempt only after having first climbed each side', Noel notes. 'Kellas would traverse nearly all his virgin mountains from one side to the other on his first ascent.'[41]

On all but his first trip to the Himalayas, Kellas climbed 'alone', which in the mountaineering parlance of the time simply meant he did not climb with other westerners, neither as guides nor as climbing partners. Like many European climbers before him, he did use Swiss guides on his first trip, but he found them wanting and never used them again. 'I have made three journeys to Sikkim in the years 1907, 1909, and 1911,' Kellas wrote. 'In 1907 Swiss guides were taken but they proved unsatisfactory, and in 1909 and 1911 only natives were employed . . . The Sherpas who come from Eastern Nepal were found to be the best and they can be recommended to travellers.' In a note on his application to join the Alpine Club, Kellas explained that his Swiss guides were timid – They 'think snow dangerous', he wrote – and they also apparently suffered from altitude sickness.[42]

Kellas's habit of climbing 'alone' can be put down in part to his introverted and reclusive nature, but another factor seems to be that he genuinely preferred to climb with Sherpas, not just as porters and in other support roles but also as fellow climbers. In one instance he singled out two Sherpas 'named Sona and Tuny [who] were found to be good at ice work, especially the latter, who is by far the best all-round coolie that I have ever met. His ice steps were admirable.'[43] While Kellas did not 'discover' the Sherpas, as is often claimed, he was one of the first to engage them and remained their tireless champion. It is said that the closest personal relationships Kellas ever formed were with a small number of Sherpas he climbed with regularly. In this respect it is noteworthy that the first place in Himalayan climbing literature where individual Sherpas are referred to by their name is in the accounts Kellas wrote of two of his expeditions.

He seems to have been especially close to a Sherpa named Anderkyow with whom he climbed on an attempt on Kangchenjhau in Sikkim in 1912. At one point on that climb, Anderkyow and two other Sherpas were sent to buy provisions, and one of the Sherpas came back to report that Anderkyow had absconded into Tibet with the expedition's cash. Kellas refused to believe ill of Anderkyow and instinctively assumed there had to be another explanation and even blamed himself for putting temptation in Anderkyow's path. He was not surprised when Anderkyow turned up later, complete with cash and supplies, and explained that he had got lost.

For most of his life Kellas suffered from auditory hallucinations – hearing voices – and while this condition was not usually debilitating, on a few occasions he would have to seek treatment and rest. In a letter he wrote to Arthur Hinks at the RGS in 1919, Kellas refers to 'a peculiar and continuous annoyance . . . a disturbance which medical men tell me is due to overwork and which takes the form of malevolent aural communications, including threats of murder'.[44] Kellas was so convinced the voices were real he believed that if he put a very sensitive microphone near his head, he could actually record them. While this condition is considered an affliction in the West, the Sherpas saw it differently. A friend recalled how Kellas once told him that 'in the mountains, when no other Europeans were there, he answered these voices, and his Sherpas had great confidence in a man who had long conversations with spirits at night'.[45]

Many qualities endeared the Sherpas to Kellas, but their happy-go-lucky temperament was especially appealing, a quality he seems to have shared with them; he was good-natured, and they were good-natured, and together they worked climbing wonders. 'Kellas found the Sherpas cheerful under all conditions,' John Noel wrote, 'willing to undertake risks, and faithful. He made friends with these rough mountaineers, and with their help he conquered virgin peaks one after another with an ease and rapidity that astonished the world.'[46] All this from a man who first started climbing in the Himalayas one year before he turned forty.

Many of those virgin peaks were conquered during what Kellas's biographers have called his *annus mirabilis*, a five-month trip to Sikkim in 1911 'which probably constituted the most successful Himalayan mountaineering expedition undertaken by anyone up to that date'.[47] Like all of Kellas's trips up to that time, his interest on this occasion lay in continuing to explore the numerous passes and glaciers around

Kangchenjunga. In mid-May Kellas and a group of Sherpas ascended the Choten Nyima Pass, the same pass Noel would use two years later to cross into Tibet, and made the first ascent of an unnamed mountain which Kellas dubbed Sentinel Peak, just over 22,000 feet high (6,705m).

The next mountain Kellas climbed in 1911 was Pauhunri, the peak that made him, unknowingly, the record-holder for the highest summit ever reached, a record he would hold for nineteen years until 1930 when Jongsong Peak, at 24,500 feet (7,482m), was climbed by Smythe and Schneider. Curiously, this fact, available to Himalayan historians since the resurvey in the mid-1980s, appears to have been overlooked for another thirty years, until 2011, when Kellas's biographers declared that the 'common wisdom that Longstaff held the world summit altitude record from 1907 till 1930 cannot now be sustained. From 1911 till 1930, that record was Alexander Kellas', and justice is served by crediting it to him posthumously.'[48]

Kellas was not a prolific writer and very few of his letters survive. Indeed, the very absence of his voice reinforces the impression of a private person who climbed for his own pleasure and to increase his knowledge but not for fame. One of the two or three writings Kellas did leave behind, an article entitled 'The Mountains of Northern Sikkim and Garhwal', is his own account of his climbs during his *annus mirabilis* of 1911 (not that he himself would ever have referred to it in such terms), including his summit of Pauhunri. The article, which he read at a meeting of the Alpine Club on 6 February 1912, is pure Kellas, a veritable compendium of the many hazards, challenges, reversals and disappointments of the earliest days of Himalayan exploration, all presented in matter-of-fact, self-deprecating prose. He writes of downed bridges; bottomless crevasses to leap over, go around, or even bridge in some cases; seracs that could collapse at any moment; raging torrents to cross; piercing cold winds; all-enveloping mists; waist-deep snowfields taking hours to wade through; snow-blindness; frostbite; headache-inducing sun glare; storms that come on in minutes; the constant risk of avalanches and rock falls; giant ice fields; stubborn and frightened porters who refuse to go on and who 'have a weakness for wanting to camp about an hour after starting in the morning'.

At one point Kellas is climbing along a path immediately below that of his porters when

> [a] few stones came down, but they went wide of me, and I thought that instead of making the coolies halt I could arrange to take a somewhat different route from theirs. This was difficult because of icy gullies requiring [cutting] steps, and the coolies doubled back until they were [again] right above me. The rocks being steep and broken, I could not see them, and the first intimation I had of their position was a stone almost 2 inches in diameter whizzing past my nose and hitting me a resounding thump on the chest. As I happened to be in a slightly awkward position, if the stone had been bigger, or if it had hit me on the head, I might have been knocked down . . . The blame was mine for not stopping them earlier.[49]

Knocked down *at the very least*. This is classic Kellas, minimising the danger and by implication his own courage, always taking the blame when things went wrong. Classic Kellas also because the article never once mentions the astonishing fact that he climbed more virgin summits on this trip than anyone had ever done before or has ever done since. Many Himalayan climbers have made entire books out of much less.

In a brief glimpse of the man early on, some of Kellas's porters lasso a mountain fox and offer to sell the animal to him, 'declaring that its skin would fetch a considerable sum in Calcutta, but [they] released it on my refusal. I was glad they did not kill the creature.'[50] Later he writes of some especially tame wild geese he comes across, 'but we only saw one young one, of which the parent birds seemed very careful. It made me annoyed to think that a certain type of gunner – one does not mean sportsman – could easily have exterminated all these geese, for they were quite easily accessible.'[51] And then there were the two young larks.

Pauhunri, it turned out, was just one of an unprecedented ten first ascents over 20,000 feet (6,100m) that Kellas made on this journey, of which the best known is probably the first ascent of Chomiomo (22,403 feet/6,828m). Kellas's achievements in 1911 are all the more remarkable for the fact that at the time he was forty-three years old, while many of his peers were as much as ten years younger. Moreover, as his biographers have pointed out, less than five years earlier, in 1907, Kellas 'was a man who had done a considerable amount of hard hill walking in Scotland and a couple of easy guided Alpine peaks', but by 1911 'this cautious, moderate mountaineer of 1907 had . . . ascended five virgin Himalayan summits of over 20,000 feet [6,100m] . . . without other European companions, including, unbeknown to even himself, the highest mountain yet ascended in the world'.[52] At the time of his death, the Scottish chemist cum mountaineer had spent more time above 19,600 feet (5,975m) than any man alive.

For Kellas, gaining elevation was not simply the aim of climbing, it was also the occasion to experience and observe the effects of altitude and oxygen deprivation on the climber, a subject of keen interest to Kellas and one he understood better than any other climber of his generation. It is 'no exaggeration', his biographers write, 'to suggest that Alexander Kellas' scientific approach to a whole range of issues concerning the possible ascent of Mount Everest . . . was light years away from the gentlemanly, amateurish atmosphere which dominated British attempts to climb Everest before the 1950s.'[53]

As a scientist and as a lecturer to medical students, Kellas would certainly have had a professional interest in and knowledge of human physiology, but his interest spiked during his first visit to the Himalayas in 1907 and his initial encounters with the Sherpas. He noticed straight away how their stamina exceeded his own – and Kellas was justly celebrated for his stamina – and he even put some numbers to their capacity, noting that from 15,000 to 17,000 feet (4,570–5,180m) a westerner could hold his own with an unloaded Sherpa, but above 17,000 'their superiority was marked'. He observed that up to 22,000 feet (6,705m) an unloaded porter could climb faster than he could and that even 'a moderately loaded' porter could keep up with him. 'Above that elevation a moderately loaded coolie could run away from me, and with an unloaded coolie one had not the slightest chance.'[54] Kellas surmised that the explanation was the greater lung capacity of people who lived all their life at high altitudes.

Over the next thirteen years Kellas devoted himself to understanding what the effects of altitude were on people of normal lung capacity – European climbers, in short – and what, if anything, they could do to minimise those effects. The starting point of his experiments was the phenomenon known as hypoxia, the lack of oxygen caused by the greatly reduced barometric pressure above a certain altitude. At 29,029 feet (8,848m), the height of Everest, barometric pressure is one third what it is at sea level, which means the body is breathing in one third as much oxygen as it needs to survive. The body can adapt, however, if certain measures are taken, principally acclimatisation, but even that, Kellas concluded, would not make any difference after 22,000 feet (6,705m). He maintained, in short, that every moment a climber spends above 22,000 feet, his body begins to shut down, which is the reason why this elevation, later amended by Kellas to 25,500 feet (7,770m), is called the danger zone or sometimes the death zone. The body can still continue to function in the danger zone, but at increasingly reduced capacity, and the question then becomes whether or not it can function long enough for a climber to reach the top of 26,250-foot (8,000m) peaks and get back down below 25,500 feet (7,770m) in the same day.

What Kellas set out to determine was just how long was 'long enough' on Everest? Was it possible that the 3,500 feet (1,066m) to the summit of the mountain from a likely last camp at 25,500 feet (7,770m) was simply too far, that climbing that distance and back at that altitude would take too long and the climber's body would give out before he could return? In short, was it in fact humanly possible to climb Everest?

To answer this question Kellas focused on calculating the volume of oxygen that would be present in the alveoli, the tiny air sacs in the lungs, on the top of Everest. Extrapolating from those calculations, from the results of a number of experiments carried out in a hypobaric chamber at the Lister Institute in London (to simulate the air pressure at high altitudes), and from the results of experiments carried out on Mount Kamet in Sikkim, Kellas concluded that above 25,500 feet (7,770m) it would take a climber an average of one hour to climb roughly 500 feet (152m). Accordingly, to climb the 3,500 feet (1,066m) from a probable high camp to the summit of Everest would take seven hours. Assuming the descent would be much faster, perhaps not even half as long, then a total of approximately ten hours would be needed to climb to the top of Everest and get back down to the high camp.

Thus the answer to the key question of how long – how long a climber's body would have to survive on depleted oxygen in attempting to climb Everest – was approximately ten hours. But whether the body *could* survive that long would not be known until someone actually reached above 25,500 feet (7,770m) and tried to keep climbing. At the time, however, most experts believed that ten hours on depleted oxygen would not be unduly dangerous. Six decades later, in 1978, Kellas's calculations proved to be remarkably accurate; in that year two climbers, Reinhold Messner and Peter Habeler, were the first people to climb Everest without oxygen, and they reported that the last 320 feet (97m), all above 28,500 feet (8,686m), took them an hour. Kellas's sixty-year-old estimate for climbing at that very altitude was 356 feet (108m) per hour.

Climbing with supplemental oxygen was also a possibility in the pre-war years, but it was highly controversial, and the equipment was notoriously unreliable. Kellas experimented at length with oxygen on Kamet in 1920 but ultimately concluded that any gains from the added oxygen were cancelled out by the increased weight of the canisters. Kellas took an oxygen canister along with him on the 1921 expedition, but it was never used. When Sherpas first caught sight of all the oxygen canisters brought along on the 1922 expedition, they laughed. 'The air in our country, sirs, is quite good,' they said. 'Why did you bring bottled air from England?'[55]

Kellas quickly became the recognised authority on the physiological effects of high altitude climbing, and he began to compose his hugely influential paper, 'A Consideration of the Possibility of Ascending Mount Everest', which he was invited to read at the annual meeting of the Alpine Congress in Monaco. This paper was later read to the Royal Geographical Society and the Alpine Club and printed in both of their journals, becoming a kind of de facto blueprint for the 1921 expedition.

If 1911 was Kellas's miracle year, his *annus mirabilis*, then 1913 was his mystery year. At the end of that year he returned from the Himalayas with a series of stunning photos of the eastern approaches to Everest, in particular the beautiful Kama Valley, photos taken from just over 10 miles from the mountain, 30 miles closer than Noel had been. If Kellas made that journey and took those photos, he would have been closer to the mountain than anyone until the 1921 expedition.

But did he? Apart from the fact that he visited Nanga Parbat that year, nothing else is known for sure about where Kellas went or what he did. On the other hand, extrapolating from the results of that trip, his intent, at least in part, is unmistakable: to gather and bring back as much information as possible about the eastern approaches to Everest, information that would be used to inform discussions then taking place about a possible Everest expedition in 1915. In addition to the photos of the Kama Valley, Kellas also brought back extremely detailed knowledge of the eastern approaches to the mountain, as John Noel documents in his book *Through Tibet to Everest*.

Noel befriended and regularly visited Kellas on his return in 1913 and throughout the war years. During these visits it was obvious to Noel that Kellas had what was almost certainly first-hand knowledge of the region around Everest. 'He told me one day of his secret knowledge of Kharta,' Noel writes, 'and the pass called the Tok Tok La over the same mountain barrier that had blocked my way on my journey to Tashirak.' Kellas explained that he could use this pass to reach Kharta, 'where he knew of a rope bridge by which to cross the Arun river and so reach the Langma La', which led into the Kama Valley and from there to the base of Everest's East Face. Kellas told Noel of a plan he had worked out 'to lay depots of food in uninhabited valleys west of Kangchenjunga . . . and of his hopes of reaching Kharta, crossing the river and going up to the eastern glaciers of Everest . . .' Noel remarked on how 'elaborately detailed' Kellas's plan was, 'thought out to the last ounce of food and water'.[56] However he acquired it, Kellas clearly had more detailed knowledge of the eastern approaches to Everest than anyone else, knowledge he must have acquired during his 1913 trip.

But the question remains: *how* did he acquire it? The strongest evidence that Kellas was in Tibet in 1913, albeit circumstantial, is that he never wrote anything about where he went that year or what he did and never told anyone except Noel. To be sure, Kellas left very few writings behind, but he did write lengthy articles about his two previous trips in 1911 and 1912, both published in the *Alpine Journal* and read by Kellas himself at two club meetings, so it is curious he never wrote or spoke about 1913. Even his biographers, who ran down numerous hitherto unknown sources of Kellas's materials, could not find any references to the trip. Information 'is almost nonexistent', they wrote. 'We simply have to confess our ignorance.'[57] Another meticulous Everest chronicler, Wade Davis, observes in his exhaustive account of the Everest story that in 1913, 'Kellas was never seen by anyone, and no one knew precisely where he had gone, or how he managed to achieve what he did.'[58] And Noel himself writes in a similar vein that 'in the long gap between my own journey of 1913 and the Everest expedition in 1921, I talked with Kellas whenever I had a chance about Everest, and he told me many things that have never been made public about his plans and work concerning the mountain', adding that Kellas 'would tell no one how he obtained the pictures . . .'[59]

Why all the secrecy? To begin with, it was illegal for westerners to be in Tibet or Nepal at this time, so if Kellas had written or spoken about his journey, he would have had to admit that he entered the country illegally. By itself, however, that would not necessarily have been something Kellas had qualms about; he had entered Nepal without permission before, on his 1909 trip to the Himalayas, hoping to get better views and photos of Kangchenjunga's West Face, and during the war years he and Noel dreamed up a scheme to embark on a 'furtive raid' into Tibet to have a go at climbing Everest. Kellas's silence about 1913 makes perfect sense, however, when considered in light of the project he had taken up immediately on his return from the Himalayas that year. He was asked by the RGS to work on a formal proposal for a two-year expedition to be carried out in 1915–16 to reconnoitre and then climb Everest, an effort to be headed by Cecil Rawling – and one Kellas very much wanted to be part of. But if the authorities in Lhasa or India or especially in London learned that Kellas had stolen into Tibet illegally in the late summer of 1913, permission for the expedition might have been withheld, or, at the very least, Kellas himself might have been forbidden to participate.

In the end it will never be known for sure where Kellas went or what he did in 1913 and whether he took the famous photos himself or, as Noel claims, he trained Sherpas to do the picture-taking. But it is beyond dispute that during the years 1913 to 1921, Kellas possessed more knowledge of the area immediately around the eastern approaches to Everest than anyone else. His vast knowledge and his secrecy about 1913 raise the intriguing possibility that the great Himalayan climber and explorer spent the late summer and autumn of that year getting closer to Mount Everest than anyone had ever been before.

Whether Kellas took the photos of the eastern approaches himself or enabled Sherpas to do the job, the fact remains that it is thanks to Kellas that those remarkable photos were taken. Those photos, even more than John Noel's, ended up playing a decisive role in that carefully choreographed meeting of the RGS in March 1919 that jump-started stalled efforts to mount an Everest expedition. For that alone, Kellas earns his place in the trio of westerners who did more than anyone before them to begin to unlock the mysteries of the world's highest mountain. When Kellas's other achievements are put alongside the ground-breaking photos – his championing of the Sherpas, his reconnaissance efforts in the general neighbour-hood of Everest, and his extensive physiological studies – a strong case can be made that, with the possible exception of Francis Younghusband, no one did more to advance the cause of finding Mount Everest than Alexander Kellas.

Which begs the question why Kellas is not better known. He was still well known and celebrated in the twenty years immediately after his death, but in the last sixty years or more his fame has faded. For one thing, his arguably greatest achievement – holding the summit record from 1911 until 1930 – could not have been ascribed to Kellas until the heights of Pauhunri and Trisul were adjusted in the 1980s. Even then, all the books published during the next thirty years, until the 2011 biography by Mitchell and Rodway, continued to assign the summit record to Longstaff. Kellas was, moreover, an especially private person who did not actively seek notoriety or acclaim. It is also the case that human physiology, one of his abiding passions and the subject of one of his greatest contributions, does not make for high drama and controversy, the stuff of many an Everest legend. Then there is the fact that Kellas left few writings and little personal correspondence behind. His biographers regularly lament how sparse the written record is, citing extensively in their writings, as if to prove the point, a few scribbled notes he made on his applications to join the Scottish Mountain Club and the Alpine Club.

But no doubt the biggest reason more is not known about Kellas is because although he knew all the great climbers of his generation, he did not climb with other Europeans, only with Sherpas. There are no stories about Kellas, in short, because he did not climb with the people who wrote the books where such stories can be found. The single exception, of course, is in books about the 1921 Everest expedition, where Kellas emerges just enough to make readers wish they could know more.

Kellas's 2011 biographers are hardly neutral observers, but at the same time it is difficult to argue with their conclusion, even allowing for hyperbole, that 'anyone [who] could achieve in Himalayan moun-taineering what Kellas did in so short a time is remarkable . . . The time has surely come for Alexander Mitchell Kellas to be recognised as what he indisputably was – one of the greatest Himalayan moun-taineers of all.'[60]

Cecil Rawling must have been pleased; after ten years, his dream of getting a chance to climb Everest was at last coming true. In late 1913 and the early part of 1914, Rawling and Tom Longstaff secured the backing of the Alpine Club and the Royal Geographical Society for the most ambitious, most comprehensive attempt yet to explore and if possible to climb the world's highest mountain. Alexander Kellas was asked to draft a detailed outline to include a description of the proposed route and recommendations for expedition members.

The proposal envisaged a two-year effort: 1915 would be spent exploring and reconnoitring the approaches to Everest, and 1916 would be the year of the summit attempt. Rawling would lead the venture. 'The expedition proposes to examine Mount Everest with a view to ascertaining the possibility of climbing it,' Kellas wrote in the proposal, or, if not, at least to reach as high as possible. But it 'may well be that Mount Everest is unclimbable on the north side by any mountaineer, however skilled, or that, even if the mountaineering difficulties are not insuperable, the altitude makes human advance impossible'.[61] The aim of the expedition was to try to answer these two questions.

Kellas and Noel met often during this period. Noel was so impressed by the details of Kellas's plan and reassured by the reconnaissance photos from 1913 that he eagerly accepted an invitation from Kellas to pursue the plan on their own – Noel said it would be their 'furtive private raid' – if the official proposal was turned down.[62]

But Noel and Kellas never went on their furtive raid, Cecil Rawling never saw Everest again, and the 1915–16 expeditions never took place. On 28 June 1914, a Serbian national named Gavrilo Princip assassinated Archduke Franz Ferdinand, heir to the Austro-Hungarian throne, and five weeks later the world was at war.

I heard that permission had just been given to Bell to go to Lhasa to see the Dalai Lama . . . This alters the situation considerably. I then saw Dobbs and asked him whether he could not wire to Bell to tell him, if he foresaw a favourable opportunity, to ask the Dalai Lama for permission for the Everest Scheme.

Charles Kenneth Howard-Bury

Younghusband seeded the audience with the right people, those establishment decision-makers who would be needed to do the heavy lifting in the discussion to follow Noel's presentation.

Aeolian Hall was full that night, with society members and a large number of newspaper reporters, as RGS president Sir Thomas Holdich rose to introduce Noel. Stepping to the podium Noel led with a brief, thirty-second prologue, striking just the right note with a touching tribute to one of the RGS's own. 'It cannot be long', he began, 'before the culminating summit of the world is visited, and its ridges, valleys and glaciers are mapped and photographed.' This would already have been done, Noel continued, 'but for the war and the lamented death of General Rawling, for whom this piece of exploration [was] his life's ambition. May it yet be accomplished in his memory.'[1] Whereupon Noel's audience rose in a prolonged standing ovation. After the audience was seated, the lights went down, save for a small spotlight shining on Noel at the lectern, while on the wall behind the speaker lantern slides of the Himalayas magically materialised in all their breathtaking splendour. At that moment, looking on from his seat on the stage, Younghusband must have realised that his ploy to get the attention of timid Raj bureaucrats was working even better than he had hoped.

Alexander Kellas was one of several members of the Himalayan climbing elite in the audience that evening – he had lent a number of his photos to Noel for the occasion – and he would be called upon after the presentation to lend his considerable prestige to the proceedings. He had, in fact, been instrumental in a number of ventures to advance the cause of Everest during the war years. While he could not explore his beloved Himalayas for the time being, he could prepare and be ready for the moment when the war was over and all attention would once again be focused on Everest. Like his countrymen, Kellas was disappointed that the other two outstanding prizes in twentieth-century exploration, the North Pole and the South Pole, had both been won without the help of anyone from Great Britain. Along with Curzon, Younghusband, Freshfield and many others, Kellas was determined that this must simply not happen again when it came to Everest. 'We missed both Poles,' he wrote to a climbing colleague, 'after having control of the seas for 300 years, and we certainly ought not to miss the exploration of the Mt Everest group after being the premier power in India for 160.'[2]

And to that end Kellas had work to do, primarily involving his altitude studies. He did some of the work in London, but Kellas needed to get back to the Himalayas to carry out experiments at altitudes above 22,000 feet (6,705m) before anyone tried to climb Everest. But before that could happen, the war would have to end. In November 1918, the war did end, and one month after that the Secretary of State for India Edwin Montagu got a letter from the RGS proposing a two-part, joint RGS/Alpine Club expedition to climb Everest. The first part, proposed for 1919, would consist of Kellas's trip to Kamet to conclude his high-altitude research, and the second part, in 1920, would be a summit attempt on Everest. Montagu forwarded the request to the viceroy in India, with a note observing that 'a task of such magnitude and geographical importance . . . should be entrusted to qualified British explorers'.[3] The viceroy's office stamped the letter as received on 17 January. After seven weeks of silence, a frustrated Younghusband convinced RGS president Sir Thomas that some prodding of the Indian government might be in order, and before long John Noel found himself behind the podium in Aeolian Hall basking in a standing ovation.

Noel's address was a somewhat subdued performance, at least as compared with the high drama that runs through the account he gives in his 1924 book *Through Tibet to Everest*. Noel began, to the delight of the journalists present, with a brief discussion of the possibility of an aerial reconnaissance of Everest, either by aeroplane or by 'the use of man-lifting kites' which thanks to 'the strong steady winds of Tibet could raise an observer 500 feet in the air which would give good observation over the plains'. Noel then went on to show his many photographs and to describe the two possible routes to Everest that he was aware of, from the east and from the north, adding that whichever of the two routes was followed, it was important to 'avoid Darjeeling and its officialdom at all costs', a probable reference to obstructionist bureaucrats.[4]

As prearranged by Holdich and Younghusband, the climbing royalty in the audience – Freshfield, Kellas and Farrar, president of the Alpine Club – then rose to respond one at a time to Noel's remarks. The highly influential Freshfield approved of what he had heard. 'I think we have got thus much forwarder tonight,' he began, and gave his opinion that while the route through Tashirak was more direct, 'we realize the best route, however, is doubtless the more northern one from Kampa Dzong through Tibet.'[5]

Next up was Kellas who 'admired [Noel's] magnificent photographs' and went on to say that he agreed with Noel and Freshfield that 'the best route is certainly along the Tista [Teesta] valley, then to Kampa Dzong and westwards . . .' He then described variant routes at some length and in great detail. He did disagree with the good major on one point, however, and his objection is typical of Alexander Kellas, the man who tried never to speak ill of anyone: 'I must venture to dissociate myself from Major Noel's remark regarding officials at Darjeeling, as I have invariably found them courteous and obliging.'[6] Farrar of the Alpine Club spoke next, observing that the expedition 'has every chance of success, and the Alpine Club is prepared . . . to recommend two or three young mountaineers quite capable of dealing with any purely mountaineering difficulties as are likely to be met with on Mount Everest.'[7]

Francis Younghusband had not been planning to speak that night, but he was completely carried away by Farrar's enthusiasm: 'The hour was late,' he wrote of the occasion, 'but I was so struck by the ring of assurance and determination in the words of the President of the Alpine Club that I could not help asking the [RGS] president . . . to let me say a few words.' Among other things, he used his extemporaneous remarks to send a not very veiled message to the bureaucrats still dragging their heels in India: 'I dare say there will be one or two attempts before we are successful; and the first thing we shall have to do is to get over the trouble with our own Government.' He then added with his usual patriotic exuberance: 'I think we are all determined that it shall be a British expedition.'[8]

John Noel's presentation had the desired result; it appears to have prompted the powers that be in India to consider the Everest proposal. Moreover, two weeks after the RGS meeting, Younghusband, seizing on the publicity generated by the event, wrote to Secretary of State Montagu to ask for a meeting to discuss where matters stood. At almost the same time and without knowing anything of Younghusband's efforts, a certain Lieutenant Charles Kenneth Howard-Bury wrote to Arthur Hinks, secretary of the RGS, to inform him that he, Howard-Bury, was on his way out to India and would be happy to seek an audience with the Panchen Lama or, failing that, with the maharajah of Nepal to ask for their cooperation for an Everest exploration. As the ward and cousin of Lord Lansdowne, a former viceroy of India, Lieutenant Howard-Bury had access where it mattered. Momentum was clearly building.

And then, suddenly, it was not. On 19 April word came from India that permission for the expedition was refused, the request having foundered on the rocks of high imperial policy. There were a number of issues, but the Chinese question was the main sticking point. After the bloody Chinese invasion and occupation of 1910–13, the Tibetans were desperate for military support and had repeatedly asked the British for artillery and other armaments. But while the British government was deeply suspicious of China's intentions towards Tibet, it preferred quiet pressure behind the scenes to overt provocation, which is how arming Tibet would have been interpreted. The situation was delicate, in short, and the government of India pointed out that 'the presence of a party of explorers on the borders of Tibet would not be likely to [facilitate] the execution of' government policy.[9] Not only was the Everest proposal rejected but also Kellas's request to carry out research on Kamet, a mountain within the confines of British India. This gratuitous slap at Kellas was interpreted as a message from the government of India to the explorers and mountain climbers back in London to mind their own business.

But it was too late. After Noel's talk, there was so much public interest in and enthusiasm about a possible Everest expedition that it had become a national cause virtually overnight, so much so that everyone recognised that it was now only a matter of time – a year, as it turned out – before an expedition would be back on track. Younghusband was everywhere that year keeping the proposal alive, an effort much abetted in June 1919 when he took over as president of the RGS. He met regularly with the president of the Alpine Club, kept up the pressure on the Secretary of State for India, established an Expedition Committee at the society, and kept in touch with Howard-Bury who stood ready to offer his services when needed. When Younghusband judged the time was right – in April 1920 – he convened a private meeting of representatives of the RGS and the Alpine Club to discuss a series of formal resolutions to establish a framework for an expedition to Mount Everest. Younghusband invited Howard-Bury to attend.

Among the resolutions that were passed were:

- That the mountain should be approached from the north, through Tibet, and that no attempt should be made to get permission to pass through Nepal.
- That Howard-Bury be asked to visit India this year with the object of obtaining the support of the government of India for the expedition and if it seems desirable of going to Gyantse to interest the Tibetan authorities.
- That the personnel of the expedition be British subjects. And that no applications for the cooperation of non-British subjects is to be entertained.

Two months later, on 23 June 1920, a joint Alpine Club and RGS deputation called on the Undersecretary of State for India to enlist his support for the proposal, which he gave on the condition that the government of India must be contacted for their approval. Howard-Bury left for India two days later on precisely that mission, and for the next six months, from June until December, the fate of the Everest expedition rested largely in his hands.

Charles Kenneth Howard-Bury was one of those polymaths England serves up from time to time, people who are expert in several different fields. In Howard-Bury's case he was an accomplished writer, photographer and naturalist, a successful horse breeder (in later years he named one of his horses Everest), an explorer, and was reputedly fluent in twenty-seven Asian and European languages. He was a Howard, the family of the earldom of Suffolk, and he himself was the great-grandson of the 16th Earl of Suffolk.

Howard-Bury attended Eton but forswore attending Oxford or Cambridge for a military career, graduating from Sandhurst in 1905, and was posted to India as a captain in the King's Royal Rifle Corps. He distinguished himself in India on two occasions: one was when he received a strong reprimand from George Curzon for crossing into Tibet without authorisation to explore the region around Mount Kailash, the holiest mountain in Tibet, sacred both to Buddhists and Hindus. The other was when he was on a pilgrimage along the Ganges and came to the holy town of Amarkantak where a tiger had recently been conducting a reign of terror, dragging off and eating twenty-one Indian holy men. Howard-Bury shot the tiger.

In 1912, when he inherited Belvedere, the Irish estate that belonged to his family, he left the army, and now, independently wealthy, he looked forward to a life of travel. It started well; in 1913 he went overland to Siberia and spent six months exploring in the Tien Shan mountains of western China, accompanied by his faithful canine companion, Nagu. In Omsk he acquired another animal, the bear cub Agu, which he brought back to Ireland with him and raised on the estate, wrestling with the bear whenever he needed exercise.

A year later the war put paid to Howard-Bury's dreams of travel. He rejoined his regiment and fought in the Battle of the Somme and at Passchendaele (where Rawling was killed). Later on he was caught in the middle of the fiercest fighting of the war, the Germans' Spring Offensive of 1918. He was captured along with most of his battalion and served out the war as a POW, escaping once for ten days only to be recaptured and thrown into solitary confinement.

He excelled at many things, but not at mountain climbing. He was drawn to mountains as a child, climbed in the Alps as a young man, and later spent time in Kashmir and in the Karakorams while stationed in India. But he was not yet a member of the Alpine Club, a box most serious climbers ticked if they could, and his mountaineering expertise is most frequently described as 'slight'. But he was a forceful personality, tactful, well connected, a good organiser, wealthy – he paid all his own expenses – and eager to help.

Howard-Bury arrived in Simla, the summer capital of British India, on 12 July 1920, to begin what turned out to be a six-month struggle over the fate of the Everest expedition, played out for the most part in a four-way contest between Howard-Bury, the viceroy, the 13th

Dalai Lama, and one Charles Bell, the British government's agent in Sikkim and unofficial envoy to the Tibetan god-king.

He wasted no time; on 15 July he had 'a long talk with the Viceroy' and came face-to-face with what would turn out to be one of the major obstacles to getting permission for the expedition: Tibet's request for arms to protect itself against possible aggression. That request had been forwarded to Whitehall some time earlier, but there had been no decision. Howard-Bury reported that while the viceroy himself was 'very sympathetic . . . and promised to give us every support possible', everything depended 'on the attitude of the Tibetans towards us, which again depends on the results of the present [arms] negotiations'. The viceroy advised Howard-Bury 'to go up to Gyantse and see [Charles] Bell and the Tibetan authorities and interest them in the project'.[10]

Five days later, in Howard-Bury's second letter to Younghusband, Charles Bell appears to have got under his skin, although the two men had still not met.

> I have just had another interview with [the deputy secretary, govern-
> ment of India] who just had a telegram from Bell . . . Bell says some
> poet-saint is buried near Everest, that the Tibetans are likely to be
> very suspicious and though we may fully explain what we want to
> do, they will not like it at all . . . Also until the present [arms]
> negotiations are settled, [Bell] is very much against any reconnaissance
> or any expedition to Mt Everest at all . . . If you could use your
> influence . . . to get the matter settled favourably, the chief obstacle
> to the expedition would be removed. (I am afraid that Bell is another
> obstacle and that as long as he is in his present position, he will put
> every difficulty he can in the way.)[11]

And the more Howard-Bury learns about Bell, the worse it sounds. 'They all say he is a most tiresome man to deal with,' he wrote to Younghusband in July, 'because he is very slow and cautious and does not make mistakes.'[12] At one point Howard-Bury met Frank O'Connor, Younghusband's translator during the 1904 invasion of Tibet and the first British agent in Gyantse, and wished 'we could get O'Connor sent as first resident to Lhasa, then there would be every chance of the expedition being allowed. The more I hear of

Bell the less I fear he will help us.'[13] Later, just before he left for Tibet to meet Bell, Howard-Bury wrote to Younghusband again: 'I am not very hopeful of getting him to look favourably on the expedition but I will do my best. Everyone seems to be quite agreed about him.' RGS secretary Hinks certainly was: '[T]he only trouble', he wrote to Kellas at the time, 'is that Bell is not a convinced believer.'[14] By the time Howard-Bury left for Tibet in the first week of August, the Everest proposal was in trouble again due to certain delicate matters regarding which the British government felt it was not 'in a position to approach the Tibetan government'.[15]

Howard-Bury wasn't bothered. He understood that while the government of India may not have been 'in a position to approach' Lhasa, Charles Bell was. If Howard-Bury could somehow make the case for the expedition to Bell, Bell might just possibly be able to rescue the mission. Such at any rate was the thin thread on which the expedition hung as Howard-Bury left for Yatung to finally meet the man he had somewhat unjustly come to regard as his nemesis.

Born in India, educated at Oxford, Charles Bell joined the Indian Civil Service in 1891 and from 1908 to 1921 served as the government's representative to the agency that oversaw the Raj's relations with Tibet, Bhutan and Sikkim, becoming in essence British India's de facto ambassador to Tibet. Bell was an academic and scholar, somewhat out of place among soldiers and bureaucrats. He loved all things Tibetan, was an expert on Tibetan culture, a renowned scholar of Tibetan Buddhism, spoke fluent Tibetan, and published the first-ever English–Tibetan colloquial dictionary in 1905. He and the Dalai Lama first met in 1910 in Darjeeling where the Dalai Lama fled when the Chinese invaded Tibet and where he lived in exile for more than two years.

'At first sight he did not look like a king,' Bell wrote of his first meeting with the Dalai Lama. 'A squat figure, somewhat pockmarked, the features showed the plebeian origin of the farmer's son . . . It was my duty to look after this most unusual refugee . . .' The Dalai Lama's attendants had arranged an elevated dais and 'a hurriedly contrived throne' in one of the largest rooms of the hotel where he was staying. The god-king always sat on a seat higher than those round him since 'in his own dominion he remains exalted and aloof. When pilgrims pass near his palace . . . they prostrate themselves three times in the dust before it; and when he passes along, eyes are turned towards the ground; they must not gaze upon divinity.' In Bell's case, however, His Holiness 'made no use of throne or dais. To show honour to the British Representative he rose from his seat and met me on the floor . . .'[16]

The government of India was in a somewhat awkward position vis-à-vis its famous exile cum guest, unwilling on the one hand to antagonise the Chinese but also keen to accord the god-king the proper respect, all without compromising a studiously neutral official posture. The viceroy decided that an official invitation for the Dalai Lama to come to Calcutta to meet him was a suitable gesture, and thus Bell found himself escorting His Holiness and some of his ministers from Darjeeling to Calcutta.

The Dalai Lama, used to the much cooler weather on the Tibetan plateau, found Darjeeling extremely warm and wondered about the weather down on the plains of India. '[In] this place in Kalikata,' he asked Bell, 'will the honourable heat be even hotter?'[17] Bell assured him it would be much hotter. Later the Dalai Lama, who until that time had had limited exposure to westerners, asked Bell another question: 'Does the great Viceroy . . . know how to speak Tibetan?' 'It had to be admitted', the ever-tactful Bell replied, 'that even viceroys are not omniscient.'[18] While the Dalai Lama was in a meeting with the viceroy, it was proposed that his ministers be entertained by a visit to the Calcutta Zoo, but they had to decline: 'This sugges-tion is wonderful,' they replied, 'but we cannot go today. It would be unfitting for us to see the elephants and tigers before His Holiness sees them.'[19]

Bell visited the Dalai Lama over fifty times during his two-year exile, each time the Dalai Lama eschewing his raised dais and sitting at a small table on a plain European chair at the same height as his guest. The two men formed an extraordinarily close relationship which lasted for the next twenty-three years, until the Dalai Lama passed away in 1933. The Dalai Lama came to rely increasingly on Bell for advice on all manner of issues he was asked to resolve, some of which Bell found exceedingly petty, such as the question of whether a Tibetan boy being sent to England for study should travel first class or second class. Because Bell spoke Tibetan, there was never any need for a translator during these meetings, so the two men usually met alone, an honour almost never bestowed on a westerner. Bell wrote that when he emerged from these one-to-one meetings, he would pass by a small group of attendants chatting at the end of a long verandah and 'they would rise and give me a friendly smile, as though to say, "Here is one who talks direct to our Dalai Lama, just the two together."'[20]

After two years and some months, the Dalai Lama returned to Tibet, and the two friends kept in touch throughout the remainder of Bell's time as the political agent for Sikkim, Bhutan and Tibet, until Bell retired in 1918. Two years later, in January 1920, the government called Bell out of retirement and asked him to return to Tibet to help facilitate the arms negotiations, among other things, during which time the Everest matter came to the fore. And now Howard-Bury was on his way up to Yatung to have a chat.

Howard-Bury met Bell for lunch on 5 August, escorted to Bell's residence by a Tibetan military band playing their version of the British national anthem. 'I have had several long talks with Bell,' Howard-Bury reported to Younghusband on 16 August, and 'he tells me that the Home Government have not yet replied about the arms question . . .' Bell told Howard-Bury that 'he did not care for the idea of the expedition until the whole of the question of the relations between China, India and Tibet had been settled . . . [a] question [that] has gone on for 14 years and may go on as long again.' Bell freely admitted that he could ask the Tibetan government 'today and he was quite certain that they would allow the expedition, but that he did not think it would be advisable at the present time and would put them in a suspicious frame of mind.'[21]

It might be asked why the Dalai Lama, after the British invaded his country and killed over 3,000 of his subjects, would even entertain requests from the British on any subject, much less grant them. Or why, for that matter, the British would even bother to approach him. But the invasion, calamitous as it was in terms of lives lost, could have been much worse, especially as compared with the recent invasion by the Chinese. Moreover, the British had paid for everything they took from the Tibetans, had for the most part refrained from looting, especially monasteries, had only fired upon Tibetans when provoked, treated prisoners humanely and released them all before they returned to India, and immediately left the country as soon as a treaty had been signed. Bell explains in his biography of the Dalai Lama that the British army left Lhasa voluntarily while the Chinese 'stayed, took all government into their own hands, and oppressed the Tibetans'. The Tibetans, Bell explained, compared the British invasion to a frog, 'symbolically regarded as a fierce animal by reason of its leaping', whereas the Chinese invasion was compared to a scorpion, 'a creature far more virulent. Tibetans quoted the proverb: "When one has seen a scorpion, one looks on the frog as divine." '[22]

Now that he had met and sat down with the man, Howard-Bury's opinion of Bell began to moderate as he came to understand why virtually everyone – the viceroy, the government of India and the home government – were so solicitous of the man and why they deferred to his views. It was clear that every decision Bell made was always in the best interests of the Tibetan people and in particular how best to protect them from the recurring threat of Chinese oppression. When the Dalai Lama was in exile in India from 1910 to 1913, the Chinese had conducted a brutal invasion and occupation, prompting the Tibetans, after the Chinese left, to ask the British government for arms. At this point it was widely believed that a party of British climbers traipsing across Tibet could compromise the sensitive arms negotiations. Even Howard-Bury agreed that if the price of helping Tibet resist Chinese aggression was a temporary pause in plans to climb Mount Everest, then that was not too much to ask. 'Now it all depends on how Bell puts it before the Dalai Lama,' Howard-Bury wrote to Younghusband in October, 'and we shall have to wait for his answer, which will not be for a couple of months.'[23]

The arms negotiations dragged on, and a deeply frustrated Bell, waiting in Gyantse, was on the verge of going back to England in September when he received an urgent letter from the Dalai Lama: 'I hear from my agent in Gyantse that you are returning to England. There is no other *Sahib* that understands every issue of Tibetan politics as you do. It will be a matter of the deepest grief to me if you leave before the issues between China and Tibet are settled. Please consider the matter.'[24] On 1 November, with permission from HMG, Charles Bell left Gyantse on his way to the Holy City, the Place of the Gods, Lhasa, for his first visit ever – the first time, in fact, that any European had ever been invited to Lhasa. Bell expected to be there for two or three months but did not leave until the following October. During those eleven months, he either worked wonders, as many have suggested, or else, more likely, a few wonders simply fell into his lap, but by the time Bell left Lhasa the British government had agreed to supply arms to Tibet, and the Everest expedition was back on.

Just how this came about, Bell does not say, but even Bell could not work wonders overnight, and initially there were no break-throughs. Indeed, after only three weeks in Lhasa, the British government announced they were pulling Bell back to India, most likely a ploy to pressure the Tibetans. And it worked, as Bell recounts in a charming passage from his biography of the Dalai Lama. 'The All Covering [Head] Abbot', Bell writes, 'said to a mutual friend, "We will first beg Lonchen Bell with folded hands to stay. If he does not agree to stay, we will throw our arms around his neck to keep him. If he still insists on going, we will hold on to him with our teeth, so that he will have to knock our teeth down our throats before he will be able to get away."'[25]

Bell stayed, and one month later he seems to have had a change of heart about Everest, deciding that the question of the relations between China, India and Tibet no longer needed to be settled before he would raise the subject of an Everest expedition with the Dalai Lama. 'I felt now that I could explain . . . the ins and outs of the question.' Bell told the Dalai Lama that he knew the Tibetans were understandably suspicious about foreigners wandering around their country, but he believed no harm would come from the undertaking. 'His Holiness knew me well enough to realise that I would not say this unless I really meant it, and that during my long service on this frontier I had always worked, as far as I could, for the welfare of Tibet.'[26] To no one's surprise, the Dalai Lama readily gave his consent.

Younghusband was delighted, naturally, and even wrote to the Dalai Lama to thank him, tactfully omitting any mention of the invasion that Younghusband had led a few years earlier. When Bell finally left Lhasa in October 1921, the Dalai Lama was standing on the roof of his palace, the Potala, to see his great friend off. Residents of the capital lined the streets, and Bell was escorted by an honour guard as far as the border with Sikkim. The two men never met again but corresponded for another twelve years until the Dalai Lama's death.

News of the permission was formally announced at a meeting of the RGS on 10 January 1921, and two days later the first meeting of the Mount Everest Committee was held, consisting of three members each from the Alpine Club and the RGS, with a secretary seconded from each organisation and with Francis Younghusband as chairman. The secretary from the RGS side was one Arthur Hinks, the indispensable man of the 1921 expedition (and of the two which followed). Hinks 'was a formidable personality' who had a hand, usually a controlling hand, in every element of the undertaking: organising, publicising, financing, fund-raising, planning, provisioning, team member selection and communications.[27] All official correspondence either originated with Hinks or at least went through him, and any that did not greatly distressed him. He was extremely hard-working – Younghusband said, 'Hinks did all the drudgery while I had all the enjoyment' – detail-oriented, thorough, completely dependable and utterly competent.[28]

Hinks was also blunt, tactless, arrogant, judgemental, insensitive, 'a manipulative civil servant' and dismissive of anyone he regarded as his intellectual inferior, of which there were legions.[29] And he did not like climbers. In the months after his appointment, he managed to alienate nearly everyone associated with the expedition, including George Mallory and, most seriously, Percy Farrar, past president of the Alpine Club and one of the most influential members of the Mount Everest Committee, a man, it was said, who was 'accustomed to have a deciding voice in anything that interested him'.[30] Hinks was certainly formidable, but in the person of 'J. P. Farrar', one observer has noted, 'Hinks had a foeman worthy of him, for Farrar was no less dogmatic in his views and trenchant in his expression of them. He proved a prickly member of the Committee.'[31]

Farrar and Hinks were from different worlds – the military and academia – and were not destined to get along. Hinks was the somewhat stuffy, consummate bureaucratic insider, while 'the great Captain Farrar' was the beloved leader, respected mountaineer and man of action. Farrar judged people by their climbing skills – 'he held that whatever a man's reputation in other fields, there could be nothing really wrong with him if his mountaineering was courageous and sincere' – which did not bode well for Hinks whose mountaineering was neither courageous nor sincere; it was non-existent.[32] But the indomitable Hinks, his lack of climbing credentials notwithstanding, was neither cowed nor threatened by Farrar; he was regularly annoyed, in fact, when everyone on the committee kept deferring to the great Captain when it came to selecting the climbers for the expedition, although that task was obviously the province of the Alpine Club and not the RGS. 'I don't think Farrar is the only authority,' he wrote. 'We have seen enough of him at the Committee to learn that he frequently talks at random, and when he differs on almost every point from Collie and Meade, who both have much Himalayan experience, I do not myself feel that Farrar is the best judge.'[33]

Hinks could be supercilious, had a tendency to pontificate and was widely considered to be without any sense of humour. He is known, however, to have made a joke on at least one occasion, in answer to a letter from George Mallory's wife, Ruth, who wrote to ask if Hinks could prevail upon the publisher of the book about the 1921 Everest expedition to send her a copy. Hinks was embarrassed that this had not been done and immediately checked with the publisher, who replied that they had already sent her one. 'Perhaps,' Hinks wrote to Ruth, 'they addressed it to the Rongbuk Valley [i.e. Tibet].'[34] Arthur Hinks was feared but not admired, indulged but not respected, tolerated rather than liked. But as everyone grudgingly admitted: he got the job done. John Noel's opinion was that all three Everest expeditions (and Noel was on two of them) 'owe[d] a large measure of their success to the organizing genius of Mr Hinks'.[35]

The Alpine Club and the RGS had been planning the expedition long before the official permission came through, discussing such issues as what the overall goal of the expedition should be, how to finance it, and who should make up the expedition team. Regarding the goal, there were, naturally, two camps. As far as the Alpine Club was concerned, the objective was obvious: to climb the mountain. But even Alpine Clubbers admitted that some reconnaissance would no doubt be needed since the mountain and the approaches to it were completely unknown; there were no maps covering the last 50 miles from the north and no photographs of the northern approaches from any closer than 25 miles. In short, there was no way of knowing whether the mountain could in fact be climbed – or even reached – from the Tibetan side. Be that as it may, the Alpine Club was mainly interested in climbing.

And so was Francis Younghusband, who saw and described the expedition in almost spiritual terms: an effort, as he put it, to dispel 'the ridiculous idea of the littleness of man'.[36] But inconveniently for him, Younghusband was not the head of a climbing organisation but of a scientific one, whose involvement he was obliged to justify. Naturally, members of the RGS would rejoice along with everyone else if Everest could be climbed, especially by the British, but for that body to be a sponsor the expedition would also have to have a clear scientific purpose, such as surveying and mapping. 'There still lingered the notion that climbing Mount Everest was sensational but not scientific,' Younghusband observed. 'If it were a matter of making a *map* of the region, then the project should be encouraged. If it were a question of merely climbing the mountain, then it should be left to mountaineers and not absorb the attention of a scientific body like the Royal Geographical Society.'[37]

In time a compromise of a sort was worked out: there would have to be considerable reconnaissance, everyone agreed, but at the same time if an opportunity should present itself to try for the summit without undermining the reconnaissance, then it should be seized. There was always going to be tension between these two competing agendas, especially when it came to deciding the make-up of the team. In the end, during the final climactic days of the expedition, these ultimately irreconcilable goals would clash at a crucial turning point, with what many observers regard as unfortunate consequences. But that was in the future.

Once the mapping/surveying vs climbing compromise had been worked out, the next order of business for the committee was to select the expedition leader, and here there was no disagreement: it would be General Charles Granville Bruce, dean of the Himalayan climbing fraternity, a man who had been part of or involved in nearly every major Himalayan climbing milestone for nearly thirty years, beginning back in 1892 when he was a member of the very first British expedition to the Himalayas, the Conway effort to climb K2. As soon as the expedition was announced, all the newspapers began referring to Bruce as 'The Man to Conquer Everest'. To not have offered Bruce the position would have been a minor scandal, but in the end Bruce turned down the offer, mainly due to war wounds from which he was still recovering. He was assured of the job the following year, however, the proposed 1922 expedition, if he wanted it, and he ultimately led that expedition and the third one in 1924.

Second choice was nearly as unanimous as Bruce: Charles Howard-Bury. He had rendered the Everest effort great service during five months of wrangling and cajoling in India, resulting in the eventual permission; he knew Hinks, Charles Bell, the viceroy and other key players; he got on well with Tibetans; he had organising experience; he had demonstrated a certain flair for diplomacy; and he offered to pay all his expenses. He had limited climbing experience, but that was deemed a secondary qualification for the position of leader, and moreover he had the all-important backing of Hinks who, suspecting criticism, wrote to Kellas that Howard-Bury was 'by no means to be despised though he does not profess to be a climber'.[38] He was a solid choice if not quite an inspired one, as Bruce would have been.

The next task the committee faced was choosing the remaining eight expedition members, a number limited by concerns over how to provision a band of westerners in an unknown region of Tibet more than a hundred miles from the closest British outpost. In the end the job came down to finding the strongest climbing and the strongest surveying teams possible. But it was not all smooth going.

There may have been eight other members, but only one name – George Mallory – is still remembered today, a hundred years later. Indeed, with the possible exception of Edward Whymper and the Matterhorn, no name is more closely associated with a mountain than Mallory with Everest. A case can be made that that distinction rightly belongs to Sir Edmund Hillary who was, after all, the first man to stand on the summit of Everest, along with Sherpa Tenzing Norgay. But even Hillary himself generously referred to Everest as 'Mallory's mountain'. Hillary's renown and reputation are certainly secure – his is the *other* name that will always be associated with Everest – but Sir Edmund was merely famous. George Mallory, on the other hand, became a legend.

'He climbed everything it was at all possible to climb,' Mallory's sister Avie recalled of her younger brother.[39] On one occasion when he was seven, Mallory was sent to his room for misbehaving at tea, only to show up a few minutes later on top of the bell tower of the church that adjoined the vicarage, having climbed up the down-spouts of the house and then up the sheer stone face of the tower. When he was accused of not going to his room as ordered, he objected; he *had* gone to his room, he replied, 'to fetch my cap'.[40] From childhood Mallory seems to have been indifferent to risk and oblivious of danger, qualities that later left him open to charges of being rash and reckless and taking needless chances when he climbed. 'That young man will not be alive for long,' an eminent Austrian climber once remarked when climbing with Mallory in Wales.[41]

George Mallory was born in 1886, the son of a vicar and of the daughter and granddaughter of vicars. Whilst his father was some-what staid, devout and dependable, his mother was free-spirited and more of a romantic, an Edwardian relative to her Victorian husband, imparting to her four children a love of adventure and a disdain for convention. When George was nine he was sent to a boarding/preparatory school at Eastbourne which he took to imme-diately. 'I had my first experience of football on Friday,' he wrote to his mother. 'It was a very nice experience. The first damage I did was to [knock] two boys over on their faces, the second was to kick the ball into a boy's nose, and the third damage was to [knock] a boy over on his ribs.'[42] Mallory was an avid athlete and later became one of the best gymnasts at his school, a skill that would serve him well as a climber.

When he was thirteen Mallory competed for and won a mathematics scholarship to Winchester College, the highly regarded public school, where he thrived. In the summer of 1904 Graham Irving, a tutor at Winchester and member of the Alpine Club, was looking for someone to climb with him in the Alps, and through another student Irving heard about Mallory, who had kept up his practice of climbing on buildings, attracting a large crowd on one occasion when he climbed to the top of a fifty-foot tower above Chamber Court in the College. Irving took the two students with him to the Alps, and after a bout of altitude sickness on his first climb – he threw up twelve times – Mallory was smitten. Irving formed the Winchester Ice Club the following year, with just four members, including himself (as president), Mallory and another student named Guy Bullock.

Irving was the first of many to marvel at Mallory's natural climbing ability, and he did not find him reckless. If he attempted dangerous routes or risky passages, it was not because Mallory sought danger or deliberately courted risk, but because for someone of his skill, the formations were simply not that challenging. 'He *was* prudent,' his friend Cottie Sanders observed, according to his own standards, though not to those of a typical 'medium-good rock climber. The fact was that difficult rocks had become to him a perfectly normal element; his prodigious reach, his great strength, and his admirable technique, joined to a sort of catlike agility, made him feel completely secure on rocks so difficult as to fill less competent climbers with a sense of hazardous enterprise.'[43] Irving remarked on his 'completely natural grace of upward movement; you knew his body to be the perfect servant of his mind, and that mind was, above all, a climbing mind.'[44] There is a well-known story of an incident that took place when Mallory was visiting America on a lecture tour after the 1922 expedition, staying in a high-rise hotel in Manhattan. A photographer chased him down and found him climbing the hotel's fire escape 'but not in the manner the builders intended. He was going up underneath the steps hand over hand, upside down.'[45] One frequent climbing companion said simply that George Mallory 'couldn't even fall if he wanted to'.[46]

Everyone who met Mallory was struck by his appearance; he was so good-looking that he was usually described as 'beautiful', as if to suggest that merely 'handsome' was somehow inadequate. His tutor Arthur Benson was struck by 'the extraordinary and delicate beauty of his face'.[47] Graham Irving wrote that Mallory 'had a strikingly beautiful face. Its shape, its delicately cut features, especially the large, heavily lashed, thoughtful eyes, were extraordinarily suggestive of a Botticelli Madonna, even when he had ceased to be a boy – though any suspicion of effeminacy was completely banished by obvious proofs of physical energy and strength.'[48] Upon meeting Mallory, the acclaimed Victorian biographer Lytton Strachey famously had a meltdown:

> Mon dieu – George Mallory . . . My hand trembles, my heart palpitates, my whole being swoons . . . Heavens! He's six foot high, with the body of an athlete by Praxiteles, the refinement and delicacy of a Chinese print, the youth and piquancy of an unimaginable English boy . . . By God! The sheer beauty of it all is what transforms me.

Strachey noted that Mallory's 'intelligence is not remarkable' and then added: '[But] what's the need?'[49]

After Winchester, Mallory went to Cambridge where his great beauty put him at the centre of a number of love triangles, as a circle of homosexuals, including his tutor, competed for his attention. Much has been written of this period of his life and whether or not Mallory returned the affection of any of his suitors, which he may have in the case of James Strachey, Lytton's brother. Most observers note that at the time 'Greek love' was something of a rite of passage in British public schools and university settings, and that for many young men it was an adventure but did not define their sexuality.

Talk of Mallory's beauty will sound very odd to those who have only seen the most commonly reproduced photographs of Mallory, those taken on the three Everest expeditions. In many of these photos he is unshaven, his hair is long and unkempt, and his clothes are well worn and dirty. In several he looks almost absurd, and in the rest he either looks quite wild or very plain; there is not the slightest suggestion of his good looks. On the other hand, a series of photos taken when he was on leave from the front in 1917 do showcase his 'delicately cut features' and his 'heavily lashed, thoughtful eyes'.

In 1909, while he was in his last year at Cambridge, Mallory met Geoffrey Winthrop Young, one of England's foremost climbers, and the two became fast friends, climbing together for the first time in Wales and then later that same summer in the Alps. In the Alps, Young observed, Mallory climbed with 'a continuous undulating movement so rapid and so powerful that one felt the rock must either yield or disintegrate'.[50] Eleven years later the influential Young would insert himself into Mallory's story at a pivotal moment and precipitate the most fateful decision of the young climber's life.

In September 1910 Mallory took up his duties as a teacher at Charterhouse School in Godalming, where he was to spend the next eleven years. He did not take naturally to teaching, did not excel at it and did not especially enjoy it. He recoiled, for example, at the prospect of having to teach Milton's *Paradise Lost* to his young charges. 'Imagine me teaching the smallest boys about the fall of man!' he wrote to a friend. 'What the devil is one to say? It was such a wholly admirable business and God behaved so badly . . .'[51] Mallory's favourite part of the teaching job by far was when he took promising young boys under his wing and taught them climbing in Wales.

In the autumn of 1913, the twenty-seven-year-old George Mallory met the twenty-one-year-old Ruth Turner, and by the following Easter, after a week Mallory spent with the Turner family in Venice, they were in love. 'What bliss!' George wrote to his mother. 'What a revolution! Ruth Turner . . . She's as good as gold and brave and true and sweet. What more can I say!'[52] Ten days later, in May, they became engaged, and at the end of July they were married. Ruth was the daughter of a successful architect and lived with her father, two sisters and a number of servants in a grand mansion her father had designed. For her dowry, Ruth's father bestowed on her an annual income of £750 and a new home. When the proud Mallory told

Ruth's father that he need not worry about his meagre salary, about whether Mallory could keep his daughter in the manner to which she had become accustomed, boasting that he, Mallory, 'couldn't possibly marry a girl if she had her own income', Thackeray Turner replied: 'You couldn't possibly marry her if she hadn't.'[53]

Ruth Mallory was progressive in her views and enormously sympathetic towards those less fortunate, so much so that one of her daughters complained that she should take better care of herself. She was exceptionally honest, often to a fault. 'She was the terror of her friends,' her daughter Clare observed, 'because she didn't have any of those little social lies that most people have, to gloss things over and make them run smoothly.'[54] She liked the outdoors, was artistic, and she was also practical and disciplined, complementing George in both respects. 'Seldom were two people more perfectly adapted', one of Mallory's friends and biographers wrote, 'to the purpose of modifying, rounding off, and completing each other.'[55]

One month after the wedding, Britain declared war on Germany, but George and Ruth's lives were not affected at that point since the government had ruled that teachers were essential to the war effort and should stay at their posts. As more of Mallory's friends joined up and more of his students graduated and went off to fight – and more of both were wounded or killed – his conscience was increasingly troubled; he wanted to avoid the front for Ruth's sake, but as the weeks and then the months passed and there were no signs that the war would be over soon, Mallory felt more and more superfluous 'as a comfortable schoolteacher'.[56] In late December 1915, when teachers were no longer exempt from service, he joined up, with Ruth's blessing.

During the war George alternated between assignments in the rear of the fighting and then in the trenches of the front line. He was initially assigned to the 40th Siege Battery, where his job was to observe the accuracy of artillery fire from observation posts, some of which were quite exposed, especially to snipers, and instruct the gunners when they needed to adjust their aim. At times he made observations directly from the trenches where he witnessed first-hand the horrors of the war; they were, as he wrote to his father, 'as harrowing as you can imagine'.[57] He was more careful when he wrote to Ruth, trying to make light of the appalling conditions at the front: 'If hereafter I say to a friend "Go to Hell" he'll probably reply "Well I don't much mind if I do. Haven't I perhaps been there?"'[58] He ended the war with a promotion to lieutenant, for which he was receiving training when the armistice was announced.

When the war ended, George returned to his teaching position at Charterhouse, but he was restless to find some work that would have more impact and meaning than simply influencing the ever-changing minds of young teenagers; he wanted to make a difference. In 1919 and 1920 he returned to the Alps where he was glad to see he had lost none of his stamina or his skill. On the 1920 trip he ran into and climbed with George Finch, whom he had met eight years earlier and who would loom large in the next chapter of Mallory's life. Coming back from the Alps that year, he arrived half an hour too late to witness the birth of his third child and first son.

It is commonly observed that Mallory was charismatic, but if he was, it was not in the usual sense of someone whose dynamic personality and arresting manner draw other people to them. Although he could be engaging when he chose, he could also be aloof and distant. Mallory's charisma was more the result of his outstanding climbing ability, in particular his seemingly effortless ease on difficult, dangerous mountains. What intrigued people about Mallory, in the end, the true source of his magnetism, was a combination of casual self-confidence and genuine fearlessness.

He was never accused of being down to earth. 'He was very vague', his friend Cottie Sanders wrote, 'and ramshackly about everything practical.'[59] Along with a related quality often associated with Mallory, his chronic forgetfulness – 'He's a great dear,' General Bruce wrote of Mallory on the 1922 expedition, 'but forgets his boots on all occasions' – there emerges the portrait of an absent-minded bumbler who also happened to be a climbing paragon. But for Tom Longstaff, another member of the 1922 team, Mallory's forgetfulness was something more serious, verging on irresponsibility. He's 'a very good stout-hearted baby', Longstaff observed, 'but quite unfit to be placed in charge of anything, including himself'.[60]

But if he was not conventionally charismatic, he could be very charming and seems to have suffered from none of the self-absorption that so often goes hand in hand with great beauty. As his tutor at Cambridge, Arthur Benson, observed: 'This was, I think, the essence of his wonderful charm, that he was so unconscious of his great personal beauty, his gifts, and his achievements.'[61] Mallory could be touchingly solicitous of others, among whom Benson was in fact one of the outstanding examples. Throughout his time at Cambridge and for years afterwards, Mallory would visit his tutor on occasions when Benson sank into severe depression, took leave from his duties, and when most of his friends stayed away. Mallory would stay with Benson, read to him, and they would go on walks together. '[H]e continued week after week to frequent the company of a man old enough to be his father,' one of Mallory's biographers writes, 'who was plunged in solitary gloom, often hardly able to sustain conversation at all – and to do all this as if it were for his own pleasure rather than for the consolation of the other.'[62] Benson was deeply touched by Mallory's selflessness and his loyalty to his old tutor. 'It is a very charming thing', he said of his former student, 'to lend a hand.'[63]

Later, on the 1921 expedition, there was a similar incident: Mallory knew that Raeburn, the oldest member and leader of the climbing team, liked to dispense climbing wisdom, and although Mallory, along with the other team members, did not like Raeburn and found ways to avoid him, Mallory also felt sorry for him. 'It was very evident at Darjeeling', Mallory wrote to Ruth, 'that he would not get on with Howard-Bury, to say nothing of the rest of us. In these circumstances I rather view myself as a soothing syrup. I had a friendly little walk with Raeburn before we left Darjeeling and rather played up to his desire to give advice.'[64]

Arthur Benson had a lot to do in forming the young Mallory and correcting some of his worst character excesses. Mallory could be very frank and direct, and Benson warned him to tone down his combativeness – '[Y]ou execute a war-dance rather easily' – and not be so prickly.[65] He also cautioned Mallory to try harder to hide the disdain he often demonstrated for people with whom he disagreed, for those he thought less intelligent – there were many – or for those who simply bored him. Mallory could be a snob, was quick to judge – in his letters home from the ship he took out to

India, he was scathing about his fellow passengers – and did not always give credit where it was due. It is telling, nevertheless, that the great Walt Unsworth, who did not think much of Mallory's climbing abilities and does not seem to have liked him much either, though they never met – it is telling that the worst criticism Unsworth can offer of Mallory is that 'his one serious weakness' was that 'he was a drifter, uncommitted and indecisive. He never seriously tried to shape events in his life; instead it was the events themselves which did the shaping. He drifted into the Everest adventure the way he drifted into everything else he did.'[66]

It may be an exaggeration to say Mallory drifted into the Everest adventure, but it's certainly true that the adventure sought him out and not vice versa. Everest dropped into Mallory's lap on 23 January 1921, twelve days after news of the expedition broke, when he received a cheeky letter from Percy Farrar of the Mount Everest Committee. 'It looks as though Everest would really be tried this summer,' Farrar wrote. 'Party would leave early April and get back in October. Any aspirations?'[67]

Mallory appears to have hesitated, primarily because he couldn't go without Ruth's blessing – he would be leaving her behind for seven months with three small children, the youngest only five months old – and initially Ruth did not approve. It was at this point that Geoffrey Young, who had recommended Mallory to the committee in the first place, intervened, travelling down to Charterhouse to visit George and Ruth. In a twenty-minute exchange he explained the significance of the invitation, how 'the label of Everest', as Young called it, being on the first-ever expedition to the mountain, would secure George's future prospects no matter what career he chose to follow. 'Ruth saw what I meant,' Young wrote later. 'She told him to go.'[68] Mallory later wrote to Young to thank him for his visit: 'I suspect I shall have no cause to regret your persuasions in the cause of Everest; at present I am elated at the prospect and so is Ruth: thank you for that.'[69]

A few days later Mallory was officially invited to join the expedition at a meeting in London with Farrar, Younghusband and the climber Harold Raeburn. Much was later made of the fact that, according to Younghusband, Mallory was not 'bursting with enthusiasm' and accepted 'with no visible emotion', but as his acceptance meant giving up his present livelihood and finding a new one upon his return, Mallory had good cause to be sobered by what he called 'a momentous step altogether'.[70] Just two months later, Mallory boarded the SS *Sardinia* in London en route to India.

George Mallory was not in fact everyone's first choice for the expedition; he wasn't even Percy Farrar's second choice. When Farrar, then president of the Alpine Club, had risen at the end of John Noel's lecture at the RGS 'to recommend two or three young mountaineers' for an Everest expedition, the first two climbers he had in mind were George Finch and his brother Max. Farrar had had Finch in mind as far back as 1918, a year before Noel's talk, when he wrote to a friend that for an attempt on Everest Finch and his brother Max were 'two of the very best mountaineers we have ever seen and much more likely to carry out a job of this kind than any other men I know'. At the time of Noel's talk, Farrar wrote to his friend again: 'If he and his brother Max . . . cannot do the job, then we have no one who can.'[71] Finch was not only a first-rate climber, he knew more about the physiological effects of altitude and the use of oxygen and oxygen equipment than anyone save Alexander Kellas. If selected, he would easily be the most qualified climber on the expedition.

Mallory and Finch had climbed together in Wales and later in the Alps, where Finch did most of his climbing and where he had much more experience than Mallory. Finch was in fact the president of the prestigious Zurich Alpine Club and was known to be especially adept on snow and ice, complementing Mallory's acknowledged skill as a rock climber. No one who had ever seen Finch climb had any doubt that he was the right man for the job. The only question was: was he the right 'sort'? Did he 'fit in'?

Finch was brash, opinionated and outspoken. He was unconventional and an outsider; he had spent far too much time in France, where he grew up from the age of fourteen and where he and his brother were once caught climbing the towers of Notre-Dame. He became something of a bohemian as a young man, even as that movement was just being born in Paris, wearing his hair long and sporting a questionable wardrobe. His private life bordered on the scandalous, and sometimes crossed the line. He was divorced and was not a gentleman, and if all that wasn't bad enough, he was Australian. None of this mattered so much to the Alpine Club – they could overlook Finch's peccadilloes if there was any chance he could get to the top of Everest – but the RGS was another matter. Younghusband, not normally prone to snobbery, objected to Finch entirely on the basis of character. While not referring to Finch by name, Younghusband wrote that 'a certain other climber in the party . . . had characteristics that several members of the Committee . . . thought would cause friction and irritation in the party and would destroy that cohesion that is so vitally necessary in an Everest expedition'.[72]

Arthur Hinks disliked Finch. When he heard that Geoffrey Young, who had recommended Mallory to the committee, was also backing Finch, Hinks thought he could shoot down the idea by enlisting Mallory in an anti-Finch crusade. But Hinks did not know his man; when he wrote to Mallory to ask him if he'd really be prepared to share his tent at 27,000 feet (8,230m) with a man like George Finch, Mallory, who had in fact shared Finch's tent on several occasions, replied that he'd 'be happy to share a tent with Finch – I'd share a tent with the Devil himself if it gave me a better chance of reaching the top of Everest!'[73] To Hinks's great annoyance, the committee invited Finch. When Younghusband met Finch to deliver the invitation, Finch was beside himself: 'Sir Francis. You have just sent me to heaven.'[74]

In all, the 1921 expedition team was to consist of four climbing members to be chosen by the Alpine Club, three surveying members to be chosen by the RGS, one doctor, plus Howard-Bury. To head the four-man climbing cohort, the committee had chosen the fifty-six-year-old Scot Harold Raeburn, a distinguished mountaineer who, although well past his climbing prime, was selected mainly because of his Himalayan experience. Raeburn, who had a strong personality and a striking presence, could be contentious and stubborn, and although he was respected, he was also the least popular member of the expedition. He announced at the time of his selection that he would not be able to go higher than 24,000 feet (7,315m).

The other experienced Himalayan climber chosen by the committee, the fourth member of the climbing cohort, was Alexander Kellas. Kellas had finally got permission to return to the Himalayas in the summer of 1920 to carry out his oxygen experiments on Kamet, experiments designed to provide information to the committee now planning the attempt on Everest. Unusually for Kellas, this time he climbed with another European, Henry Morshead of the Survey of India, who would later be asked to join the 1921 expedition. Kellas's experiences on Kamet convinced him that men could climb above 25,000 feet (7,620m) without oxygen, but only for a limited number of hours. After his experiments on Kamet, Kellas returned to Darjeeling in the late autumn of 1920 and rented a bungalow at the Pines Hotel in nearby Ghoom. In the spring he undertook yet another expedition, this time to Kabru, principally to get photos of Everest for use in the planned reconnaissance.

Kellas, who was delighted when he received his invitation, was as dubious a choice as Raeburn in some ways. He was fifty-three and, like Raeburn, was not expected to go above 25,000 feet (7,620m). Moreover, before he left England on his Kamet expedition, he had suffered from a serious recurrence of his auditory condition, which eventually became so severe he was obliged to resign his position at Middlesex Hospital and take a complete rest. Hinks, a great admirer of Kellas, agitated strongly for his selection, although he was worried about the state of his health.

Percy Farrar was not in Kellas's corner and was in fact alarmed that Kellas was even under consideration – Freshfield had actually proposed Kellas for expedition leader – and tried his best to undermine the groundswell that otherwise would almost certainly propel someone of Kellas's formidable reputation onto the climbing team: 'Now Kellas, besides being fifty, has never climbed a mountain,' Farrar charged, unkindly and inaccurately, 'but has only walked about on steep snow with a lot of coolies, and the only time they got on a very steep place, they all tumbled down and ought to have been killed!!'[75] But the momentum for Kellas was unstoppable, much to Hinks's delight. 'We send you all good wishes for a triumph,' he wrote to Kellas upon his selection, 'and we all assured Farrar that we would sooner put our money on you to get to the top than upon his nimble young climbers.'[76]

In fact, the make-up of the climbing team was strongly criticised at the time. Many people, including Mallory, thought there should have been more climbers, six or even eight. '[I]n my judgement,' Mallory wrote to Hinks, 'the party is weak . . . It may be a judgement with very little [behind it] but it is one of the precious stars I have to steer by. In mountaineering the ultimate safety lies in reserve strength; no amount of experience or judgement can create that.'[77] Then there was the fact that almost everyone thought Kellas and Raeburn were simply too old; if their ages, fifty-three and fifty-six, were combined with that of the two younger climbers, the average age of the climbing party was just over forty-four, ten or even fifteen years past the age when most climbers reached their prime.

It is notable that the only two climbers with Himalayan and high-altitude climbing experience were by their own admission too old to climb higher than 24,000 feet (7,315m) on Everest, 5,000 feet (1,525m) below the summit, and the two climbers who were fit enough to climb that high – on whom all the hopes for the summit attempt were ultimately pinned – had never climbed in the Himalayas and had never climbed anything more than half the height of Everest. To be fair, Raeburn and Kellas were not chosen for their fitness but because they were wise in the ways of the Himalayas, and while Mallory and Finch (and, later, Guy Bullock) had never climbed in the Himalayas or at altitude, they were nevertheless two of the best English climbers of their generation. All the same, much was made at the time of the fact that a number of outstanding English climbers who would otherwise have been strong contenders for the expedition, stronger, in fact, than the finalists, had been either wounded if not killed in the war, Geoffrey Young the most prominent among them.

Three of the four other members of the expedition team were surveyors; Henry Morshead and Oliver Wheeler were from the Survey of India, and Alexander Heron was from the Geological Survey of India. Morshead was an accomplished surveyor who, along with Frederick M. ('Hatter') Bailey, had solved one of the great geographic puzzles of the era: whether the Tsangpo in Tibet and the Brahmaputra in India were one and the same river. Morshead was famously stoic, thriving in appalling conditions, never complaining about – or even noticing – adversities that defeated the average person. Bailey once saw him covered in leeches, bleeding out of his boots, apparently unaware. 'I never met a harder man,' E. F. Norton said of him later, 'his shirt open at the chest to the dreadful Tibetan wind – a heart-breaking man to live with.'[78] Morshead most recently had been on Kamet with Kellas.

Oliver Wheeler, a Canadian and the youngest person ever elected to the Alpine Club, was chosen largely for his expertise in the new technique of photo-surveying which his superior, the Surveyor General, was keen to try out in the Everest region. While Morshead's job was to map several thousand square miles of the approaches to Everest, Wheeler's was to survey and photograph the last 200 square miles in the immediate vicinity of the peak itself, a task he under-took mostly alone, in some of the most formidable geography in the world, discovering the route to Everest in the process. Wheeler had begun climbing in the Canadian Rockies at the age of twelve and later climbed there with Tom Longstaff, who called him one of the best climbers he had ever seen. Later Sir Oliver Wheeler would become the Surveyor General of India.

Poor Alexander Heron, the geologist, did his job too well and managed to get himself barred from Tibet. His job was digging and rock collecting, and it turned out that both activities were deeply alarming to the Tibetans, whose prime minister complained mightily about Heron to Charles Bell, among others. 'It was agreed that Mount Everest might be explored,' the official wrote to Bell, 'but if this is used as an excuse for digging earth and stones from the most sacred hills of Tibet, inhabited by fierce demons, the very guardians of the soil, fatal epidemics may break out amongst men and cattle.' Heron finished the expedition, but when the government of India proposed Heron for the second expedition in 1922, Charles Bruce vetoed the idea.

The ninth member of the team was the forty-one-year-old doctor-naturalist Alexander (Sandy) Wollaston, who was also an ento-mologist and a friend of Hinks. Wollaston in fact had no interest in medicine – in the one hospital job he accepted, he lasted all of two days – and only took it up so he could indulge his real passions: travelling, exploration and collecting (plants, birds and insects). He had travelled extensively in Africa and Asia, including in New Guinea with Cecil Rawling. Wollaston was somewhat shy but he had the ability, his friend Maynard Keynes observed, to 'unlock hearts with a word and a look, and break down everyone's reserves except his own'.[79]

This, then, was the team for 1921 and, although there were only four official climbers, the two surveyors Morshead and Wheeler were highly experienced mountaineers; Morshead, in fact, would be chosen as one of the climbers for the 1922 expedition. Having two additional members with climbing skills must have been some solace to Mallory, worried as he was that the team was so small and so old. But if this did give Mallory some small comfort, it didn't last very long.

George Finch may have been sent to heaven by the invitation to join the expedition, but his sojourn among the angels turned out to be cruelly circumscribed. No one seems to know why, but in the middle of March, just two weeks before Mallory and Finch were scheduled to depart, it was decided they should each undergo a medical; Mallory passed and Finch did not, owing, perhaps, to his recent exposure to malaria. The medical reports, from two different doctors, were reviewed by Wollaston who agreed with the conclusion that Finch should be disqualified and a replacement named.

There has been endless speculation about whether the medical, coming as late as it did, was part of a scheme by Hinks and possibly Bruce, who also did not like Finch – he would later call him 'an absolute swine' – to get around the committee and kick Finch off the team.[80] Naturally, the news stunned Finch, who had already reserved berths on the SS *Sardinia* for himself and Mallory. Finch complained bitterly to Hinks, but Hinks was unmoved and even asked Finch to return his equipment allowance. Farrar was predictably outraged, for Finch (along with his brother) had always been his first choices for the team. A few days before Finch's disqualification was announced, Farrar had observed Finch when he was taking part in oxygen experiments in a vacuum chamber at Oxford to test his endurance at simulated high altitudes. 'I saw [Finch] in the vacuum chamber,' Farrar wrote to Hinks as soon as he heard

Finch had been disqualified, 'without oxygen at 21,000 feet and with a load of about 30 pounds on his back [going] through all sorts of evolutions. This is the weakling we are throwing out.'[81] Percy Farrar eventually resigned from the committee, in part over this incident.

Finch was to get a measure of satisfaction later that summer in the Alps when he pioneered a new route on Mont Blanc. A delighted Farrar, who had been climbing with Finch on this occasion, immediately informed Hinks of Finch's triumph: 'Our invalid Finch', he wrote, 'took part in the biggest climb in the Alps this season . . .' Farrar, who could not resist goading his desk-bound nemesis, continued: 'You will be pleased to hear that I lost 1 stone in weight. I should recommend you to take a similar course . . . [Y]ou could easily afford to lose 3 stone!!'[82] Finch would in fact be the first person, after Mallory, selected for the 1922 attempt on Everest, during the course of which he would apply his vast knowledge of the oxygen apparatus used on that expedition to save the life of another team member, General Bruce's nephew. Eventually in 1959 Finch would be elected president of the Alpine Club.

Although he had some reservations about Finch, Mallory became alarmed when replacements for Finch began to be suggested, especially the name of one William Ling, the forty-eight-year-old president of the Scottish Climbing Club and a friend of Harold Raeburn. Mallory immediately wrote to Hinks to express his view that success on the upper reaches of Everest came down to a question 'purely of endurance' and that

> for the final push we want men who can last . . . I have all along
> regarded the party as barely strong enough for a venture of this kind
> with the enormous demands it is certain to make on both nerves and
> physique. I told Raeburn . . . I wanted to have Finch because we
> shouldn't be strong enough without him.

Mallory ends his letter with a mild threat, saying he will have to reconsider his position. 'You will understand that I must look after myself in this matter. I'm a married man and I can't go into it bald-headed.'[83]

The ever-tactless Hinks responded with a letter that was patronising even for him:

I don't think you should feel any anxiety about your own position because you will be under the orders of very experienced mountaineers who will take care not to call upon you for jobs that can't be done. The fact that you have been in close touch with Farrar all along has no doubt made you imbibe his view, which is hardly that of anybody else, that the first object of the expedition is to get to the top of Mt Everest this year.[84]

Mallory was furious at this condescension, but Wollaston talked him out of firing off an angry letter to Hinks:

I got hold of Mallory alone to myself this afternoon and told him a number of things. He was evidently hurt in his pride by your letter, which was perhaps just as well, and said that he was going to write to you, but I persuaded him not to do so, at all events in the way that he intended, and I don't think you or we will have any trouble with him.[85]

Mallory instead turned his attention to finding a replacement for Finch and believed he had the ideal candidate in his old Winchester schoolmate and frequent climbing partner, Guy Bullock. He wrote to Younghusband about Bullock immediately, before Hinks could find another forty- or fifty-year-old: he was 'a tough sort of fellow who never lost his head and would stand any amount of knocking about . . . I can think of no one else . . . that would probably last longer than myself . . . level-headed and competent all around – a man in whom one would feel confidence in an emergency as one of the least likely to crack.'[86] In this letter Mallory mentioned that he knew Bullock kept himself fit, as he had been playing soccer as recently as six months previously and was a strong runner.

Neither Hinks nor Farrar was reassured by Bullock's running and soccer exertions and distanced themselves from the decision to invite him, explaining that they had interviewed far more experienced candidates but none of them could commit at such short notice to a seven- or even eight-month absence. Farrar was especially blunt in a note he wrote for the Mount Everest Committee book: '[T]he remaining climbers, Mr Mallory and Mr Bullock, whose mountaineering experience is limited and not of recent date, do not form a party sufficiently qualified to continue [safely] the reconnaissance beyond the point where Mr Raeburn finds himself unable to lead.'[87]

At the time Bullock was serving as a consular officer in Lima, but he happened to be on vacation in London. When Younghusband asked the Foreign Office to grant him leave, they declined, where-upon Younghusband went directly to the Foreign Secretary, who happened to be Lord Curzon, who approved Bullock's leave. Although he was a last-minute choice, the thirty-four-year-old Bullock was a stalwart on the expedition and proved popular with the other members, in part because of his genial disposition and in part because he took it upon himself to keep a close eye on the absent-minded Mallory and regularly cleaned up after him.

As a rule, world-class mountaineers do not suffer fools gladly. They have unusually healthy egos, tremendous drive and ambition, and no lack of self-confidence; they are justly celebrated for their 'splendid independence and colourful bigness'.[88] They can, accordingly, be difficult under the best of circumstances, and the members of the 1921 team were no different. While there were a few exceptions – everyone liked Kellas, and most members liked Wollaston and Morshead – for the rest it soon became the 'expedition where almost everybody actively disliked someone else'.[89]

From the beginning, nobody liked Raeburn; Howard-Bury thought Raeburn was 'a fool' and Mallory lamented Raeburn's 'total lack of calm and sense of humour . . . He is dreadfully dictatorial about matters of fact and often wrong.'[90] Mallory found Heron dull and also seems to have had it in for poor Wheeler, whose only apparent flaw was that he was Canadian: 'You know my complex about Canadians,' he wrote to Ruth. 'I shall have to swallow before I like him, I suspect. God give me the saliva.'[91] He later complained that Wheeler was sick most of the time 'on top of which he grouses a good deal'. Mallory tried to like Howard-Bury – 'He knows a great deal about flowers,' he wrote to Ruth, grasping at straws – but he did not succeed: 'I can't get over my dislike for him.'[92] And Howard-Bury didn't think much of either Mallory or Bullock. '[They] have been perfectly useless to me,' he wrote to Hinks. 'They have never attempted to help in anything.'[93] Later in the expedition,

even Bullock and Mallory got on each other's nerves. As the great
Himalayan climber Chris Bonington noted, it was 'a team . . . of
cantankerous individuals'.[94] Needless to say, sentiments such as these
never made it into official expedition accounts, and Howard-Bury's,
in which he heaps praise on the 'happy family [where everyone]
pulled together', was no exception.[95]

In truth the 1921 expedition team was probably no less cohesive
than most other teams of its kind. But given the unusual circumstances – the first-ever attempt to climb the highest mountain in
the world, if they could but find it – expectations were impossibly
high and the resulting pressure was enormous. If members of the
'happy family' sniped at each other rather more than in most happy
families, it was perhaps understandable. Moreover, this expedition
required much less teamwork than many of its kind, since the
surveyors – Morshead, Wheeler and Heron – generally worked
independently of the climbers and of each other. And as for the
climbers, Mallory and Bullock climbed only with each other until
the very last month of the effort.

As the team was being put together, the other major task facing
the committee was financing the expedition, which was expected
to cost £10,000 over two years. Alpine Club and RGS members
were solicited for pledges; King George V pledged £100, and the
Prince of Wales £50. Hinks led and completely dominated all aspects
of the fund-raising effort, alienating many people in the process, as
usual – he asked Mallory whether he expected the committee to
pay his boat ticket out to India – and also getting the job done, as
usual. He was responsible for selling exclusive print rights to two
newspapers, *The Times* and the Philadelphia *Public Ledger*, although
he loathed journalists, and also selling rights to the photographs and
films. Beyond that he made sure the committee received all revenues
from numerous secondary sources, such as maps, images, public
lectures, exhibition receipts, magazine articles by team members and
proceeds from all film showings. With regard to the latter, when
the Invalid Children's Aid Association – Her Majesty the Queen
was its patron – wrote to ask for permission merely to set up a
collection box for the children outside a cinema showing a film of
the 1922 expedition, Hinks refused. On another occasion, when

Ruth Mallory asked Hinks if he could provide free tickets to an Alpine Club photo exhibition to twenty members of the Working Women's College, Hinks replied that her request was 'altogether irregular, but the [AC] President has a soft heart and consents to your 20 students going to [the exhibition] without payment'.[96] It is said that in four years, 1921–5, Hinks 'gave away only two items: a small packet of seeds to the king and a single photographic image of Everest to the son of the maharajah of Nepal'.[97]

It only remained now, in late March 1921, for the team to assemble in Darjeeling. The three surveyors were stationed in India and were already in place, as was Kellas who had been in the country since June 1920. Raeburn arrived in April and Howard-Bury a few days later. Wollaston and Bullock arrived only on 9 May after an exhausting journey across India from where they had disembarked at Bombay, the other side of the country from Darjeeling.

Mallory was the last to arrive, leaving England on the *Sardinia* on 8 April for the five-week trip to Calcutta, with thirty-five trunks of the expedition's equipment. He found his fellow passengers intolerably dull, kept in shape by walking thirteen circuits (one mile) of the ship every day, cited possible routes up the Rock of Gibraltar as they steamed past. In Sri Lanka he bought lace collars for his children and sent them home. He arrived in Calcutta on 10 May where Hinks, with his usual foresight and organising genius (along with his low opinion of Mallory), anticipated that Mallory might have trouble with his luggage, to say nothing of the expedition's trunks, and made arrangements accordingly: '[H]e seems to be a very innocent traveller,' Hinks wrote to Howard-Bury, 'who can hardly be trusted to get his own luggage aboard, so that I am writing to the Survey of India to ask them to send an officer down on the arrival of the *Sardinia* at Calcutta to help him get his ton or so of personal luggage on the train for Darjeeling.'[98]

In the end the Survey's man did not make an appearance, and Mallory quite competently oversaw the onward shipping of his own and the expedition's trunks. He then boarded a train for the fourteen-hour, 350-mile journey to Siliguri, where he caught the famous narrow-gauge Darjeeling Himalayan Railway (affectionately known as the toy train) for the 50-mile, 7,000-foot (2,130m) climb up to

Darjeeling. At Kurseong, 19 miles below Darjeeling, Mallory got
off and walked for some distance, making better time than the train
and getting better views of the mountains, especially Kangchenjunga,
his first breathtaking Himalaya.

Mallory arrived in Darjeeling a few hours before Lord Ronaldshay,
the governor of Bengal (and a friend, of course, of Howard-Bury),
was hosting a formal dinner party to mark the official start of the
Everest expedition. Mallory described the event in amused detail in
a letter to Ruth. It was, he said, 'a swagger party' of twenty-five
couples and altogether 'a wonderful show'.[99] There were embossed
invitations, an orchestra playing softly so as to permit conversation,
the expedition members chatting quietly in groups, several meeting
each other for the first time. Everyone stopped talking when His
Excellency entered, wearing full-dress regalia and accompanied by
his two aides-de-camp, and proceeded to circle the room, greeting
each small group. The two aides then ushered everyone into the
drawing room where numerous native servants in long red coats
with gold and silver braids pulled out everyone's chair, filled and
refilled champagne glasses 'after every sip' and where the entire party
rose during dessert when the governor toasted the health of the
King-Emperor, and the band played God save the King. 'Everything',
Mallory told Ruth, 'went with a click.'[100]

Or almost everything, save for an entirely unscripted moment
heralding the arrival of Alexander Kellas, who had walked the four
miles in the rain from where he was staying at Ghoom and arrived
for dinner ten minutes late and dripping wet. Mallory, smitten
immediately with Kellas, described the moment for Ruth:

> Kellas I love already. He is beyond description Scotch and uncouth
> in his speech – altogether uncouth. At the great dinner party he
> arrived ten minutes late after we had sat down, and very dishevelled,
> having walked from [Ghoom] . . . His appearance would have formed
> a good model for the stage for a farcical representation of an alchem-
> ist; he is very slight in build, short, thin, stooping, and narrow-chested;
> his head is a very curious shape, and made grotesque by veritable
> gig-lamps of spectacles and a long, pointed moustache. He is an
> absolutely devoted and disinterested person.[101]

Howard-Bury and Wollaston had in fact been quite concerned about Kellas, who had not been seen in Darjeeling, even as late as the day before the governor's dinner party, since he had left several weeks earlier to climb on Kabru. With his arrival, all the team members were now present and accounted for.

Meanwhile, the Dalai Lama, via an official notice sent to all the district headmen, along the expected route to Everest, had done all he could to tee up the expedition for success:

> You are to bear in mind that a party of Sahibs are coming to see the Chha-mo-lung-ma mountain and they will evince great friendship towards the Tibetans. On the request of the Great Minister Bell a passport has been issued requiring you and all officials and subjects of the Tibetan Government to supply transport, e.g. riding ponies, pack animals and coolies as required by the Sahibs, the rates for which should be fixed to mutual satisfaction . . . All the people of the country, wherever the Sahibs may happen to come, should render all necessary assistance in the best possible way, in order to maintain friendly relations between the British and Tibetan Governments.
>
> Dispatched during the Iron Bird Year,
> Seal of the Prime Minister[102]

Now at last the party of 'sahibs' were all assembled in Darjeeling, and in a few days they would set out on one of the grandest adventures of the twentieth century.

We paused here in sheer astonishment . . . We asked no questions
and made no comment, but simply looked.

George Mallory

IT MUST BE remembered that they did not know where they were going. 'The position of the mountain had been fixed from a distance in 1849, its height established in 1852. But . . . no Englishman had been anywhere near [Everest] or had any precise idea how to reach it.'¹ Or as Tom Longstaff put it, rather more succinctly: 'They will have a big enough job to find the mountain.'²

If they did not quite know how to get there, they did at least know where they had to get *to* – the base of the mountain – and they knew roughly where it had to be: in that tangle of giant peaks and massifs, some of the most formidable geography on earth, that stretches for 20 miles or so along the Tibet–Nepal border 50 miles south-east of Tingri. But no one knew for certain if Everest could even be reached from Tibet. Even as the team assembled in Darjeeling, it was still possible that the entire expedition might turn out to be nothing more than a fool's errand.

Plans were for the expedition to set out as early as possible in May, before the monsoon set in, but eighty-seven trunks of supplies shipped from England were delayed in Calcutta and did not arrive in Darjeeling until the 14th, and another four days passed before all preparations were complete. Darjeeling, meanwhile, did not appeal to everyone, though it offered many distractions. It rained every day, although this was not yet the monsoon but what the locals called the *chota bursat*, the little monsoon, a distinction without any meaningful difference. (The 1922 and 1924 expeditions would both start several weeks earlier to avoid the *chota bursat*.) 'Darjeeling is like many other Indian "Hill Stations",' Wheeler observed, 'except for its weather, which is atrocious . . . I should have liked to visit Sandakaphu . . . from which a fine though distant view of the

Everest group is obtained, but the weather . . . made it quite useless.'³ Although panoramic views of Kangchenjunga are the highlight of the Darjeeling skyline, every day was overcast, and none of the expedition team ever mentioned seeing the mountain from there. Mallory called Darjeeling 'a devastating place – or rather it is a wonderful beautiful place almost incredibly bedeviled [sic] by fiends'.⁴ The 'fiends' were no doubt members of that same 'officialdom' John Noel had advised climbers to avoid at all costs.

Raeburn, who had been in Darjeeling since 23 April, was responsible for interviewing and selecting porters, forty of whom were eventually chosen, mostly Sherpas from north-eastern Nepal, a few from villages just south of Everest. Four cooks were selected and two translators. One of the expedition's most important elements were its pack animals, a hundred mules, all supplied by the Indian army and just recently sent up from the plains below Darjeeling.

In a meeting on 12 May with the Himalayan newcomers – Wollaston, Mallory and Bullock – Howard-Bury explained that there were two routes to Khamba Dzong, the last marked place on the map they carried and the jumping-off point for western Tibet and Everest. The first, the route Younghusband had taken in the summer of 1903, was due north from Darjeeling, following the Teesta River to the pass known as Serpo La, the border between Sikkim and Tibet, and on to Khamba Dzong. This route was shorter than the alternative, by nine days, it turned out, but not suitable for a large expedition, with many porters and pack animals, due to the sweltering heat of the Teesta Valley, the lack of villages along the way where they could stop, and the need in some spots to negotiate extremely narrow paths carved out of rock cliffs high above the Teesta.

The alternative was to follow the traditional trade route from Darjeeling to Lhasa, the one the Tibet invasion force had taken in 1904. The Lhasa road goes through Kalimpong, north and east over the Jelep La into Tibet and the Chumbi Valley, on to Yatung and Phari, thence via Tuna, Guru and Gyantse to Lhasa. The expedition would follow this well-travelled route to a point 30 miles north-east of Phari, where it would make a sharp turn to the north-west just after Guru (sight of the massacre in 1904), cross over the Dug La, and then head directly west across the Tibetan plateau to Khamba Dzong. On this second route the climbs and descents, although rigorous, were less steep, the trails for much of the way were at higher, hence cooler, elevations, and there were many villages where supplies could be obtained and additional transport arranged if necessary. This second route, also taken by the two follow-on expeditions, offered the additional advantage of dak bungalows, a series of government rest houses a day's march from each other to accommodate mail carriers and other official travellers, which meant that the team members, as long as they were on the Lhasa road, could have a roof over their heads at night for the first two weeks and, in some cases, proper meals prepared by the bungalow cook.

Howard-Bury's plan was to send Morshead and his small party of two assistant surveyors and a cook along the direct route and the other eight members by the second route, divided into two parties of four each, leaving Darjeeling one day apart so as not to overcrowd the sleeping quarters in the small bungalows. The first party would consist of Wollaston, Wheeler, Mallory and Howard-Bury, and the second was made up of Raeburn, Kellas, Bullock and Heron.

Morshead left first, on 13 May, to begin the surveying work that would in the end add 15,000 square miles to the map of Tibet. Morshead and his survey partner Wheeler were so efficient at what they did that they actually finished their new map of Tibet before the expedition members left India for home at the conclusion of the 1921 effort. Too efficient, it might be said, as Morshead's surveying activities in fact far exceeded what the Tibetans had agreed to when they gave permission for the expedition; Wheeler was only supposed to survey along the actual route the expedition would take to reach the mountain and the area immediately around Everest and nothing else. Indeed, back in March, a worried Charles Bell had dispatched specific instructions to the Survey of India that Morshead should not go 'off the beaten track and away from the vicinity of Everest to avoid arousing Tibetan suspicions'.[5]

In fact, both Morshead and Wollaston, the latter in his capacity as the expedition naturalist, veered far off the official track, more or less as it struck their fancy. Wollaston freely admits in his report on the expedition that as he and Morshead were operating under a 'liberal interpretation of the expression "Mount Everest", we considered it necessary to explore the surrounding country as far as a hundred miles or more from the mountain, East, North, and South, in all directions, that is excepting towards the forbidden territory of Nepal'.[6]

When Charles Ryder, the head of the Survey of India, received Bell's letter, he suspected that Bell's worries were well founded. A very worried Ryder immediately wrote to Younghusband to ask him to make sure no mention of any 'exploration' got into the press back home, and then back to the Tibetan authorities. But the RGS had an exciting story to tell – via regular dispatches carried by runners to Calcutta and thence to the two newspapers in London and Philadelphia – and a public eager to hear it. When the Tibetan prime minister inevitably learned of Morshead's activities, he protested strongly to Charles Bell to ask that he '[k]indly prevent officials wandering about' and even requested that Bell 'effect their early return'.[7] A frustrated Bell, whose honour and integrity were at stake, was furious, and not for the last time. The Dalai Lama might trust Bell implicitly, but Bell knew that most Tibetans had no reason to trust the British – and good reason not to – and would not react well when they heard the invaders were back and once again marching in force through their country. Before the expedition was even out of Sikkim, there were already rumours in Tibet that 500 'sahibs' were on their way, along with 1,000 mules. Due to these unauthorised explorations by Morshead and Wollaston in 1921, the Tibetan government refused to allow any surveyors on the two following expeditions, and a naturalist was only approved at the last minute under certain limited conditions.

The first party left Darjeeling on 18 May, with 40 mules, 20 porters, two cooks and one translator, and the second party followed the next day with an identical entourage, plus his 'personal Indian servants' in the case of Wheeler.[8] They descended gradually past the neat rows of tea plantations on the upper slopes and then began the steep 5,000-foot (1,525m) plunge to the bottom of the Teesta Valley, 750 feet (230m) above sea level.

For the first two weeks, making their way north across Sikkim, they struggled mightily with the elements, their mood alternating between exhaustion and exhilaration. The elements in question, all magnified by the monsoon, were threefold: the heat, the rain and, because of the rain, the worst element of all – the mud. As for the heat, the Teesta Valley was the epitome of a teeming tropical rain-forest, brutally humid and oppressive, the canopy so thick the men never saw the sun or the sky when they were down by the river. Both Howard-Bury and Wheeler commented on how the stunning butterflies the valley was famous for 'made us forget the fact that we were dripping with perspiration from every pore'.[9] They would have stripped off much of their clothing but for the threat of mosquitoes and leeches.

The rain was to be expected, but it was almost non-stop, often more than an inch in a single day. The men got used to being drenched and looked forward to the late afternoons when they could at last get under cover in the bungalows. At night the downpours often continued. '[T]his land of marvellous scenery has a terrible drawback in weather,' an earlier British traveller along the Teesta observed.

> The traveller has really to undergo great hardships. The mist and rain are provoking beyond the power of description. He has to march in the wet, to unpack his tent in the wet, to lie down to sleep in the wet, to pack up again in the wet; and for hours and sometimes for days together he lives in the wet . . .! It will be seen, therefore, that Sikkim rejoices in a climate which, though extremely favourable for vegetation, is particularly rigorous as regards mankind.[10]

Men can still walk when they're sweating and they can walk when they're drenched, but when the trail becomes mud, walking turns into tumbling, falling and sliding. In some places the Lhasa route was covered in smooth stones precisely to prevent mudslides, but in other places it was just dirt, which the monsoon torrents turned into rivers of mud in minutes. 'The best description I can give of the spot at the time we passed', Douglas Freshfield wrote of his passage through the Teesta Valley a few years before the 1921 expedition, 'would be *a moving hillside*. The whole surface of the mountain was more or less in motion; mud was slipping and sliding in streams, along which rocks rumbled and tumbled at intervals in an extremely disagreeable and somewhat hazardous manner . . .'[11]

Another challenge were the famous Teesta leeches at the lower altitudes, which no traveller who ever walked along the banks of that river ever failed to mention. The surveyor Wheeler called them 'nasty little brutes about the thickness of a match and three-quarters of an inch long, they sit on the stones in the thousands and wave at you as you pass and crawl through the boot-lace eyelets of the unwary'.[12] The renowned botanist Dr Joseph Hooker encountered 'legion[s] of leeches' on his trip through the valley. '[T]he bite of these blood-suckers gives no pain, but is followed by considerable effusion of blood. They puncture through thick worsted stockings, and even trousers, and, when full, roll in the form of a little soft ball into the bottom of the shoe . . .'[13] For his part, Howard-Bury was more worried about the threat to the mules. The leeches sat on 'most of the stones and blades of grass beside the path . . . waiting for their meal of blood and clung on to any mule or human being that passed by. The mules suffered severely and drops of blood on the stones became frequent from the bleeding wounds.'[14]

Serrated by numerous east–west ridges, the terrain of Sikkim was yet another challenge. Most days saw a descent of two or three thousand feet, sometimes even more, often followed by an ascent of equal length. '[W]e had a very wet and trying march to Rongli,' Howard-Bury wrote of their third day out. 'The distance was only 12 miles, but this included a very steep descent of over 3,000 feet to the bottom of a steamy valley, followed by a climb of 3,000 feet across an intervening ridge, and then down another 2,000 feet to the . . . bungalow.'[15]

The terse entries in Guy Bullock's diary tell the story:

21 May: Gradual rise to 9,400 [2,865m] and descent to 4,800 [1,463m] at Pedong.
Sunday 22 May: Pedong to Ari. Steep descent down rough paved road from Pedong and equally steep to Ari which is two or 3,000 feet [914m] below the pass.

Tuesday 24: Ari to Padamchen 6,500 feet [1,981m]. Pleasant descent to Rongli. From there follow valley to Padamchen. Steep ascent last 2,000 feet [609m] after crossing stream.

Wed. 25: To Gnatong 12,000 feet [3,657m]. 9 miles walked. Steep climb about 4,000 feet [1,219m].

Thursday 26: Gnatong to Kupup, 5 miles, 12,000 ft [3,657m]. Very stormy night of rain.[16]

Taxing and trying as they were, the heat, the rain, the leeches and the roller-coaster terrain were all anticipated and not new for most of the team members, except Mallory and Bullock who had no experience of the tropics. What was not anticipated and potentially more serious was the complete and almost immediate breakdown of the entire cohort of government mules. Simply said, lowland mules used to the relatively flat plains of India were completely unsuited to the elevation, the heat, and the steep climbs and precipitous descents of Sikkim, and they began to suffer from the first day. In some places the slopes were said to be as steep as the sides of a house. 'When you put 160 pounds (or more) on a mule's back,' Mallory wrote, 'and ask him to go 4,000 feet [1,220m] up and 4,000 feet down, unless he is very fit, he doesn't like it.'[17] On the sixth day Howard-Bury ordered all the mules sent back to Darjeeling. After Sedongchen (day 6) the expedition used a combination of Tibetan mules, ponies, bullocks, yaks, zohs (hybrid yak and cow) and donkeys, depending on what was locally available.

If exhaustion and frustration were major themes of these first few days, exhilaration was another, inspired by the spectacular flora of the Sikkimese valleys and hillsides. At the lowest elevations, along the banks of the Teesta, the men marched through the impossibly lush tropical rainforests with two hundred kinds of ferns and where 'every inch of soil is fought over by flowering weeds and shrubs . . . and every forked bough or hollow trunk is seized on by parasitical ferns and orchids'. Here the trail was so overgrown it was often hard to make out, a plush carpet of moss, creepers, pothos, pepper vines, primulas, caladiums, colocasias, convolvulus (morning glory) and begonias growing out of every rock. Overhead was a towering canopy of rainforest trees: palms, pandanus, stands of bamboo, banana trees, sal trees, terminalia, giant tree ferns, orange trees.

'The magnificent forests of Sikkim are rightly famous,' one chronicler writes.

> Arborescent ferns grow literally to the stature of trees, and the trees themselves rise to a height of 150 feet [46m]. Some of them are smooth-trunked, others are covered in thick, fleece-like masses of white [flowers]. Pepper plants and tropical creepers twine together and sprawl from branch to branch, curl themselves into tangled skeins and then reach out again, coil here and there around festoons of blossom or hang down to the ground like long ropes. So dense is the foliage that it forms a sort of natural crypt, within which everything is shrouded in a semi-darkness made still more eerie by a mist which makes solid objects appear to recede and blurs every outline, while general humidity turns the entire forest into a soggy, dripping mass of reeking vegetation.[18]

And there were orchids everywhere, over 450 varieties – most from the *Coelogyne*, *Dendrobium* and *Cymbidium* families – mauve, white, yellow, pink, scarlet, some on the forest floor but most spilling out of forks in the trees, dangling from the climbing vines, creepers and trailing mosses, or poking out from beneath the maiden ferns, many with sprays of blossoms a foot and a half long. There were also purple irises, white roses, scarlet hibiscus and Himalayan blue poppies. 'It has been *the* day for flowers,' Mallory wrote to Ruth on the 24th, 'so much beyond words to describe that it . . . makes me weep to think I convey nothing to you, or almost nothing.'[19]

Above 5,000 feet (1,525m) and up as far 12,000 feet (3,660m) it's the turn of the rhododendron, the uncontested star of Himalayan flora, blanketing entire hillsides in a profusion of blossoms. 'Then came rhododendrons of every colour – pink, deep crimson, yellow, mauve, white or cream coloured. It was impossible to imagine anything more beautiful and every yard of the path was a pure delight.'[20] Some, like the white *R. argenteum*, were great trees, 40 feet (12m) high, while others, at higher elevations, were dwarves of only 5 or 6 feet. 'I know of nothing of the kind', writes Joseph

Hooker, director of the Royal Botanical Gardens at Kew in London, 'that exceeds in beauty the flowering branch of *R. argenteum*, with its wide spreading foliage and glorious mass of flowers.' Hooker goes on to say that in 'the months of April and May, when the magnolias and rhododendrons are in blossom, the gorgeous vegetation is, in some respects, not to be surpassed *by anything in the tropics*' (italics added).[21] This unsurpassed flower show lasted for eight days.

There was yet one more source of breathtaking colour in the valleys of Sikkim: the butterflies. Everyone commented on them: Wheeler, Howard-Bury, Bullock and Mallory: 'One of the best moments on our last march', Mallory wrote, 'was when we sat on a bridge waiting for our ponies, and I saw and watched any number of gorgeous butterflies, arching about like gently moving birds, dark objects shimmering about with vivid colour.'[22] Younghusband, who had come through the valley in 1904, observed that when the butterflies landed, the show was even better: '[T]o see one of these gorgeous insects alight in front of us, slowly raise and lower his wings and turn himself about almost as if he was showing himself off for our especial pleasure, compensates us for every worry his fellows in the insect world may cause us.'[23] Bullock, an avid collector, was out chasing butterflies every day with his net (he also used it to catch fish), adding his own colour to the scene with his vivid pink umbrella. He chased butterflies all across Tibet and all the way to the base of the North Face of Everest, pink umbrella in tow.

By 26 May, nine days after setting out, everyone had completed the first and most trying leg of the journey, having crossed over the Jelep La (at 14,009 feet/4,270m) into Tibet and descended to Yatung in the beautiful Chumbi Valley. At an average elevation of 9,400 feet (2,865m), the Chumbi reminded most of the team of Alpine valleys in Switzerland, with their hillsides covered in European species such as silver fir, birch, sycamore, spruce, mountain ash, larch and elder. The valley, on the north side of the Himalayas, receives only a quarter of the amount of monsoon rain as the Sikkim side, so the party saw the sun and sky again, for only the second time since leaving Darjeeling.

The new scenery, the diminishing rains, the levelling out of the terrain, success with the new Tibetan mules – these changes came just in time, for the arduous journey through the Teesta Valley had tried everyone's patience and caused friction among team members. 'Wheeler . . . very easily grumbles when things aren't going well,' Mallory wrote to Ruth.[24] And Raeburn, as expected, got on nearly everyone's nerves. He annoyed Mallory, Bullock and Wheeler no end by criticising their kit and did not get along with Howard-Bury. Mallory and Bullock also had a run-in with Howard-Bury, who made them send their Indian mules back to Darjeeling after crossing the Jelep La and hire cheaper local ponies 'to save a few rupees', he wrote to Ruth. 'It turns out we would have been very glad of [the Indian mules] as Bury, who knows the journey, could have told us. He is not a kind man.'[25]

As soon as the party entered Tibet, Howard-Bury sent a telegram announcing their arrival to Younghusband who received it a few minutes before the start of an anniversary dinner at the RGS, where it was duly read out and received a prolonged standing ovation. Interest in the expedition was intense. Younghusband had put Howard-Bury in charge of composing and sending regular updates on the progress of the expedition back to London, to RGS and Alpine Club members eager for the latest news and, more importantly, for reprinting in *The Times* and Philadelphia *Public Ledger*, and runners were used to get the telegrams out as quickly as possible.

Younghusband gave Howard-Bury detailed instructions on how long the telegrams should be (no more than 1,000 words), what they should contain, and especially the style in which they should be written. 'You will literally have the whole world for an audience, so we want the thing exceedingly well done, hitting the right mean between sensationalized "high falutin" and dry dreary matter-of-fact chronicling.'[26] Mallory, who fancied himself a writer, was not impressed with Howard-Bury's prose; when he read one of the dispatches in a newspaper much later in the expedition, he called it 'a deplorably incompetent performance'.[27] The disdain was mutual. Howard-Bury was supposed to forward Mallory's periodic reports from his explorations of the North Face along with these dispatches, but after Howard-Bury read the first two of Mallory's efforts, he stopped asking for them. 'They were so full of nonsense and often unintelligible that I thought it better not to [send them].'[28] Meanwhile, Hinks, who had negotiated the exclusive contracts with the two newspapers, complained regularly to Howard-Bury and later to Mallory that they weren't sending reports back nearly often enough nor quickly enough. On one occasion Hinks wrote to Ruth in desperation to ask her if she could pass on any letters she had received from her husband.

Once in the Chumbi highlands, the men enjoyed the expansive views and the cool, clean mountain air. But the Teesta Valley had not been kind to the party, the orchid and rhododendron extravaganzas notwithstanding; by the time the eight men arrived in Yatung, almost all of them were already sick or on the verge of becoming so. Everyone but Bullock and Mallory, it seemed, was suffering from dysentery and indigestion, whilst they both suffered from headaches. The dysentery, which they blamed on the poor hygiene and insanitary habits of the cooks, was debilitating under the best of circumstances but especially so to men who were already exhausted. 'Wheeler has constantly been suffering more or less from indigestion,' Mallory wrote, 'and has been sufficiently bad these past two days to make it a real difficulty to come on. Raeburn seems frail . . . We're cursed . . . by . . . abominable cooks.'[29] One Everest historian has called Sherpas 'undoubtedly the world's best porters . . . and probably the world's worst cooks'.[30]

The food was so disgusting that Howard-Bury wanted to send all the cooks back 'as they were very bad and usually drunk . . . but I could not let them all go, so it was necessary to find out which were the most useless'.[31] Mallory took to eating a quarter pound of chocolate every afternoon so he did not have to face 'the nasty messes' the cooks prepared each evening.[32] Stories about the food and sickness on the 1921 expedition were so notorious that on the 1922 expedition General Bruce made a point of carefully auditioning his cooks ahead of time. 'Our cooks had to be chosen with a great deal of care,' Bruce wrote. 'Captain Bruce [the general's nephew] and myself took the most likely candidates out into the hills and gave them a good trial before we engaged them . . .'[33]

From time to time the expedition members were invited out for a meal, either by local Tibetan dignitaries or by British expats who lived along the route. The meals prepared by Tibetans posed a host of culinary challenges. At Phari, for example, Howard-Bury and others were invited for a meal by the dzongpen: '[T]hey presented us with a dried sheep,' he writes, 'which looked mummified and smelt very strongly.' This was almost certainly one of the dried, decomposed and very ripe 'salaaming sheep' Cecil Rawling had been presented with on his expedition. 'It proved very acceptable to our coolies,' Howard-Bury adds.[34]

As bad as the Tibetan food could be, what came next was often worse: the dreaded Tibetan tea. Tea ended every formal meal and was also regularly brought out and served with cakes during brief courtesy meetings with Tibetans. Tibetan tea is mostly water, lots of salt, a generous dollop of butter and the merest hint of tea leaves, everything cooked over a fire of yak dung and served with great formality to the foreign guests, most of whom could not abide 'the vile concoction'.[35] The British suffered more than most, growing up as they did in a culture where tea was part of the very fabric of daily life. Tibetan tea was variously described as 'distinctly nasty', 'horribly rich', 'hot, greasy, tasty slime', and as that compared with which the taste 'of castor oil is pleasant'.[36] Tea was an ongoing trial for British climbers in the Himalayas, all the more so because in most cases it was difficult to decline the drink without causing offence.

This was especially a problem for dignitaries, such as Howard-Bury and General Bruce, who were feted more often than the rest of their teams. 'I never much took to it as a beverage,' Howard-Bury recalled, 'though I had to take many cups of it during the next few months and had to pretend to enjoy it.'[37] For his part Bruce, on at least one well-known occasion in 1922, devised a plan to forestall 'the dreadful imposition of having to drink Tibetan tea', though he may have used the stratagem at other times. He knew the head lama at the Rongbuk monastery would almost certainly offer him tea during the expedition's obligatory visit to receive the lama's blessing. And he also knew that while he could decline tea with lesser figures, it would be highly inappropriate on this formal occasion at Rongbuk, especially as he would be surrounded by his Sherpas whom he did not want to offend. So he had his interpreter Paul explain to the lama that he (Bruce) had taken a vow never to touch butter until he reached the summit of Everest. Bruce notes that his interpreter was greatly amused by this ploy and that 'Paul's effort to repress his smiles . . . must have strained him to his last ounce of strength'.[38]

Partly to augment the 'nasty messes' the cooks came up with and partly because they were avid 'sportsmen', that is hunters, Howard-Bury and Bullock went shooting whenever they could, bringing back hares, geese, wild ass, gazelles, pheasants. Bullock also snared fish with his butterfly net. In fact the expedition had been expressly instructed to refrain from hunting and killing due to the strict Buddhist injunction against taking life, but the only concession Bullock and Howard-Bury made to Tibetan sensibilities was never to hunt near monasteries or villages. When an angry Charles Bell learned of all the shooting, he wrote to Howard-Bury to urge him to stop. On the two subsequent expeditions, the Tibetans reluctantly permitted a naturalist only on the condition that no animals, birds or butterflies would be harmed. In a postscript to this story, the head lama at Rongbuk, in his autobiography, wrote of his interview with Bruce in 1922: 'We will not harm the birds and wild animals of this area,' the lama quotes Bruce as saying. 'I swear our entire weaponry consists of this little penknife.'[39]

Kellas's health was the worst affected by the journey, including the unhygienic cooking, and Howard-Bury had been worried about him ever since Darjeeling.

> Dr Kellas had unfortunately in the early spring of this year tried his constitution very severely by climbing Narsing and had also spent several nights at very low temperatures at camps over 20,000 feet [6,100m] at Kabru, so that when he arrived at Darjeeling a few days before the Expedition was due to start, he was not in as fit a condition as he should have been.[40]

He might have added that before Narsing and Kabru, Kellas had spent nearly three months on the Kamet expedition, along with Morshead, carrying out oxygen experiments and hoping to make a summit attempt on that peak. By the time Kellas left Darjeeling on 19 May, he had been climbing in the Himalayas, often above 20,000 feet (6,100m), for almost nine months and had lost fourteen pounds off his modest frame.

Kellas was in fact well known for his stamina – Morshead had marvelled at his strength on Kamet – and it must have been that which got him through the first leg of the trip to Khamba Dzong when no mention is made of his condition. After he arrives in Tibet, however, Kellas can no longer walk or even ride a pony or a yak – he tries but falls off repeatedly – and there are daily references in the sources to his deteriorating condition, although Kellas himself always put on a brave face. Howard–Bury, for example, was becoming increasingly worried:

> *May 28*: The . . . bad cooking had affected the stomachs of all members of the Expedition and none of us was feeling very well. Dr Kellas was the worst and as soon as he arrived at Phari, he retired to bed.
> *May 29*: Dr Kellas was no better; he refused to take any food and was very depressed about himself.
> *May 30*: Dr Kellas was not well enough to ride and was carried in an arm–chair all day. Dr Kellas, though rather better the next day, was still too weak to ride.
> *June 3*: Dr Kellas had had a very trying day. He had been rather better and had started riding a yak but he found this too exhausting and coolies had to be sent back from Tatsang to bring him on in a litter.[41]

Affection for Kellas was unanimous among the team members, and concerns about 'the old gentleman's' health weighed heavily. 'Yesterday he was in a state of collapse on route,' Mallory wrote, and 'Heron and I got him down to a shelter while Bullock went off and got Wollaston who administered Bovril and brandy, but except for such incidents one scarcely saw him and he went to bed the moment he came in and never had a meal with us.' Mallory wanted to stay with Kellas, but Kellas wouldn't have it: '[He] was obliged to retire a number of times en route and could not bear to be seen in this distress, and so insisted that everyone be in front of him.'[42] After making sure Kellas's tent was prepared, one or two team members would go out to meet him at the end of a day's march and walk the last mile into camp with him.

After Yatung, the first stop in Tibet, the party moved on to Phari, 'the most incredibly dirty warren that can be imagined,' Mallory called it, while Bullock's diary summary read 'a filthy place . . . All people excessively dirty.'[43] From Phari it was 20 miles to Tuna over a pass at 15,200 feet (4,632m), still on the road to Lhasa. By now the entire character of the journey had changed: they were marching through a series of wide valleys and open plains; the road was level or gently sloping in most places, rising gradually to the passes. When they weren't above the tree line, the vegetation was mostly pines and other evergreens, with dwarf rhododendrons and Alpine primulas tucked in the undergrowth. They were at an average elevation of more than 11,000 feet (3,350m), the sky was clear and there were views of the Himalayas throughout the day.

The main event of this part of the route, all by itself and dominating the skyline, is Chomolhari, 24,035 feet (7,325m), at some points as close as three miles across the Tibetan plain. No one who ever marched past Chomolhari failed to be enchanted by it. It was 'a magnificent sight all day', Howard-Bury noted, 'with its 7,000 feet [2,130m] of precipices descending sheer into the plain'.[44] Colonel Edward Norton, who led the 1924 expedition, spoke of 'the joy of doing a whole march under that most beautiful mountain Chomolhari, whose isolated position and perfect shape combine to produce a picture from which one can hardly take one's eyes'.[45] When the members of the 1922 expedition got their first view of the storied mountain, looking on in awed silence, General Bruce quietly reminded the men that one of the lower camps they were planning to establish on the upper slopes of Everest would be only 600 feet (180m) lower than the summit of Chomolhari. 'We all admired [Chomolhari] enormously,' Bruce writes, 'but the enthusiasm of the party was somewhat dampened when I pointed [this] out to them . . .'[46]

The expedition left Phari on 31 May. Normally the trip to Khamba Dzong took three days, but the Tibetan guides told Howard-Bury that it was too early in the year to take the shorter route and they would have to take the long way round. 'We afterwards found out that this was a lie, and that they had sent us the long way round in order to be able to charge us more. We had not yet got accustomed to Tibetan ways.'[47]

It was a very costly detour. The long way round would take six days, involve crossing the two highest passes of the entire route and be a severe strain on Kellas's health. The day the party set off from Phari, Wollaston spoke with Kellas, suggesting he stay back and rest until he was stronger and offering to make arrangements to have him escorted back to Sikkim where he could be looked after in Lachen by missionaries. At first Kellas resisted, insisting he was fine, but he later reconsidered; by that time, however, Wollaston and the others had all left, and Kellas set out from Phari alone in a litter borne by six porters.

The group made 20 miles that day, most of it across a gentle plain, dotted with herds of Tibetan wild ass and gazelles. 'We were now in the true Tibetan climate,' Howard-Bury notes after they crossed over the Tang La, the main Himalayan watershed, 'with brilliant sunshine, blue skies, still mornings, and strong winds all the afternoon.'[48] At Tuna, where Younghusband had spent a miserable winter in 1903–4, they all crowded into the rest house. The next day they rode from Tuna to Dochen, 13 miles, and spent the night at the rest house on the shore of Lake Bamtso. Here they turned north, finally leaving the Lhasa road behind, along with the comfort of its rest houses, sleeping from now on in tents. They crossed over the Dug La (16,500 feet/5,029m) and then made straight west for Khamba Dzong.

Two days later, on 4 June, Kellas passed out just short of the top of the 17,100-foot (5,212m) Tatsang La, and Wollaston was summoned. He managed to revive Kellas and bring him into camp, but Howard-Bury and Wollaston decided that as soon as the expedition reached Khamba Dzong the next day, they would make arrangements to send Kellas back to Lachen in Sikkim. Mercifully, Kellas seemed better on the 5th and was reportedly even cheerful, though he still had to be carried and lagged behind everyone else by nearly two hours. By four o'clock that afternoon, everyone but Kellas had arrived at Khamba Dzong, and Howard-Bury was sitting down to tea with the dzongpen, who had come to offer 5 sheep, 100 eggs and a carpet as gifts to the expedition. Suddenly a man came running up with the news that seven miles back, just short of the top of the last pass, alone save for his litter bearers, Alexander Kellas had collapsed and died.

The party was devastated. Howard-Bury and Wollaston were the most shocked by the news as each of them had had contact with Kellas only a few hours earlier. Howard-Bury had visited a nearby nunnery first thing in the morning, hitting the trail after Kellas had left and overtaking him mid-morning, when Kellas seemed fine. And Wollaston had had even more recent news – a note in the afternoon from Kellas saying he had reached the last pass, was resting for an hour or two, and would then proceed on to Khamba Dzong. Wollaston rushed back to verify the sad news, determining that Kellas had died from heart failure, most probably brought on by exhaustion and enteritis.

Wollaston was deeply upset and blamed himself, but Howard-Bury was doubtless closer to the truth when he said that 'his very keenness' was Kellas's undoing, pointing to the three expeditions he had undertaken in the past twelve months, which had all been carried out to gather information in support of the Everest reconnaissance but had left Kellas weak and debilitated. Younghusband agreed: 'The Scottish mountaineer', he wrote, 'had in fact, with the pertinacity of his race, pursued his heart's love till he had driven his poor body to death.'[49] For his part, Mallory deeply regretted that he had agreed to leave Kellas behind, albeit at Kellas's own insistence, and was especially saddened by the fact that the 'old gentleman' had died alone. 'The most tragic and distressing fact about his death', he wrote to Geoffrey Young, 'is that no one of us was with him. Can you imagine anything less like a mountaineering party?'[50]

Mallory was fond of Wollaston and anticipated that his friend was likely to face criticism in climbing circles when word of Kellas's death reached England. To his great credit, Mallory immediately wrote to Geoffrey Young to describe the mitigating circumstances of Kellas's death in order to provide Young with facts to mount a defence of the doctor. 'Wollaston is more my friend than any one in the party', he wrote, 'and has been greatly distressed. I am afraid some folk at home may be inclined to criticise him, and this you may be able to prevent.'[51]

Mallory was also worried about how Ruth would react when she read about Kellas in the newspapers, which would carry the story at least a month before any letter from Mallory could reach her. He sat down just a few hours after Kellas's death to offer comfort, however late it would be in arriving. 'Kellas died this afternoon,' he began. 'You will have seen the news a month or so before you receive this, and my sadness at this event makes my thoughts fly to you and wonder what your thoughts will have been.' He knows Ruth is bound to be worried and wants to reassure her that he is fine and that Kellas's circumstances were unique. 'I know it is no use saying don't be anxious because anxiety is unreasoning and comes upon us unbidden. But it can be dispelled by reason . . . The plain fact about Kellas is that he had worn himself out before the expedition started.' Mallory explained that all the other members of the expedition, save himself, had suffered from dysentery and diarrhoea as bad or worse than Kellas, but because they were in good form to begin with, they had quickly recovered. 'The great personal fact is that I am very fit.'[52]

The funeral for Kellas was held the next day, 6 June. '[W]e buried him on the slopes of the hill to the South of Khamba Dzong,' Howard-Bury wrote,

> in a site unsurpassed for beauty that looks across the broad plains of Tibet to the mighty chain of the Himalayas out of which rise up the three great peaks of Pawhunri, Kanchenjhow, and Chomiomi, which he alone had climbed. From the same spot, far away to the West – more than a hundred miles away – could be seen the snowy crest of Mount Everest towering far above all the other mountains. He lies, therefore, within sight of his greatest feats in climbing and within view of the mountain that he had longed for so many years to approach – a fitting resting place for a great mountaineer.[53]

'It was a very touching little ceremony,' Mallory observed. 'I shall never forget the expression, more wonder than anything else, of four of his own special boys who sat on a great stone a yard away from the grave while Howard-Bury read the passage from the Corinthians.'[54]

In an article he later wrote for *The Times*, Howard-Bury noted that the four porters looking on made a rough cross out of some flowers they found nearby and laid it on Kellas's grave. We do not know for sure just who these 'four boys' sitting on the stone were, but it is likely that among them was at least one if not more of Kellas's old Sherpa climbing friends – Sona, Tuny or perhaps Andyerkow – 'his own trained mountain men', as Mallory calls them. If even just one of them was present, then Kellas may not have died quite such a lonely death after all.

Kellas's death so early on in the expedition, just three weeks out of Darjeeling, is surely another factor contributing to his undeserved and unfortunate obscurity. This was the biggest stage even someone as renowned as Kellas was ever likely to play on, and he was gone before most of the drama unfolded. Moreover, his early death also meant that he was not present when virtually all of the best-known and most widely reprinted group photographs of the 1921 team members were taken. As his two biographers have aptly noted, Kellas is 'the man not in the photograph'.

Harold Raeburn now had to be sent back. Twice since Phari he had been thrown from his horse, rolled on, and kicked in the head and in one knee. Moreover, he had not been well since Darjeeling, suffering from indigestion and dysentery, growing weaker every day. Raeburn didn't want to go: 'Raeburn has become very old,' Howard-Bury noted, 'and has become a great responsibility, and like all Scotch, he is very obstinate.'[55] But Wollaston wasn't taking any chances; the day after Kellas's funeral he and one of the translators left to escort Raeburn back to Sikkim. In the end, Raeburn was away for nearly three months, only rejoining the group late in the expedition in their camp at Kharta.

Upon Raeburn's departure, the now six-man team (until Wollaston returned from escorting Raeburn) would continue on towards Everest minus the two most experienced Himalayan climbers on the expedition, including one, Kellas, who doubtless understood more about the effects of altitude on climbers than any man alive. Their knowledge and experience of the Himalayas would be sorely missed. Moreover, in their absence George Mallory became the de facto head of the climbing team, one of the only two men on the expedition who had never been in the Himalayas nor ever climbed anything higher than Mont Blanc which, at 15,774 feet (4,808m), is 40 feet (12m) lower than the place at Khamba Dzong where the expedition was now camped. 'It is a bad business,' Hinks wrote to Howard-Bury, 'having lost Raeburn as well as Kellas because I can quite believe that Bullock and Mallory are somewhat children in those parts . . .'[56]

Mallory took it all in his stride. In point of fact, the climbing team, at least in Mallory's mind, had never been more than two in the first place, in the sense of men who could actually go above 24,000 feet (7,315m); hence Mallory had in effect been the true climbing leader from the beginning. He had always thought the size of the climbing team woefully inadequate, however, and now the very situation he had warned Hinks about had come to pass; but in assessing the skills of the remaining party members, he was realistic and cautiously optimistic. Bullock was solid, 'my stable-companion, a very placid one. I think he's going to turn out very useful.' Morshead, who had more Himalayan climbing experience than anyone still on the expedition, would be stronger even than Mallory if he could be freed up from his surveying responsibilities. He 'has been walking everywhere on the hills up to 18,000 all the way from Darjeeling', Mallory wrote, 'and looks as fit and strong as possible – a very nice keen man'.[57] Mallory knew that Wheeler too had extensive climbing experience, in his case in the Canadian Rockies, but did not think he could rely on Wheeler who had been suffering from stomach problems almost since Darjeeling. Heron, Wollaston and even Howard-Bury might be useful in some situations.

As of 6 June 1921, one day before Raeburn was sent back to Sikkim, George Mallory had never set eyes on Mount Everest. The mountain can be seen from Darjeeling, albeit poorly, but not during the monsoon, nor can it be seen from along the route the expedition took through Sikkim and the Chumbi Valley to Khamba Dzong. But it was well known that Everest could be seen from Khamba

Dzong; in 1903 Younghusband saw it almost every morning as he shaved. To get the best possible view, much better than Younghusband had had, Mallory and Bullock set out early on the morning of the 6th to climb to the top of the 1,000-foot (304m) hill which towered over their campsite. They passed by the great fort and kept on climbing until they reached the top of the ridge and gazed to the west, out over the Tibetan plain. The man and the mountain were about to meet.

'It may seem an irony of fate', Mallory observes in one of the three much-celebrated and best-known descriptions he wrote of Everest,

> that actually on the day after the distressing event of Dr Kellas' death we experienced the strange elation of seeing Everest for the first time. It was a perfect early morning as we plodded up the barren slopes above our camp and . . . behind the old rugged fort which is itself a singularly impressive and dramatic spectacle; we had mounted perhaps a thousand feet [304m] when we stayed and turned, and saw what we came to see. There was no mistaking the two great peaks in the West; to the left must be Makalu, grey, severe, and yet distinctly graceful, and the other away to the right – who could doubt its identity? It was a prodigious white fang excrescent from the jaw of the world.[58]

Bullock was more subdued: 'Mallory and I went up hill to right of *jong* and above the older building higher up, nearly 1,000 feet [304m]. And had excellent view of Everest range.'[59]

Mallory and Bullock's first glimpse of Everest was a memorable moment for the two men, but the personal resonance of the incident notwithstanding, the actual view of Everest from Khamba Dzong is quite limited. For one thing, Everest is 100 miles away to the south-west and for another, the mountain, as seen from this position, sits behind the intervening Gyangkar range, which obscures all but the very top of Everest, the last 5,000 feet (1,524m) or so. Thus the view Mallory and Bullock had on 6 June did not reveal any of the mountain below 24,000 feet (7,315m) nor any other, lower mountains that might be hidden behind the Gyangkar range and closer to the mountain, girding Everest, as it were, and possibly preventing access to anyone approaching from the north. The members of the expedition would have to wait until they were well west of Khamba Dzong, beyond where the Gyangkar range ended, to have a less obstructed view of the mountain.

The often-quoted description of his first view of Everest given above, as well as the two other well-known passages from later in the journey, are taken from Mallory's chapters in the official account of the expedition, *Mount Everest: The Reconnaissance, 1921*, of which Howard-Bury was the lead author. It is well-known that Mallory, who gave up his teaching position to go to Everest, was worried about what he would do to support his family when he returned, especially as he had become disenchanted with the teaching profession and was loath to take it up again. Even before he left for Everest, he had entertained the notion of becoming a writer, and in fact he had accepted the invitation in part because he saw it as a possible platform for a writing career.

Whether Mallory would have found much success is an open question. In many of his formal attempts, when he was writing for an audience, unlike in his letters to Ruth, Geoffrey Young and others, Mallory's prose was often florid and overwrought. While there is genuine beauty to be found, especially in parts of his official expedition account, clarity was often sacrificed for the sake of effect. Even before the expedition, Mallory regularly submitted articles to the *Alpine Journal*, but George Yeld, editor at the time, confessed that he often couldn't make any sense of them. Rather than a straightforward description of the terrain and the details of a particular climb, Mallory tried to evoke 'the feelings and emotions of climbing . . .'[60] A typical Mallory effort was an infamous essay comparing an alpine climb to a symphony. On one occasion Yeld forwarded one of Mallory's articles to the president, Percy Farrar, who returned it saying he couldn't understand a word. Even Mallory had his doubts: 'I can't think I have sufficient talent to make a life work of writing,' he wrote to Robert Graves.[61] That did not stop him, however, from passing judgement on Howard-Bury's prose in the official expedition account; his chapters, Mallory told Ruth when he read them, 'are worse than I expected, dreadfully bad', a reaction no doubt triggered by Howard-Bury's insistence that

Mallory rewrite some of his sections of *Mount Everest: The Reconnaissance, 1921.*[62]

Khamba Dzong marked the end of the first phase of the expedition, which had covered 260 miles in twenty-two days. The second phase, from Khamba Dzong to Tingri, a journey of 120 miles, would take them another eleven days. They spent two days at Khamba Dzong, arranging ongoing transport, respecting a laborious local process for selecting pack animals that often took one or two hours and meant late starts in the morning. They left on 8 June, and while they were indeed 'just about to walk off the map', as Mallory famously observed, referring to the map made by the 1903 mission to Tibet, they did in fact have another map, one drawn two hundred years earlier at the request of the Chinese emperor Kangshi. While this map was certainly of dubious value, even so the expedition was not heading out into complete terra incognita; the road from Khamba Dzong to Tingri was well travelled, with several major villages, at least one famous monastery, at Shekar Dzong, and a number of smaller villages and hamlets. That said, the mood that morning was celebratory; these six men were about to go where no westerners had ever gone before. 'Geoffrey,' Mallory wrote to Young, 'it's beginning to be exciting!'[63]

Their route took them across the Tibetan plateau, where the elevation ranges from 14,000 to 18,000 feet (4,265 to 5,485m), higher in many places than the highest of the Alps and higher too than any of the expedition members had ever been before, except for Morshead. The Tibetan plateau is a high-altitude desert, treeless except for a few willow shrubs that grow briefly in the spring. It is a place of 'vast empty spaces, [of] brown barren hills, tracts of loose and crumbling sand, the cloudless skies, the penetrating light, the wide extremes of temperature, the scanty rainfall, the dry air, the fierce winds, the low, scanty vegetation'.[64] The temperature on the Tibetan plateau fluctuated by as much as 50 degrees in a single day; at midday it could be 55° or even 60° Fahrenheit and by night as much as 10 degrees below freezing. During the day, as Mallory wrote to Ruth, 'the sun is always scorching and threatens to take our skin off', whilst by late afternoon the men could not wait to get into their tents and climb into their sleeping bags to get warm.[65]

On most days the main event on the plateau is wind, which comes up in the late morning and blows for the rest of the day, so hard in some places that it etches cracks in the surface of boulders. In most Everest accounts, beginning with 1921, the wind on the plateau comes in for so much comment – and so much colourful imagery – that it almost becomes a character in the narrative, just another member of the expedition. Noel called it 'an incessant, piercing gale'[66] and elsewhere writes that '[w]e had our first encounter with the Tibetan wind. It is more than a wind. It is a thousand knife-points . . .'[67] In 1922 Finch observed that the 'icy blasts invariably met one straight in the face . . . [W]e marched in the teeth of a wind that gnawed . . . at our weather-beaten, hardened skins and was the most generous contributor of . . . discomforts that Tibet meted out.'[68] In 1921 Wheeler called it simply 'the curse of the country', adding that 'your face simply goes to bits'.[69]

Even then, in a few spots the icy blasts and sheer force of the wind were not the worst of it; that distinction belonged to the ferocious sandstorms the wind whipped up as it swept across the mostly barren plains. In places there were dunes 20 feet high and in other places quicksand. After crossing the Chiblung river, the expedition had to camp on some nearby dunes. Wheeler wrote that 'the dry sand . . . was blowing off so strongly and continuously that it seemed as though the whole river bed, about a mile wide, was shifting. Our dinner that night . . . seemed to consist mostly of sand dune.'[70] In the most sandy stretches there was not even any respite when the wind stopped, for then the sandflies and midges swarmed in their millions about the men and the animals. 'We were plagued with midges,' Bullock wrote in his diary.[71]

The wind, the sand, the cold, and the glaring sun of Tibet all took their toll, but there were also compensations. Every morning before the clouds moved in and the wind came up, there were stunning vistas of the Himalayas stretching for over 200 miles to the south and west. 'Tibet has at least one good trait,' Younghusband observed, 'the mornings are usually calm. The sky is then of transparent, purest azure. The sun is warm. The snowy summits of some distant peaks are tinged with delicate pinks and primrose. And the heart of man warms even to Tibet.'[72] Another compensation was the simple fact that every day brought the team 10 miles closer to Everest. And there was the growing sense of anticipation and excitement about what would happen once the expedition reached Tingri, which was to be the base for the northern reconnaissance. The plan, as everyone knew, was to dispatch Mallory and Bullock (and also Wheeler, although separately and by himself) into the final 50 miles of unexplored territory south-west of Tingri. And there, somewhere, they would either find the mountain or determine that it could not be reached from the north. A moment of reckoning was now just days away.

On 13 June, near a place called Shiling, the expedition rounded the northernmost ridge of the Gyangkar range, the mountains that had partially hidden the earlier view of Everest, prompting Mallory and Bullock to ride some distance off the main trail to climb a hill they hoped would at last give them an unobstructed view of the mountain. '[W]e were penetrating a secret,' Mallory wrote to Ruth. 'We were looking behind the great barrier running north and south which had been as a screen in front of us ever since we turned our eyes westwards . . .' He explained that for several days, ever since the morning they left Khamba Dzong, 'the ultimate tops of these great mountains had been invisible. What were we to see now? Were they really to be revealed to us in their grandeur?'[73]

They left their Tibetan ponies to graze at the foot of the ridge and climbed for an hour. What they observed from the top of the ridge, a sight no westerner had ever seen, inspired the second of Mallory's celebrated descriptions of the mountain:

We were now able to make out where Everest should be; but the clouds were dark in that direction. We gazed at them intently through field glasses as though by some miracle we might pierce the veil. Presently, the miracle happened. We caught the gleam of snow behind the grey mists. A whole group of mountains began to appear in gigantic fragments . . . A preposterous triangular lump rose out of the depths; its edge came leaping up at an angle of about 70° and ended nowhere. To the left a black serrated crest was hanging in the sky incredibly. Gradually, very gradually, we saw the great mountainsides and glaciers and arêtes, now one fragment and now another through the floating rifts, until far higher in the sky than imagination had dared to suggest the white summit of Everest appeared.[74]

The writer and climbing historian Robert Macfarlane believes that from this moment Mallory was never quite the same, that Everest became the central focus in his life, supplanting even his family. It was 'a turning point. For from this day forth Everest, more even than Ruth, becomes the focus of Mallory's letters. The mountain starts to intrude into his thoughts like a lover. The third point of the love triangle which will destroy both Mallory and Ruth is put in place.'[75] Mallory himself also seems to have sensed that this sighting was especially significant. 'I have dwelt upon this episode at some length,' he writes in his account of the expedition, 'because in all our travels before we reached the mountain, it is for me beyond other adventures unforgettable . . .'[76]

Nearly every day after this sighting on 13 June Mallory and Bullock would wander off from the direct route in search of a hill or some other vantage point that promised a better view of Everest. It had begun to 'haunt the mind', he admitted to Ruth. 'Where can one go for another view, to unveil a little more of the great mystery? From this day that question has always been present.'[77] One of his biographers writes that Mallory began to perceive that he had now become part of something that was 'a greater matter than the joyous mountain climbing of the past', that 'an unbreakable link had been forged' between him and the mountain and that '[h]enceforth Mallory belonged to Everest'.[78] In a letter to Young, Mallory plaintively asked his friend: 'Geoffrey, when am I going to stop?'[79]

The party camped at several smaller towns along their route, always greeted and normally feted by the officials through whose districts they were passing. They were routinely offered gifts of eggs and sheep and often invited for a meal. The largest and most important town, famous for its monastery, was Shekar Dzong, a village clinging to the steep slopes of a towering ridge, with the town itself near the bottom, the great monastery (destroyed by China during the Cultural Revolution) perched halfway up the cliff, home to 400 monks, and the elaborate *dzong* or fort commanding the summit. 'On our arrival,' Howard-Bury writes, 'the whole town turned out and surrounded us . . . for we were the first Europeans they had ever seen.'[80] The villagers had erected a ceremonial tent to receive the party, one reserved for visiting dignitaries, but the group erected their own tents inside a stone enclosure in the shade of a grove of young willows.

Several members of the party climbed up narrow, almost vertical streets to the monastery and were given a tour of various court-yards and temples, using steep and slippery ladders for access in some places. The temples contained statues of various guardian deities, with the foremost temple housing a statue of the Buddha which was 50 feet (15m) high; the face had to be re-gilded every year. Howard-Bury took photographs of a number of the resident monks who urged him to also take a picture of their head lama. He was believed to be the reincarnation of a former abbot and was revered throughout Tibet as a kind of saint, responsible, it was said, for a number of miracles. The lama was reluctant as he only had one tooth – clearly a tenacious one, it should be noted, in a man who gave his age as 137 – but '[a]fter much persuasion the other monks induced him to come outside and have his photograph taken, telling him that he was an old man and that his time on earth was now short, and they would like to have a picture of him to remember him by'.[81] The lama was dressed in beautiful Chinese brocades and placed on a raised dais in front of which there was an elaborately carved Chinese table holding his *dorje* (a representation of a thunderbolt) and his bell. For all his toothlessness, the old abbot 'had a very pleasant smile'. The 'fame of this photograph spread throughout the country', Howard-Bury wrote, 'and in places hundreds of miles away I was asked for photographs of the Old Abbot of Shekar, nor could I give a more welcome present at any house'.[82] Indeed, the picture survives to the present day and is regularly reproduced in almost any book about the 1921 expedition.

After leaving Shekar Dzong, the party spent one night at Tsakor, and then covered the final 20 miles to Tingri. On that last day, they encountered a Mongolian pilgrim making his way, one prostration at a time, from Lhasa to Kathmandu. Now three months out of Lhasa, the man was engaging in a time-honoured religious custom of purifying oneself by a ritual of extreme exertion. He would stand straight with his arms raised high over his head and then lower himself to the ground and stretch out full length. He would then stand up and repeat the process from the spot where his fingertips had reached, making his way one body length at a time for the more than 650 miles to Kathmandu. The lamas in Lhasa prescribed just such a ritual for the inhabitants of that city, declaring that devout individuals should annually purify themselves by circling one prostration at a time the hill on which the Dalai Lama's residence sat. Pious Lhasa residents who were well meaning but otherwise busy with worldly affairs often hired professional crawlers to do the deed for them.

The expedition reached Tingri on 19 June, exactly one month after setting out from Darjeeling. It was still a party of only six westerners, but Wollaston would return in three days, on the 22nd. Although no one could have known it – no westerner had ever been to Tingri before – Tingri was an especially unpleasant place, and yet it was to be the base and headquarters of the expedition for the next month. The village of 300 houses sat on top of a hill 300 feet (91m) high in the middle of an otherwise flat salt plain. It sat astride two major trade routes: an east–west one from Lhasa to Kathmandu and a north–south one from Tingri over the Himalayas to Solu Khumbu in Nepal, the home of the Sherpas. Like frontier trading posts the world over, with single men passing through in great numbers, Tingri had a reputation as a den of vice, with drinking and whoring foremost among them, and one of the highest rates of illegitimate births in all of Tibet. Wollaston was appalled by the hygiene, calling it a place of 'unimaginable filth inhabited by people vile in their habits'.[83] It was their good fortune that most of the expedition members, except for poor Wollaston, would spend very little time in the place.

The first order of business was to set up the expedition's head-quarters. They were offered a large Chinese-built rest house at the base of the hill, just below the village, with a number of small rooms arranged around three concentric courtyards. The building was in poor repair, with mud floors, leaking roof, and peeling murals of flying dogs and demons painted on the walls; but within hours the place was cleaned up and the first priority, a functioning darkroom, had been created to develop photographs. In all, over 600 photos were taken during the expedition, the majority by Wheeler as part of his photographic survey, but many were also taken by Mallory, Bullock and by Howard-Bury himself, an accomplished photographer. They would prove to be invaluable to the two follow-on expeditions in 1922 and 1924.

On the afternoon of the 20th, the expedition members had a piece of information that greatly excited them. In a courtesy call on the acting governor, Howard-Bury was told that there was a long, almost flat glacial valley that led in a straight line for 25 miles from the base of Everest north to a monastery at the head of that valley, called the Rongbuk. If there was such a monastery, then there had to be a way to get to it, and if it did indeed sit at the entrance to such a valley, then that valley was the highway to Everest.

After the end of June the monsoon could arrive at any time in the Himalayas, and when it did the climbing season would end for the next few months. One fact the 1921 group had begun to realise was that they had left Darjeeling at least a month too late, and they were now racing the monsoon. To get the most out of the few weeks they might have left – if the monsoon was late – Howard-Bury decided to send three teams out simultaneously from Tingri, one each to explore the approaches to Everest from the east, from due north and from the west. Mallory and Bullock would head straight for the base of the North Face. Morshead and his team of surveyors would go east; Wheeler and the geologist Heron would head for the west side of the Everest group, but in separate parties.

Later Howard-Bury would single Wheeler out for special recognition, noting how he spent nearly the entire summer 'in lonely camps 18–20,000 feet [5,486–6,096m] high' waiting day after day 'in bitter cold and driving snow . . . for the clouds to lift' so he could take his pictures. In all Wheeler would spend forty-one nights on glaciers and moraines above 18,000 feet (5,486m), almost always alone since his porters did not have the clothes or the warm tents to pass the nights at those altitudes. 'I think that he had the hardest and most trying time of all of us,' Howard-Bury noted.[84] Later Wheeler himself wrote that the worst part of the experience for him was 'the loneliness, all by myself at high altitudes, waiting and waiting for the clear day that seldom came'.[85] And surely the best part, although Wheeler himself does not say so, was the day he made the most significant discovery of the entire expedition.

Nearly everything after Tingri was true terra incognita; the men were venturing where no westerners had ever gone before. Mallory and Bullock were probably the luckiest because the Rongbuk monastery was regularly supplied from Tingri, which meant there had to be a well-travelled route known to a few locals who went in and out. Even then, in all three of the explorations Howard-Bury now set in motion, there was no way of knowing how difficult these excursions would prove to be or how long they would take. Another unknown was how the extreme elevations they were about to enter would affect men who had already spent two weeks above 14,000 feet (4,265m), who would now be going up to 20,000 feet (6,095m) or higher, and who might even have to sleep at that altitude on occasion. Several members had already exhibited signs of altitude sickness even before they reached Tingri, and in the coming weeks frostbite would become another potential health hazard. The doctor, Wollaston, had his hands full with two very sick porters as soon as he arrived in Tingri, and he was asked by Howard-Bury to remain at headquarters so as to be available in an emergency. Upon hearing Wollaston had returned, Mallory's comment was, 'I only hope he won't have to amputate our toes.'[86]

Mallory and Bullock, who arrived in Tingri one day after the others, were electrified by the news of the Rongbuk monastery. They were certain it had to be the same one John Noel had been told of in 1913, the one that sat at the base 'of the lofty Pherugh mountains' and from which he could 'look across, as I hoped, to Mount Everest'. This was the monastery Noel was heading for when he was unceremoniously booted out of Tibet.

The two men made plans to leave immediately. Already, even before reaching Tingri, they had carefully selected the members of their expedition: sixteen Sherpas, each of whom they provided with climbing boots – Mallory had hammered nails into the boots to create primitive crampons – an ice axe and warm underwear; a sirdar or head man (Gyalzen by name); and a cook (Dukpa). Fifteen yaks would carry their provisions, enough for a two-week excursion, which later turned into four. Only one thing was missing: a means of communication between the sirdar and the two 'sahibs'; or, as Mallory put it: 'Our equipment was seriously deficient in one respect: we were short of words.'[87] Back in Darjeeling Mallory had copied 150 words of Tibetan into a note-book, planning to memorise them on the march; it would have to be enough. On the morning of 23 June, their preparations complete, yaks all loaded, two local guides engaged, George Mallory and Guy Bullock were ready to depart. Their next stop, with any luck, would be Mount Everest.

In some ways Guy Bullock is the missing man of the 1921 expedition. He went everywhere Mallory went, usually just a few steps behind, climbed every hill and mountain Mallory climbed, including Everest, demonstrated the same strength and endurance – Mallory himself says at one point that Bullock will 'probably last longer than myself' – and was, if anything, more skilful at managing and communicating with the porters.[88] His name ought to loom larger in the annals of 1921, but he remains obscure, in part because he was by nature self-effacing, in part because he left no record behind, save a very bare-bones diary, and in part because he had the bad luck – although he would never have called it that – to be paired with the most colourful and charismatic member of the enterprise. Very few people, certainly not the self-effacing Guy Bullock, ever shone next to George Mallory.

That said, by the time the expedition reached Tingri, if not before, all its members realised that Guy Bullock had turned out to be a very happy accident indeed. Hastily chosen for the expedition at the last minute, just two weeks before he would have to be on a boat for Calcutta, having received minimal vetting, opposed by Farrar and Hinks, selected almost exclusively on the recommendation of Mallory, Bullock's main qualification appears to have been that he was available. He was a member of the Alpine Club, to be sure, and had climbed as high as 14,000 feet (4,265m) in the Alps, but he had not climbed recently and had never been to the Himalayas. He would acquit himself admirably – and then some – in the weeks ahead, but his climbing skills paled beside another quality that would turn out to be much more important: his even temperament.

It was the first thing everyone noticed about Bullock, that he 'never lost his head', as Mallory had written to Younghusband.[89] Howard-Bury, who could at times be highly critical of both Mallory and Bullock, nevertheless recognised and valued Bullock's easy-going personality. 'It was of the greatest importance on an enterprise of this kind', he wrote some years later, 'to have people that got on well with each other. At high altitudes men tend to become irritable, but Bullock had . . . a placid temperament . . . [He was] always ready to help, a companion cheerful and unassuming.'[90]

The noted Alpine climber Graham Irving, tutor of Mallory and Bullock at Winchester College, thought highly of Bullock's climbing skills but even more highly of his 'perfect steadiness'.

> Bullock was, in many ways, an ideal companion for Mallory that year. In nearly all the climbs he did with me he was last on the rope and I believe it was the position that he liked best, and he was admirably fitted for it, strong, imperturbable and exceptionally safe. In all the years we climbed together, I cannot remember his ever slipping. Mallory was always eager to jump into the lead, and Bullock was just the man to ensure the climb [was] carried out safely, for he was a good judge of conditions as well as an assurance of support in difficulty. His part in the [Everest] reconnaissance does not catch the light as that of Mallory does, but his staying power and cool, controlled efficiency were just what was needed.[91]

The essence of dependability, the great enabler of others' achievements, Guy Bullock was the perfect man for the role he was destined to play for the next three months: the faithful Sancho Panza to the mercurial, idealistic, impatient and reckless Don

Quixote who was George Mallory. It is difficult to imagine anyone else on the expedition, with the possible exception of Kellas, who could have got along so well with Mallory or tolerated so cheerfully his wild mood swings.

And now they were off.

Whatever else they might have felt, we do know that Mallory and Bullock were not delusional. 'The task before us was not likely to prove a simple and straightforward matter,' Mallory wrote, 'and we had no expectation that it would be quickly concluded. It would be necessary in the first place to find the mountain; as we looked across the wide plains from Tingri and saw the dark monsoon clouds gathered in all directions, we were not reassured.'[92] And Howard-Bury likewise had both of his feet on the ground: 'Looked at from here,' he wrote, meaning Tingri, 'it is certainly a very wonderful mountain, as it seems to stand up all by itself, but from this side it looks far too steep to be climbed.'[93] But first, as Mallory said, they would have to find it.

The party left Tingri at 7 a.m. on 23 June, having been told they should reach the Rongbuk monastery and valley in two days. Things got off to a bad start almost immediately as the yak drivers headed off in what Mallory and Bullock believed was the wrong direction. 'An almost interminable three-way argument followed,' Mallory observed, 'a horrible crisis in two tongues I could not understand', as he and Bullock, talking through the sirdar Gyalzen, sought an explanation from the drivers, who merely said the destination would take five days to reach, not two.[94] The two sahibs, who suspected the locals of a scheme to line their pockets, decided to go their own way, leaving Gyalzen behind to accompany the drivers to Nazurga where he would hopefully find new transport and new drivers. Mallory and Bullock reached their campsite by mid-afternoon and spent two anxious hours waiting for Gyalzen and the new pack animals to arrive, which they did just before nightfall. Mallory was proud of having 'foiled the natives, whose aim was to retard our progress'.[95] Bullock's diary describes his 'rotten pony' and then records another arrival: 'Mail. Letters and chocolate and fudge.'[96]

The next day, the 24th, they crossed the Dzakar Chu over the bridge at Nazurga, climbed over a 16,000-foot pass (4876m) and camped at Zambu where, Bullock noted, the 'top of Everest [is] just visible'.[97] From Zambu they would proceed on the following day to where the Dzakar Chu met the Rongbuk Chu at a place called Chobuk, whence they would cross the Rongbuk which 'we knew we had but to follow . . . up to reach the glacier at the head of the valley', the celebrated Rongbuk Glacier which they now knew led directly to the foot of Everest.

Crossing the Rongbuk on the 25th was somewhat fraught. 'Tibetan bridges are so constructed', Mallory wrote, 'as to offer the passenger ample opportunities of experiencing insecurity and contemplating the possibilities of disaster. This one was no exception.' The yaks were unloaded, lest they be swept downstream with all the excursion's provisions, and goaded to swim across by a crowd of yelling onlookers. The two men were now on the right bank of the river and proceeded for some time through a limestone gorge lined with high red cliffs below which

> a green ribbon stretched along the margin with grass and low bushes, yellow-flowering asters, rhododendrons, and juniper . . . It was a day of brilliant sunshine, as yet warm and windless . . . I was filled with the desire to lie here in this 'oasis' and live at ease and sniff the lean fragrance of mountain plants. But we went on, on and up . . . At length we followed the path up a steeper rise crowned by two chortens [stone shrines] between which it passes. We paused here in sheer astonishment. Perhaps we had half expected to see Mount Everest at this moment. In the back of my mind were a host of questions about it clamouring for answer. But the sight of it now banished every thought . . . We asked no questions and made no comment, but simply looked.[98]

Viewed from the north, Everest sits at the head of the Rongbuk Valley (Tibetan for the valley of precipices), rising nearly 10,000 feet (3,050m) – just under two miles – straight up from the valley floor in what is called the North Face. The upper, southern part of the 25-mile-long valley is the Rongbuk Glacier, essentially a 15-mile, very rough highway to the mountain, rising ever so gently to the base of the North Face. Seen from the north, the very top of Everest, the last 2,000 feet (610m) or so, is a not-quite-perfect triangle, with two sides or ridges descending due east and west, the right or west side at a steeper pitch than the east. After 1,500 feet (457m) or so, a branch splits off from the ridge on the east side (the North-east Ridge), curves slightly to head due north, continues for over two and a half miles, dips slightly to form a saddle called the North Col, and then climbs steeply to the top of Changtse or North Peak at 24,730 feet (7,537m). This offshoot from the North-east Ridge is called the North Ridge. The right or West Ridge of Everest (seen from the north) also extends northwards in a gentle curve but in a more westerly direction. Where the two ridges begin their curve to the north and north-west respectively, they create the two steep sides of a great bowl at the foot of the North Face.

Seen from the bottom or north end of the Rongbuk Valley, near the Rongbuk monastery, the bulk of Changtse, sitting midway up the valley, extends halfway out into the valley itself on the left side, obscuring the view up to the North Face. But from the right side of the valley, where Mallory and Bullock were now standing, the view is unobstructed past Changtse, open all the way back to the bowl at the base of Everest, with all 10,000 feet (3,048m) of the mountain from summit to base exposed. It is one of the most dramatic spectacles on earth.

Such is the topography. For the poetry, here is George Mallory in almost perfect pitch:

The Rongbuk Valley is well constructed to show off the peak at its head; for about 20 miles it is extraordinarily straight and in that distance rises only 4,000 feet [1,219m], the glacier, which is 10 miles long, no more steeply than the rest. In consequence of this arrangement one only has to be raised very slightly above the bed of the valley to see it almost as a flat way up to the very head of the glacier from which the cliffs of Everest spring. To the place where Everest stands one looks along rather than up. The glacier is prostrate, not a part of the mountain, not even a pediment; merely a floor footing the high walls. At the end of the valley and above the glacier, Everest rises, not so much a peak as a prodigious mountain-mass. There is no complication for the eye. The highest of the world's great mountains, it seems, has to make but a single gesture of its magnificence to be lord of all, vast in unchallenged and isolated supremacy. To the discerning eye other mountains are visible, giants between 23,000 [7,010m] and 26,000 feet [7,925m] high. Not one of their slenderer heads even reaches their chief's shoulder; beside Everest they escape notice – such is the pre-eminence of the greatest.[99]

It is one of the most celebrated passages in the literature of climbing and one of the great moments in the history of mountaineering. Privately, in a letter to Ruth, Mallory can barely contain himself: '[W]e saw the great mountain standing up from its base at the end of [our valley], a more glorious sight than I can attempt to describe. My darling, this is a thrilling business altogether. I can't tell you how it possesses me, and what a prospect it is. And the beauty of it all!'[100]

For seventy-one years, ever since it was discovered in 1850, Everest had been a mystery, a symbol, a metaphor, more dream than reality. But now on this day, as Mallory and Bullock gazed up at it in astonishment from the floor of the Rongbuk Valley, Everest became something which, oddly enough, it had never quite managed to be before: a mere mountain.

The unflappable Bullock was also moved. He was not given to emotional outbursts, nor were his diary entries susceptible to poetry; indeed, they are barely susceptible even to prose, laden, instead, with four- and five-word phrases rather than complete sentences. In fairness to Bullock, however, who was university-educated and almost certainly a competent writer, he is not writing for anyone but himself in his diary; indeed not writing at all, merely jotting down notes. Nevertheless, his matter-of-fact diary note for 25 June 1921, is, in its own way, just as apt – and just as perfect – as Mallory's more effusive effort, and pure Guy Bullock: 'From Chobuk, up the valley across stony flats, then turning southwards and at the junction of torrents again almost due south. Finally [the] valley turns a little east and Everest appears full in view at the end – with nothing in between.'[101]

'With nothing in between.' In the lore of hunting, the hunt is said to conclude when the hunter has the quarry in his sights and there is nothing between them, when the hunter, if he chooses, can claim his prize. With these four words in his brief diary entry, Guy Bullock announces, if only to himself for the moment, that after seventy-one years the West's hunt for the world's highest mountain has finally ended. Mount Everest has been well and truly found.

The world would find out soon enough.

Epilogue

'The col of our desires'

From the mountaineer's point of view, as far as we have seen it, no more appalling sight could be imagined.

George Mallory

O N THE MORNING of 24 September, during the final week of the 1921 expedition, after spending the night on the East Rongbuk Glacier just below the North Ridge, three men – George Mallory, Guy Bullock and Oliver Wheeler – along with ten Sherpas, began the 1,500-foot (455m) climb to the North Col. Twenty-three porters had been planned for this excursion, but all except ten had dropped out the day before, too weak to continue. 'It was with great difficulty', Mallory wrote, 'that we could get 10 coolies to come on, [and] three who declared they were too ill drew lots for the last place.'[1] If all went well, the party of three sahibs and ten Sherpas would reach the col around mid-morning, establish a camp, and that day or early the next begin man's first attempt to climb Mount Everest.

But the men were all tired that morning after a sleepless night on the glacier. 'It might have been supposed', Mallory wrote of their campsite, that in an area 'sheltered on three sides by steep mountain slopes, we should find tranquil air and the soothing, though chilly calm of undisturbed frost. Night came clearly indeed, but with no gentle intentions.'[2] What with the heroic effort to ascend the nearby Lhakpa La one day earlier and after spending nearly three months above 18,000 feet (5,486m), longer than any Europeans ever had – the men who set out to climb to the North Col on the morning of the 24th had no business, Mallory wrote to Geoffrey Young, being 'on a mountainside anywhere'.[3]

Three months earlier, just after emerging from the spell cast by their first view of Everest on 25 June, Mallory and Bullock set out to do what they had come 8,000 miles for: to find a way to the top. It was never going to be easy. Indeed, Mallory's initial reaction, after studying the mountain through his binoculars for hours on 28 June, was distinctly sobering: 'The mountain appears not to be intended for climbing.'[4]

From this remove, after a hundred years of pictures and films, it is difficult to imagine just how confused and bewildered Mallory and Bullock were by the landscapes they now entered. For two men whose only point of reference was the Alps, the sheer scale of the Rongbuk Valley was overwhelming, bordering on incomprehensible. Veteran climbers though they were, almost nothing in their experience enabled them to make sense of what they saw around them. If they could only have studied a photo, looked at a crude drawing or consulted a map, then they could have at least constructed a mental picture of their surroundings and located themselves therein. Just two aerial photos, had they been available, would have revealed what it would take them three months to piece together.' We simply looked', Mallory said, meaning with no clear sense of what, precisely, they were looking at.[5] 'The aim of the reconnaissance', one Mallory biographer writes,

> was a correct understanding of the whole form and structure of the mountain, and a detailed knowledge of the accessibility of all the faces and arêtes of which it was formed. This is an easy thing to picture now it is done, but in the doing it was like asking an ant to make a plan of a cathedral . . .[6]

And so the ants got to work. They established two camps: their base camp at 16,000 feet (4,875m) not far from the monastery, and a second smaller camp another five miles up the valley, at 17,500 feet (5,335m), near the foot of the glacier.

When climbers reconnoitre a mountain, they study the top, examining all the lines or ridges that lead down from the summit to identify one or two with the most reasonable pitch or angle of ascent. Then they look for a way to get onto that ridge and follow it to the summit. Two such ridges descend from the very top of Everest as seen from the north, one to the left or east and one to the right or west. The two men could see these ridges from both of their camps, but they needed to get closer for a better view. (A third line, the North-east Ridge, was mostly hidden from down on the valley floor.) Their plan, which they expected to be a relatively straightforward proposition, was to proceed up the glacier to the great bowl at the base of the North Face and have a look. They knew this would require a vigorous effort on their part, not because they expected the glacier itself to pose any problems but because of the altitude, whose effects they had already begun to feel. Their 'lower' camp, after all, at 16,000 feet (4,875m), was higher than the highest mountain in the Alps, and their upper camp was another 1,500 feet (455m) higher still. Indeed, at the second camp, 17,500 feet (5,335m), Mallory and Bullock were already more than halfway to the top of Everest.

There are glaciers – and then there are Himalayan glaciers, also known as 'densely clustered forests of ice pinnacles', 'icy version[s] of the shell-pocked battlefields of the First World War' and 'slow route[s] to purgatory'.[7] While Alpine glaciers are often relatively smooth highways to the base of the mountains from which they flow, with crevasses the only serious obstacles, Himalayan glaciers are nothing like that. They are a maze of giant stone hummocks, melted ponds and highly unstable pinnacles or towers of ice 40–50 feet high, alternately melting and freezing in the blazing sun, liable to collapse at any moment and crush the unwary climber. Glaciers in the Himalayas are often much more difficult – and considerably more dangerous – to climb than the mountains they issue from. Altitude, the two climbers were about to learn, would be the least of their worries.

Writing of their first morning out on the Rongbuk Glacier on 27 June, Mallory noted that in 'the Alps the main glaciers are . . . usually highways . . . offered to the climber for his travelling', but this was clearly not the case with the Himalayas. 'No feature of what we saw so immediately challenged this comparison as the glacier ahead of us . . . [T]he hummocks of ice covered with stones of all sizes, like the huge waves of a brown angry sea, gave us no chance of ascending [it] . . . The White Rabbit himself would have been bewildered here.'[8] The glacier 'was no use for travelling in any part we had seen, not a road but an obstacle'.[9]

The best way to climb a Himalayan glacier is to stay off it, climbing instead along the moraine, the relatively uncluttered strip of land at the sides of the glacier where it comes up against the mountain. Mallory and Bullock learned this lesson after a very hard morning, eventually reaching a height of 18,500 feet (5,640m). On their return down the valley to their camp, following the moraine down the east side of the glacier, they crossed a modest stream coming in from their right and, in one of the most infamous incidents of the 1921 expedition, they noted the stream but failed to understand its significance.

After three days spent exploring the lower, northern parts of the Rongbuk Glacier, Mallory and Bullock took a half day of rest on 30 June to prepare for a big push they planned for 1 July to proceed up the top half of the glacier and into the great bowl or cwm at the foot of the North Face. After dinner on the 30th, Bullock announced he was feeling 'pretty slack . . . and so we decided that Mallory would go without me tomorrow'.[10] Accordingly, on the morning of 1 July, Mallory set out with five Sherpas to reach the head of the glacier, in the process almost certainly becoming the first humans ever to set foot on Mount Everest.

It would have happened like this. To reach the cwm or basin, Mallory and the five Sherpas proceeded south up the Rongbuk Glacier until they were directly beneath the 10,000-foot wall of Everest's prodigious North Face, with the North Ridge towering over them on their left and the West Ridge looming on their right. While they would have been out on the glacier at certain points as they trudged up towards the cwm, hence not technically on Everest itself, they would also have hugged the moraines on either side of the glacier wherever they promised easier going. But moraines, unlike glaciers, are part of the mountain, and anyone who walks along a moraine on the lower slopes of Everest, no matter how low, is standing on the mountain. And it is inconceivable that the party could have reached the cwm without occasionally making their way along the moraines to get there.

While there is no actual record of who was the first man on Everest, Mallory or one of the Sherpas, it is extremely unlikely to have been a Sherpa because the 'sahibs' always led when they were climbing. This was not so much because of any elitism on the part of the sahibs, but rather due to the fact that in these early years of

Himalayan exploration, Sherpas were not yet climbers – they were porters – and thus were rarely if ever given the job of blazing the trail, and especially not on snow and ice where they were considerably less experienced than westerners who had climbed in the Alps. Indeed, even when he was climbing with Bullock, Mallory was almost always in the lead by virtue of being much the better climber. Which did not keep him from complaining on occasion: 'The whole thing is on my shoulders,' he says in one letter to Geoffrey Young; 'Bullock follows well and is safe, but you know what it means on a long, exhausting effort to lead all the time.'[11]

To be sure, Tibetans lived in the Rongbuk Valley – monks at the monastery and other monks in seclusion in caves closer to the mountain but well below where the glacier starts – but only in the realms of sheer fantasy would the monastery monks or the cave-dwelling ones decide one day to become climbers, ascend the tortuous Rongbuk Glacier and stand on Mount Everest. Another possibility, of course, is that someone approaching Everest from the south or Nepalese side was the first person to stand on the mountain, but the closest village to the mountain is more than 15 miles away, no Nepali would have had any reason to climb on the mountain (and no westerners were allowed in until 1949) and anyone who did want to stand on Everest would first have to climb up the treacherous Khumbu Icefall. If someone did beat Mallory to Everest, that person did not come from the Nepalese side.

Arriving at the cwm, Mallory had his first close-up views of both the North Ridge and the West Ridge, although clouds obscured certain features. It was a stunning – and sobering – sight. In a letter to Ruth, Mallory wrote that '[f]rom the mountaineer's point of view, as far as we have seen it, no more appalling sight could be imagined'.[12] And in a letter to Farrar at the Alpine Club, he was even more blunt:

> You'll be wanting to know something of the mountain, and in one respect it is very easily told. It's a colossal rock peak plastered with snow, with faces as steep as any I have ever seen . . . I've hardly the dimmest hope of reaching the top, but of course we shall proceed as if we were meant to get there.[13]

No one had ever assumed that the North Face itself could be climbed, but the two ridges (or arêtes) that descend from the North Face – the North Ridge and the West Ridge – were another matter. When these two ridges curve around, to the north and west respectively, they form the steep sides of the bowl Mallory now stood in and from which he gazed up at them, studying their contours and taking numerous photos. Examining the West Ridge, Mallory was not optimistic: '[F]rom a near inspection of the slopes below the North-west arête, I was convinced that they could be chosen for an attack only as a last resort.'[14]

But Mallory had in fact been pinning his hopes on the North Ridge ever since the two earlier tantalising views he had had of the mountain, first from Khamba Dzong and later from Shiling. On those two occasions, when he did not have a clear view of the entire North Ridge, what he could see and what had greatly excited him was the North-east Ridge, an arête leading gently down from the summit for 2,000 feet (610m) to a point where it splits, one spur continuing almost directly east and the other, the North Ridge, turning due north, ending in Changtse or the North Peak. What had excited Mallory about the two earlier views was the fact that the North-east Ridge, the final 2,000 feet (610m) to the summit, rose at a gentle angle and was eminently climbable; indeed, to all appearances it was walkable. If one could reach that ridge, one could reach the summit. And if the North Ridge – at the base of which Mallory now stood, seeing it in its entirety for the first time – also lay at a gradual pitch, with no other obstacles, then as long as there was a way to get on the North Ridge, there was a way to the top of Everest.

What Mallory now saw encouraged him. To begin with, he determined that the North Ridge did indeed rise at a gradual pitch for approximately two miles to the spot where it joined the North-east Ridge, with no apparent obstructions. He also saw that at its lowest point the North Ridge dipped to a saddle or col at 23,000 feet (7,010m), before climbing abruptly to the top of the North Peak. He concluded that if that col could be reached, then perhaps one or two additional high camps could be established along the North Ridge, and the summit of Everest could be won. '[T]he upper parts of Everest's North face had been clearly visible for a long time,' Mallory wrote, 'and we could now be certain that they lay back at no impossibly steep angle, more particularly above the North col and up to the North-east shoulder.'[15]

But not everything Mallory saw encouraged him. He believed that the North Ridge 'might go if one could reach the col', as he wrote to Farrar, but from where he now stood in the bowl, at the foot of and looking up the western side of the ridge, he found it 'impossibly steep . . . [with] great buttresses of rock and snow gullies; we have no hopes there.'[16] Hope now hung on the possibility that the eminently climbable North Ridge (as Mallory conceived it) could perhaps be reached from its other side, the back of the side he was now looking at. 'I was now sure that before attempting to reach this col . . . we should have to reconnoitre the [east] side and if possible find a more hopeful alternative . . .'[17] There had in fact been a plan all along to move the reconnaissance from Tingri around to Kharta, on the east side of Everest, after the north side had been fully explored, and now that plan had just taken on greater urgency.

Back at camp, meanwhile, even as Mallory was quietly making history up in the cwm, Bullock was enjoying a lie-in that morning. He felt better when he finally did get up, at 8.15, 'had a good wash' and went out butterfly collecting. He caught three butterflies that day, along with 'some flies and bees', and finished up with a bit of bird-watching. If he was disappointed at not making it up to the cwm himself, Bullock does not mention it. He listened late in the afternoon to an excited Mallory as he described what he had seen of the North and West Ridges, arguably two of the most important findings of the entire northern reconnaissance, and then wrote in his diary that evening that 'Mallory had a good day'.[18]

After reconnoitring and photographing various aspects of the northern approaches to the mountain, the two men turned their attention to their other assignment: to explore the west face of Everest to see if there was a route to the summit from that side. Mallory had already concluded that climbing up the West Ridge from the bowl at the base of the North Face was 'a last resort'. But what lay behind that ridge on its west side? If the two men could get around the ridge – which they could by following the West

Rongbuk Glacier that intersected the Rongbuk not far above their upper camp – could there be a path to the summit up that face of the mountain?

Mallory and Bullock spent nearly two weeks on the task, taking photos wherever they went and climbing several peaks to get better views, even naming a few of them, one after Kellas and another after Mallory's daughter Clare, deeply annoying Hinks in the process. 'He must not go on calling mountains by personal names,' Hinks wrote to Ruth, 'like "Kellas" and "Clare", for they certainly will not be allowed to stick. The idea is enough to make poor Kellas turn in his grave at Kampa Dzong . . .'[19] But it became clear that climbing the West Face of Everest was a non-starter, 'practically out of the question', Bullock noted.[20] By 19 July they had finished the northern reconnaissance 'and moved [their] tents and provisions back down to base camp, and "we" . . . said good-bye to the West Rongbuk Glacier'.[21]

At base camp, things were not running smoothly. The sirdar or headman, Gyalzen, had not been bringing up enough food and other supplies for the porters, and Mallory was furious. The organisation '. . . never did run smoothly so long as we employed, as an indispensable Sirdar, a whey-faced treacherous knave whose . . . incompetence was only less disgusting than his infamous duplicity. It was hopeless . . .'[22]

But if Mallory was angry with Gyalzen, he was even more annoyed with himself. In a few days, the two men were scheduled to head over to the new camp Howard-Bury was setting up in Kharta, the base for the reconnaissance of the East Face of Everest, the final phase of the expedition. Meanwhile, Mallory and Bullock had planned to take a closer look at the modest stream they had come across on the east side of the Rongbuk Glacier on their first day out. 'It had always excited our curiosity,' Mallory noted, 'and I now proposed to explore it . . .'[23]

But this plan, which could have altered the entire course of the expedition if it had been carried out, was now spoiled by a letter Mallory received from Howard-Bury containing 'an extremely depressing piece of news that all my photos taken with the quarter-plate cameras had failed – for the good reason that the plates had been inserted back to front, a result of ignorance and misunderstanding', for which Mallory blamed poor instructions he received from Wheeler. Mallory was devastated. 'It was a depressing evening,' he writes. 'I thought of the many wonderful occasions when I had caught the mountain . . . just at the right moment, moments of most lovely splendour – of all those moments which would never return.' Instead of following the little stream to see where it led, Mallory and Bullock had to spend the next two days 'repair[ing] this hideous error', rushing up and down the Rongbuk Valley ('pounding' is Bullock's verb), retaking as many photos as they could.[24] They would learn later that the little stream they had had no time to explore in fact issued from the as yet undiscovered East Rongbuk Glacier – a glacier destined to become the highway to Everest.

During the four weeks the two men spent in the Rongbuk Valley, Mallory's spirits rose and fell, soaring at times as he was dazzled by the sheer scale and beauty of the surroundings, and plummeting at others as he encountered the appalling cliffs, treacherous glaciers, hazardous overhanging snowfields and lethal rock bands that in one place after another made climbing either impossible or simply too dangerous. Wherever he looked, the mountain was unyielding, adding immensely to the pressure Mallory felt due to his sense that in the end the success of the reconnaissance rested almost solely on his shoulders. 'All the driving power comes from me,' he wrote to Ruth, 'and it makes me a little dispirited at times to be giving out so much.'[25]

Confronting the duplicity of Gyalzen and the debacle of the photos on the same day was too much for Mallory, who went into a tailspin. 'I sometimes think of this expedition as a fraud from beginning to end,' he wrote to a climbing friend,

> invented by the wild enthusiasm of one man, Younghusband, puffed up by the would-be wisdom of certain pundits in the A[lpine] C[lub] and imposed upon the youthful ardour of your humble servant. The long imagined snow slopes of this northern face of Everest with their gentle and inviting angle turn out to be the most appalling precipices, 10,000 feet [3,048m] high . . . The prospect of ascent in

any direction is almost nil, and our present job is to rub our noses against the impossible in such a way as to persuade mankind that some noble heroism has failed once again.[26]

After two more days, Mallory had become more reflective as he and Bullock got ready to leave the Rongbuk Valley. Reviewing what he and Bullock had learned during the previous four weeks and speculating on what lay ahead, Mallory was optimistic, especially regarding the North Ridge, which 'is comparatively smooth and continuous. We had still to see other parts of the mountain but already it seemed unlikely that we would find more favourable ground than this.'[27] Unless those other parts of the east side of Everest offered a different route, which no one expected, the three-month-old 1921 expedition had all come down to a single factor, what Mallory called '[t]he great question before us . . . Could the North Col be reached from the east and [if so] how could we attain this point?'[28] From this time on Mallory began referring to the North Col in all his letters as 'the col of our desires'.[29]

At just over 12,000 feet (3,655m) the new camp in the Kharta Valley was a kind of paradise of flowers and crops for men who had spent the last month above 16,000 feet (4,877m) in and around the naked, boulder-strewn moonscape of the north side of Everest, 'a contrast full of pleasure', Mallory said, from 'nature's niggardli-ness in arid, wind-swept Tibet'.[30] There were forests of fir and birch; the noon temperature was often 70° Fahrenheit. Mallory and Bullock arrived in early August and spent four days luxuriating in the freshness of it all. 'To see things growing again,' Mallory wrote, 'as though they *liked* growing, that has been the real joy.'[31] The change in scenery and weather completely revived Mallory's spirits. 'Be not anxious,' he wrote to Ruth from Kharta. 'I've got the hang of this game.'[32]

Even as Mallory and Bullock were rejuvenating at Kharta, Wheeler had entered the Rongbuk Valley to begin his photo-survey, during which he would make his celebrated discovery of the East Rongbuk Glacier. On 30 July Wheeler noticed there was a small opening on the east side of the valley – it was the spot where Mallory and Bullock had seen the modest stream coming in from the east – and Wheeler decided to explore it. He spent the next week pushing his way up what is now known as the East Rongbuk Valley, navigating the many twists and turns of its glacier, and from views he got along the way Wheeler estimated the glacier extended for at least 15 miles up the east side and below the North Ridge. Although he could not get far enough up the glacier to confirm this, Wheeler was convinced from what he could see that the glacier passed under the foot of the North Col. If it did, then Wheeler's discovery answered Mallory's question: the col could be reached – or at least attempted – from the east side, and the point of access was the East Rongbuk Glacier. On or about 9 August Wheeler sent a note and a crude, hand-drawn map to Howard-Bury, describing his findings and sketching the geography. The note would arrive in Kharta six days later.

Meanwhile, the reconnaissance of the east side of Everest had begun in earnest – and in error. The whole object of the expedition now was to determine if the North Col, which had been established as the key to the summit, could be reached from the eastern slopes of the North Ridge. But the locals gave the team confusing information about the geography in the area, and the men now spent more than a week looking in the wrong place for those slopes, one valley too far to the south, albeit discovering in the process, as ample compensation, the magnificent Kama Valley.

No one who has ever seen the Kama Valley has failed to be stunned by it. It sits at the base of three of the five highest mountains on earth, including Everest, Lhotse and the undisputed star of the valley: the majestic Makalu. 'Among all the mountains I have seen,' Mallory wrote, 'and, if we may judge by photographs, all that have ever been seen, Makalu is incomparable for its spectacular and rugged grandeur.'[33] Mallory added that he was 'altogether beaten for words', and that if the photos he took 'don't come out well, I shall weep'.[34] Howard-Bury called the whole valley 'a mountain wonderland such as few men have ever been privileged to see'.[35] These paeans to the beauty of the Kama Valley are a reminder that along with the enormous physical, emotional and psychological challenges of the first-ever reconnaissance of some of the most demanding geography anywhere in the world – along with all the dangers and hardships of the expedition – there were compensating interludes of sheer wonder.*

Beautiful, to be sure, but the wrong valley; they could see no possible route from the Kama to the summit of Everest. At the very end of their misadventure, however, as the team was returning to their base camp in Kharta, they noticed a ridge slightly to the west and north of where they stood that appeared to look directly over at the North Ridge and the North Col. They could not see the back side of that ridge and whether they would be able to get down it, but if they could, then at the bottom of that ridge there must be direct access to the eastern slopes of the North Ridge, hence to the North Col. In short, if they could get to the pass at the top of that ridge – it was called Lhakpa La (they nicknamed it the Windy Gap) – and get down the other side, there was every likelihood they would find themselves at the base of the North Col. Whether the route up to the col from there was climbable was still an open question, but from the moment the team spotted the Windy Gap, reaching that pass became the sole focus of all their efforts.

Poor George Mallory. At this crucial juncture – 'the climax of our whole reconnaissance', he called it – he fell ill on the morning of 13 August and had to stay back and wish Bullock well as he headed off to reconnoitre approaches to the Windy Gap and perhaps even climb it and discover the elusive route to the North Col. 'It was a depressing moment for me when I reflected that from the first I had been [at the heart of] all that had been done to reconnoitre Everest, and now at the last it seemed that I was going to miss the climax, the joy of wresting from the mountain its final secret.'[36]

In the end, Bullock did not make it to the top of the Windy Gap, but he did make it far enough to confirm (in a note he sent back to Mallory) that there was a glacier in the valley on the other side of the gap, that that glacier ran along the bottom of the North Ridge, right under the North Col, continued on northwards, beneath Changtse, and emptied into the Rongbuk Glacier. Mallory was astonished when

* In his book *Snow in the Kingdom*, Ed Webster notes that while in the Kama Valley, Mallory and Bullock passed the home of the then seven-year-old Tenzing Norgay. He might very well have been watching as the first-ever westerners in his valley walked past, one of them carrying a pink umbrella.

he read the note and not completely convinced. 'Into the Rongbuk Valley!' And then, referring to 'the little stream which we had but just failed to cross [on] the afternoon of our first expedition', he asks: 'How could so little water drain so large an area of ice . . .?'[37]

Any lingering doubts Mallory may have had about Bullock's speculation proved much harder to entertain the next day when Howard-Bury received the letter and sketch map of the East Rongbuk Glacier that Wheeler had sent on 9 August. Wheeler's drawing, which confirmed Bullock's impression, was the second piece of evidence in two days that the East Rongbuk Glacier did indeed drain the east side of the North Ridge and then swung around to empty into the Rongbuk at the very spot where the two men had passed it a few weeks earlier. The glacier the two men had missed was almost certainly a direct route from the Rongbuk Valley up to the base of the North Col – and much easier than the approach from Kharta.

Even then Mallory hesitated. 'It was, unfortunately, a very rough map,' he wrote in his expedition account, 'professedly nothing more, and was notably wrong' with regard to some of its features. Neither Mallory nor Bullock was yet convinced that 'the head of the East Rongbuk Glacier was really situated under the slopes of Everest . . . Still, we had some more pickings to digest.'[38] To Ruth, Mallory wrote that the 'obvious inaccuracies' in Wheeler's map 'made us discount his conclusion, perhaps too much'.[39] Later Mallory admitted he had been too quick to dismiss Wheeler's map, credited the Canadian with the discovery, and confessed that his own efforts with regard to the East Rongbuk had been 'lamentably incomplete'.[40]

The fact that Mallory and Bullock missed the East Rongbuk Glacier is not simply because they did not have time to explore it, but also because they misinterpreted the meaning of the modest stream when they came across it and dismissed its significance. In the Alps such a small stream could not possibly drain a glacier of any size, but in the Himalayas, where melted snow is more likely to evaporate than it is to feed a stream, even a modest stream could announce a large glacier. John Noel among others has noted that if Kellas had been along on the reconnaissance of the Rongbuk Valley, he would never have made such a mistake, and the East Rongbuk Glacier would have been discovered several weeks earlier and perhaps changed the entire outcome of the expedition. 'It is a pity', Noel writes, that 'in this first exploration [Mallory] did not have the cooperation of Kellas who had such a wide experience of the Himalayan Mountains . . .' Noel goes on to say that 'I . . . believe that if [Kellas] had not died, Everest would have been conquered [in 1921], and by nothing other than this – the combination of Kellas's Himalayan knowledge and Mallory's dash.'[41] When Hinks, always prepared to think the worst of Mallory, heard that he and Bullock had missed the glacier, he was scathing: 'I regret more than ever the death of Kellas,' he wrote to Farrar, 'who would have shown Mallory in two days how far he was negligible as a mountaineer.'[42]

Bullock's note and Wheeler's map ignited considerable discussion. Should the expedition go back round to the Rongbuk Valley and try to approach the mountain up the East Rongbuk Glacier (as in fact the two following expeditions would)? Or should they climb up to the Lhakpa La, descend onto what they now knew was the East Rongbuk Glacier, and then climb up from there to the North Col, assuming, of course, that the east side of the North Ridge could in fact be climbed? As it would take at least a week to move the whole camp back to the Rongbuk Valley, and as all food and fuel, unlike in Kharta, would have to be carried into the valley, it was decided to stay on the east side for the moment and try their luck with the Lhakpa La. 'Our business was to reach the nearer pass,' Mallory wrote, referring to the Windy Gap, 'and I felt sure that once we had looked over it to the other side . . . we should have discovered one way to Chang La [the North Col], and a sufficiently good one' – a way, it should be said in fairness to Wheeler, that had already been discovered.[43] In his mind Mallory had concluded that if a possible route to the North Ridge had not been found by 20 August, there would not be time that year to plan and prepare an actual summit attempt.

This was the moment when the tension between the two competing agendas of the 1921 expedition, reconnaissance and climbing, finally came to a head – and for better or for worse, climbing won. There is no question that if the team had returned to the north side and reconnoitred the East Rongbuk Glacier, most likely sacrificing the summit attempt in the process, they would have gathered invaluable information about that approach to the mountain and quite possibly altered the outcome of the 1922 expedition. John Noel, who was on the 1922 expedition, was certain of this, writing that if the glacier had been reconnoitred in 1921, then the 1922 expedition, which approached Everest via the East Rongbuk, would not have had to 'do this exploration work and thus los[e] valuable time and exhaust the native porters and themselves. In the early spring season there is so little time before the monsoon breaks that every moment is needed for the actual business of climbing.'[44] Reconnaissance seems the right choice in hindsight, but after two months of non-stop exploring, with the looming peak a constant, daily presence, and facing the spectre of returning to the decidedly inhospitable Rongbuk Valley – under the circumstances, a summit attempt from Kharta, no matter how remote the chances of success, must have been an irresistible lure. In any event, there is no suggestion in the record that the decision to try for the Lhakpa La was in any way controversial. 'We remained content with the way we had found,' Mallory wrote, 'and troubled our heads no more for the present about the East Rongbuk Glacier.'[45]

On 18 August, Mallory, Bullock, Morshead and three porters headed out for the Windy Gap on what Mallory called 'the most critical expedition' undertaken thus far.[46] At 1.15 that afternoon, the party reached the Lhakpa La, and although they had poor views of the North Ridge itself, they could see down to the East Rongbuk Glacier, could see that it was an easy walk across that glacier to the foot of the North Ridge, and could make out the slope leading up to the North Col. Mallory was greatly excited. 'We have found our way to the great mountain,' he wrote to Ruth. 'I don't know when I have allowed myself so much enjoyment of a personal achievement, for this success brings our reconnaissance to an end . . . and we are now planning the attack.'[47]

But due to extremely bad weather, the attack could not even begin for an entire month, a frustrating interlude of almost complete inactivity, although it did allow the men ample time to acclimatise. 'Now about my eventful life,' Mallory wrote to Ruth at this time, 'the tragic thing, my dear, is that there are no events.'[48] No mountaineering events, perhaps, but it was during the first three weeks of September that the entire eight-member team was gradually reunited at the base camp in Kharta, anticipating the climax of their extraordinary adventure. 'The party has been gathered for the great assault,' Mallory wrote to Graham Irving, 'mountaineers and surveyors, the chief himself, the man of medicine, the geologist, who demands a piece of the top [a rock], even old Raeburn.'[49] All that was missing was favourable weather. 'We're all waiting for the indispensable friend,' Mallory wrote, 'who never shows himself, the sun, to melt the snow for us.'[50] And they were all deliberately trying not to count 'the days so as to avoid any painful thoughts of the hurrying month'.[51]

The sun finally came out on 22 September and the long-delayed attack finally began. The route was back up the Lhakpa La, down onto the East Rongbuk Glacier, across the glacier, and up the side of the ridge to the North Col. And if they actually reached the col, then a summit attempt might just be possible. Along with twenty-six Sherpas, all the members of the expedition except Raeburn climbed up to the Windy Gap on the 22nd where they spent an anxious night. 'Visited by malicious gusts from the North-west,' Mallory wrote, 'the pass was cheerless and chilly . . . I was not very happy about the prospects for the morrow.'[52]

With good reason, for the next morning only Mallory, Bullock and Wheeler felt fit enough to continue – there was 'no great sparkle of energy or enthusiasm among my companions' – and sixteen of the twenty-six Sherpas were also too exhausted to go any further.[53] This much-diminished party of three sahibs and ten Sherpas made their way down the west side of the pass on the 23rd, crossed the East Rongbuk Glacier, and set up camp at the foot of the North Col, where they suffered yet another sleepless night. 'Fierce squalls of wind visited our tents and shook and worried them with the disagreeable threat of tearing them away from their moorings.' During the early hours the winds 'scurried off, leaving us in wonder at the change and asking what next to expect'.[54]

It was a greatly fatigued group of three Europeans and three Sherpas (seven others stayed behind for the time being) who headed out at 7.30 on the 24th to begin the climb up to the North Col; 'a pitiful party,' Mallory wrote to Young, 'not fit to be on a mountainside anywhere'.[55] They made the relatively easy climb up the 1,500 feet (455m) of the North Ridge and reached a protected spot just below the col where, Wheeler observed, '[we] were met by suffocating eddies of snow which warned us, if the "smoking" north ridge had not already done so, to expect a howling gale . . . on top'.[56] Just before 11.30 the three men climbed the last few feet and set foot at last on the col of their desires.

Their reception was not friendly. Here is George Mallory on the final few moments of man's first attempt to climb Mount Everest:

> My eyes had often strayed, as we came up, to the rounded edge above the col and the final rocks before the North-east arête. If ever we had doubted whether the arête were accessible, it was impossible to doubt any longer. For a long way up those easy rock and snow slopes was neither danger nor difficulty. But at present there was wind. Even where we stood under the lee of a little ice cliff, it came in fierce gusts at frequent intervals, blowing up the powdery snow in a suffocating [vortex]. On the col . . . it was blowing a gale. And higher was a more fearful sight. The powdery fresh snow on the great face of Everest was being swept along in unbroken spindrift, and the very ridge where our route lay was marked out to receive its unmitigated fury . . . To see was enough; the wind had settled the question; it would have been folly to go on.

Folly or not, Mallory wanted to go on 'to put the matter to the test', so the three men continued on for another 200 yards or so, exposing themselves on the col 'to feel the full strength of the blast, then struggled back to the shelter'.[57] The ever-faithful, exhausted Bullock wrote that while he 'was prepared to follow M. if he wished to try and make some height', he was relieved when Mallory decided not to. 'It was lucky he didn't as my strength proved to be nearly at an end.'[58] Wheeler was frostbitten and could not continue. And Mallory, too, was now done with the mountain: 'Nothing more was said about pushing our assault any further.'[59]

Some time after midday, the three men and the Sherpas began their descent back to their camp at the foot of the col. At one point, in a measure of just how drained Bullock was – and how compromised his and Mallory's judgement – he told Mallory to push on with Wheeler while he, Bullock, stopped for a brief rest. This was a violation of one of the fundamental codes of climbing – to never leave anyone behind – but Mallory, deeply alarmed at

Wheeler's condition, went on ahead and later spent an hour rubbing Wheeler's feet and lower legs with whale oil to restore circulation, saving them in the process, and, according to Wheeler, saving his life.

The next morning, 25 September, there was some desultory discussion about whether to try moving the camp up to the col and make another summit attempt or to turn back. But the wind was if anything stronger than on the previous day, and a heavy snowfall seemed imminent; there was no support for continuing. The party struck their camp, headed back up and over the Lhakpa La in a fierce blizzard – the porters, at Mallory's suggestion, joyfully hurled several loads of surplus stores over a precipice – and returned to Kharta. 'The real weakness of the party', Mallory wrote, 'became only too apparent in the course of our return journey over Lhakpa La on this final day . . . None of the climbers has ever felt a spasm of regret about the decision to go back or a moment's doubt about its rightness.'[60] In a letter he wrote to Geoffrey Young, Mallory explained that he too was clearly at peace with the decision to turn back on the North Col. It was not 'a question of what might have happened [if the men had tried to climb] higher, but of what *would* have happened with unfailing certainty'.[61]

And so it transpired that 1921 was not the year Mount Everest would be climbed.

The expedition members were frustrated, but there was no sense of failure, as even Mallory himself had to admit. 'It is a disappointment, there's no getting over it,' he wrote to Ruth,

> that the end should seem so much tamer than I had hoped. But it wasn't tame in reality; it was no joke getting to the North Col. I doubt if any big mountain venture has ever been made with a smaller margin of strength. I carried the whole party on my shoulders to the end, and we were turned back by a wind in which no man could live for an hour. I had plenty of reserves personally and could have carried on another 200 feet anyway with ease had the conditions been favourable. As it is, we have established the way to the summit for anyone who cares to try the highest adventure.[62]

Francis Younghusband agreed. 'Nothing further then was possible,' he wrote. 'And nothing further was necessary; for they had already accomplished what they had been sent out to do. They had found a . . . route to the summit.'[63]

Within a week, everyone had departed the Kharta Valley to begin the return journey back to India. Several members of the party (but not all) retraced the original route across Tibet, over the pass into Sikkim, through the Teesta Valley, and on to Darjeeling, where they arrived one month later. On 11 October, this group reached Khamba Dzong, and that afternoon, during a fierce blizzard, they participated in a small ceremony to honour their fallen comrade. '[W]e put up over Dr Kellas' grave the stone which the Jongpen had had engraved for us during our absence,' Howard-Bury recalled. 'On it were inscribed in English and Tibetan characters his initials and the date of his death, and this marks his last resting place.'[64] The next morning, they rose early, took one last look at Everest and, mounting their Tibetan ponies, rode east towards home.

Years later Younghusband put the 1921 expedition in context, declaring in his uplifting, quasi-spiritual register that

> The doom of Everest is sealed, for the simple and obvious reason that man grows in wisdom and stature, but the span of mountains is fixed. Everest fights stoutly with her many terrible weapons, but she fights blindly . . . She cannot learn from experience . . . This doom can be seen to be relentlessly closing in on Everest. Man is remorselessly overtaking her. Forty years ago he was very humble, and did not presume to think of anything higher than 21,000 feet [6,401m]. Twenty years ago he had reached 23,000 feet [7,010m]. . . Arithmetic alone shows that 29,000 feet [8,839m] must follow and Everest be vanquished.[65]

★

Today, apart from George Mallory, none of the names of the other westerners on the 1921 expedition are remembered. As it happens, they had a range of unusually dissimilar after-lives: two were murdered; one went mad; two rose to the pinnacle of their respective professions; and two, Howard-Bury and Guy Bullock, had a more quiet second act. Howard-Bury served in Parliament off and on between 1922 and 1931, when he retired to restore his estate, Belvedere House, raise race horses, and wrestle with his pet bear Agu. He died in 1962. Guy Bullock rotated through a number of overseas posts, serving for a time as British Consul in Lyons. When he was stationed in Ecuador in 1938 he climbed Cotopaxi and was the first person to take a picture of its crater. He died in 1956.

The Canadian Oliver Wheeler eventually became Surveyor General of India in 1941, returning to Canada upon retirement and serving as president of the Canadian Alpine Club. The geologist Heron, the disturber of rocks and unleasher of plagues and evil spirits, was refused permission to join the 1922 expedition. He later became the director of the Geological Survey of India, and after that president of the Calcutta Geological Society. He died in 1971 in Nilgiri, aged eighty-six.

Henry Morshead, the surveyor, was one of only two men to return on the 1922 Everest expedition, where he reached 25,000 feet (7,620m), the site of Camp V. On the way down, Morshead slipped and nearly pulled two other climbers off the mountain; Mallory heard a noise above him, planted his ice axe, and saved all three of them from almost certain death. Morshead was appointed Director of Surveys in Burma in 1929, where two years later he went out riding one afternoon and did not return; when his body was found the next day, he had been shot at close range. No one was ever charged with his murder. Alexander Wollaston, the doctor, was asked by John Maynard Keynes to become a tutor at Cambridge University where in 1931 a student shot Wollaston, along with a police officer, and then shot himself. Harold Raeburn never fully recovered from his encounter with Everest, in body or in mind. His behaviour became erratic on his return voyage from India, and thereafter he descended slowly into madness. At the time of his death five years later in 1926, he had become convinced for some time that he had murdered Alexander Kellas.

George Mallory passed into legend early on the afternoon of 8 June 1924, when he and his climbing partner, Sandy Irvine, disappeared in cloud as they climbed past 27,500 feet (8,382m) on their way to the summit of Everest. The two men were never seen again;

Irvine's body has never been found, but Mallory's was recovered seventy-five years later in 1999. There was always the hope that recovering the body and whatever might be found with it would answer the now nearly hundred-year-old question of whether Mallory and Irvine – not Tenzing Norgay and Edmund Hillary – were the first to the top of Everest, but the discovery was inconclusive. Many who knew Mallory well believed he would never have risked a perilous descent, which would have had to come very late in the day. He would have been 'the last man to press on' beyond the point it was safe to continue, the 1924 expedition leader Edward Norton wrote to Ruth. Yet Geoffrey Young, who knew Mallory perhaps even better, wrote to Younghusband that 'far from being "the last man to press on", he was on the contrary, of all the great mountaineers I have known, the *most* likely to have decided [to] advance at all hazards . . .'[66]

In the end the British would send another eight expeditions against Everest after 1921. On the one that finally succeeded, in the spring of 1953, there was always a chance, however slim, that if the attempt on Everest that year were to succeed, it might just be possible to get the news back to London in time for Queen Elizabeth's coronation on 2 June. To that end *The Times* sent the journalist James Morris (later Jan Morris) to Nepal to accompany the expedition. When Morris learned on the morning of 30 May that Norgay and Hillary had reached the summit of Everest at 11.30 the previous day, he was himself at the top of the Khumbu Icefall and had just over two days to get down to Base Camp, compose the story (in a brief code) and get it to the British Embassy in Kathmandu where it could be wired to London.

After a harrowing descent through the icefall, Morris reached Base Camp late on the 30th and sent the coded message the next morning with a runner to the main Sherpa village of Namche Bazaar. There was a radio in Namche from where the news was sent to Kathmandu and on to London, arriving at 4.14 p.m. on 1 June. Much of the British public – and the world – either heard the news on the BBC late on the 1st or read about it in the newspapers on the morning of 2 June. Many others heard it from loudspeakers lining the route the

Acknowledgements

I would not have had the courage to start this book if it were not for Wade Davis and his magnificent achievement *Into the Silence: The Great War, Mallory, and the Conquest of Everest*. Even before I had the final plan for my book, I knew that the last one or two chapters, the climax, would only work if they could be filled with details, a kind of granular recreation of the 1921 expedition. And *Into the Silence* showed me that that degree of detail was indeed available in the sources.

In the UK I was helped by very kind people at three key institutions: Nigel Buckley at the Alpine Club, who answered numerous requests and showed me every consideration when I was on site, as did the AC archivist Glyn Hughes; Julie Carrington at the Royal Geographical Society library; and Tilda Watson at Magdalene College library, Cambridge. I'm sure these people thought they were just doing their jobs, but to me it felt like kindness itself.

At Hachette/John Murray, Nick Davies supported the book from the outset, and Joe Zigmond was the editor a writer dreams of having but never gets. Joe did not actually make that many suggestions, but the ones he did make were so astute, I'm afraid to think how the book would have read without them. It's a cliché, but I really can't thank Joe enough. Caroline Westmore was a true stalwart throughout the various aspects (and author crises) of the multi-faceted production process. The copy-editor, Martin Bryant, does not deserve to toil in obscurity as his kind so often does; thank you Martin for catching so many of my potentially embarrassing missteps. I am also very grateful to Joe Wilson for his bewitching jacket design, to Rodney Paull for his two maps and mountain drawing, and to Juliet Brightmore for all her help with the photos.

I also owe a debt (one of many) to my mother-in-law Charlotte Zelenkov, who read John Hunt's *The Conquest of Everest* to her children sitting in the back of the car on a road trip the family took in the late 1950s. One of her daughters (now my wife, Charlotte) was inspired and eventually went to Nepal where, among other things, she worked for Sir Edmund Hillary's Himalayan Trust as a nurse in a Trust clinic in Solu Khumbu. I met Charlotte in Kathmandu in 1979 and we lived there during the early 1980s where I first had the idea for this book, some forty years ago now. That idea was to write a book that *ended* in 1921, where all the other Everest books inevitably began. And now it's done.

Picture Credits

Alamy Stock Photo: 1 above, 2 above and below left, 3 centre right and below left, 4 above/Photo J. C. White, 6 below left and right. Getty Images: 1 below/SSPL, 2 below right/Photo De Agostini, 6 above left/Library of Congress/Corbis. Public Domain: 3 above left. Royal Geographical Society via Getty Images: 4 below/Photo G. I. Davys, 5 above left, 5 centre right/Photo A. M. Kellas, 5 below left/Photo J. B. Noel, 6 centre right, 7 above left/Photo A. F. R. Wollaston, 7 centre right/Photo C. K. Howard-Bury, 7 below/Photo A. F. R. Wollaston, 8 above/Photo G. L. Mallory, 8 below/Photo C. K. Howard-Bury.

Notes

Abbreviations

EA Everest Archive
GLM George Leigh Mallory
RGS Royal Geographical Society
RM Ruth Mallory
FY Francis Younghusband

Unless otherwise indicated, all letters of George Mallory (GLM) are from the Mallory Papers at Magdalene College, Cambridge.

Prologue: 'I could stand it no longer'

1. Fleming, P., p.130.
2. Younghusband, *The Light of Experience*, p.89.
3. Hopkirk, *Trespassers*, p.162.
4. Younghusband, *The Light of Experience*, p.90.
5. Younghusband, *India and Tibet*, p.163.
6. Allen, p.87.
7. Younghusband, *The Light of Experience*, p.90.
8. Twigger, p.217.
9. Younghusband, *India and Tibet*, p.164.

10. Ibid., p.166.
11. Markham, p.247.
12. Younghusband, *India and Tibet*, pp. 166–7.
13. Ibid., p.167.
14. Ibid.
15. Allen, p.87.

Chapter 1: Peak XV

1. Wilford, p.126.
2. Markham, p.44.
3. Keay, *The Great Arc*, p.xx.
4. Ibid., p.22.
5. Ibid., p.23.
6. Ibid., p.27.
7. Everest, p.28.
8. Keay, *The Great Arc*, p.64.
9. Ibid., p.59.
10. Markham, p.52.
11. Wilford, p.192.
12. Markham, pp.53–4.
13. Wilford, p.190.
14. Markham, p.89.
15. Keay, *The Great Arc*, pp. 75–6.
16. Ibid., p.94.
17. Ibid., p.3.
18. https://www.tandfonline.com/doi/abs/10.1179/003962678791965228.
19. Phillimore, p.155.
20. Ibid., p.29.
21. Ibid., p.30.
22. Ibid., p.37.
23. Martyn, p.26.
24. Phillimore, p.15.
25. Markham, p.79.
26. Phillimore, p.11.
27. Keay, *The Great Arc*, p.39.
28. Ibid., p.47.
29. Ibid., p.124.
30. Martyn, p.28.

31. Phillimore, p.32.
32. Ibid., p.434.
33. *Gleanings in Science*, p.35.
34. Phillimore, p.135.
35. Ibid., p.389.
36. Ibid.
37. Ibid., p.402.
38. Mukhopadhyay, p.3.
39. Gulatee, 'Mount Everest'.
40. Dickey, p.699.
41. Ibid.
42. Ibid.
43. Ward, *Everest: A Thousand Years of Exploration*, p.9.
44. Tilman, p.754.
45. Waugh, p.104.
46. Ibid., p.102.
47. Ibid., p.104.
48. Ibid., p.110.
49. Ibid., p.111.
50. Ibid., p.112.
51. Keay, *The Great Arc*, p.169.
52. Tanner and Freshfield, p.453.
53. Freshfield, 'Mount Everest v. Chomolungma', p.67.
54. Unsworth, *Everest*, p.546.
55. Ibid., p.547.
56. Ibid., p.548.
57. *Morning Post*, 9 November 1920.

Chapter 2: 'Nature's rough productions'

1. Fleming, F., p.9.
2. De Beer, p.90.
3. Macfarlane, p.15.
4. Ibid., p.14.
5. Goethe, p.21.
6. Macfarlane, p.206.
7. Ibid., p.75.
8. de Saussure, p.429.
9. Ibid., p.219.

10. Freshfield, *The Life of Horace Benedict de Saussure*, pp. 203–4.
11. Fleming, F., pp. 38–9.
12. Ibid., p.43.
13. Ibid., p.45.
14. Unsworth, *Hold the Heights*, p.34.
15. Mathews, pp. 254–5.
16. Smythe, p.114.
17. Fleming, F., p.214.
18. Smythe, p.56.
19. Whymper, 1871, p.82.
20. Smith, p.94.
21. Whymper, 1985, p.301.
22. Ibid.
23. Unsworth, *Hold the Heights*, p.84.
24. Smith, p.100.
25. Whymper, 1985, p.310.
26. Ibid., pp. 313–14.
27. Ibid., p.318.
28. Ibid., p.322.
29. Unsworth, *Peaks, Passes and Glaciers*, p.50.
30. Dangar and Blakeney, 'The First Ascent of the Matterhorn', p.491.
31. Whymper, 1985, p.327.
32. Ibid., p.332.
33. Ibid., p.314.
34. Isserman and Weaver, p.27.
35. Davis, p.32.
36. Isserman and Weaver, p.49.
37. Hinchcliff, p.91.
38. Isserman and Weaver, p.42.
39. Ibid., p.43.
40. Ibid., p.61.
41. Ibid., p.44.
42. Dent, p.16.
43. Isserman and Weaver, pp. 74–5.

Chapter 3: 'An absurd response to a ragbag of rumours'

1. Dalrymple, p.79.
2. Ibid., p.80.
3. Stewart, p.40.
4. Hopkirk, *The Great Game*, p.28.
5. Ibid., p.15.
6. Ibid., p.118.
7. Meyer and Brysac, p.52.
8. Hopkirk, *The Great Game*, p.174.
9. Ibid., p.190.
10. Ibid., p.171.
11. Dalrymple, p.90.
12. Hopkirk, *The Great Game*, p.191.
13. Dalrymple, p.141.
14. Keay, *When Men and Mountains Meet*, p.157.
15. Hopkirk, *The Great Game*, p.254.
16. Ibid., p.415.
17. Ibid., p.429.
18. Ibid., p.431.
19. Fleming, P., p.25.
20. Hopkirk, *The Great Game*, p.446.
21. Ibid., pp. 25–6.
22. Meyer and Brysac, p.284.
23. Ibid.
24. Fleming, P., p.28.
25. Ibid., p.39.
26. James, p.390.
27. Ibid.
28. French, p.187.
29. Meyer and Brysac, p.261.
30. Fleming, P., p.48.
31. Ibid., pp. 59–61.
32. Meyer and Brysac, p.292.
33. Younghusband, *The Heart of a Continent*, p.155.
34. Ibid., p.56.
35. Allen, p.17.
36. Younghusband, *But in Our Lives*, p.255.

37. French, p.64.
38. Ibid., pp. 135–6.
39. Ibid., p.137.
40. *Nature*, 17 May 1888, p.41.
41. Younghusband, *The Heart of a Continent*, pp. 57–8.
42. Ibid., p.156.
43. Ibid., pp. 161, 167, 168.
44. Parker, p.69.
45. Keay, *When Men and Mountains Meet*, p.95.
46. Younghusband, *India and Tibet*, p.331.
47. Younghusband, *The Heart of a Continent*, p.214.
48. Younghusband, *The Light of Experience*, pp. 69–70.
49. Ibid., p.79.
50. Allen, p.19.
51. Verrier, p.183.
52. Younghusband, *The Light of Experience*, pp. 81–2.
53. French, pp. 175–6.
54. Younghusband, *India and Tibet*, p.122.
55. Ibid., p.118.
56. Ibid., p.122.
57. French, p.184.
58. Allen, p.29.
59. Younghusband, *India and Tibet*, p.128.
60. Allen, p.28.
61. Younghusband, *India and Tibet*, p.137.
62. Ibid., p.128.
63. Fleming, P., p.84.
64. Ibid., p.85.
65. Allen, p.31.
66. French, p.193.
67. Fleming, P., p.95.
68. Younghusband, *The Light of Experience*, p.84.
69. Younghusband, *India and Tibet*, p.133.
70. Fleming, P., p.96.
71. Younghusband, *India and Tibet*, p.161.
72. Allen, p.77.
73. Ibid., p.79.
74. Ibid., p.96.
75. Ibid., p.212.
76. Hopkirk, *Trespassers*, p.182.

77. Meyer and Brysac, p.300.
78. Allen, p.177.
79. French, p.224.
80. Younghusband, *The Light of Experience*, p.97.
81. French, p.233.
82. Meyer and Brysac, p.301.
83. French, p.234.
84. Fleming, P., p.173.
85. Meyer and Brysac, p.301.
86. French, p.238.
87. Younghusband, *India and Tibet*, p.299.
88. Ibid., p.334.
89. Hopkirk, *Trespassers*, p.188.
90. Younghusband, *India and Tibet*, p.299.
91. Fleming, P., p.272.
92. Ibid.
93. Younghusband, *India and Tibet*, p.vii.
94. Younghusband, *The Light of Experience*, p.105.
95. French, p.253.
96. Fleming, P., p.269.
97. Ibid., p.267.

Chapter 4: 'Close quarters'

1. Kellas, 'The Mountains of Northern Sikkim and Garhwal', p.116.
2. Ibid.
3. Rawling, p.164.
4. Ibid., p.163.
5. Ibid., p.7.
6. Ibid., p.219.
7. Ibid., p.173.
8. Ibid., p.310.
9. Ibid., pp. 212–13.
10. Ibid., p.214.
11. Ibid., p.215.
12. Ibid., p.270.
13. Younghusband, *India and Tibet*, p.331.
14. Rawling, p.306.
15. Curzon, *Alpine Journal*, 24, 1909, p.190.

16. Blakeney, 'The First Steps Towards Mount Everest', p.43.
17. Unsworth, *Everest*, p.17.
18. Ibid., p.18.
19. Curzon, *Alpine Journal*, 24, 1909, p.191.
20. Noel, *Through Tibet to Everest*, p.30.
21. Noel, 'A Journey to Tashirak', p.292.
22. Noel, *Through Tibet to Everest*, pp. 30, 31.
23. Ibid., p.34.
24. Ibid., p.35.
25. Ibid., pp. 35–6.
26. Ibid., pp. 46–7.
27. Ibid., p.30.
28. Ibid., pp. 52–3.
29. Ibid., pp. 55–6.
30. Noel, 'A Journey to Tashirak', p.299.
31. Ibid., p.300.
32. Ibid., pp. 300–1.
33. Ibid., p.301.
34. Noel, *Through Tibet to Everest*, p.58.
35. Ibid., pp. 58–62.
36. Isserman and Weaver, note 71, p.462.
37. Rodway, p.25.
38. Unsworth, *Hold the Heights*, p.246.
39. Davis, p.76.
40. Noel, *Through Tibet to Everest*, p.88.
41. Ibid., pp. 88–9.
42. Mitchell and Rodway, p.98.
43. Kellas, 'The Mountains of Northern Sikkim and Garhwal', p.116.
44. RGS/EA, Kellas to Hinks, 21 October 1919.
45. Mitchell and Rodway, p.103.
46. Noel, *Through Tibet to Everest*, p.88.
47. Mitchell and Rodway, p.98.
48. Ibid., p.108.
49. Kellas, 'The Mountains of Northern Sikkim and Garhwal', p.128.
50. Ibid., p.114.
51. Ibid., p.131.
52. Mitchell and Rodway, p.123.
53. Ibid., p.151.
54. Kellas, 'The Mountains of Northern Sikkim and Garhwal', p.130.
55. Noel, *Through Tibet to Everest*, p.163.

56. Ibid., pp. 89–90.
57. Mitchell and Rodway, pp. 121–2.
58. Davis, p.76.
59. Noel, *Through Tibet to Everest*, p.89.
60. Mitchell and Rodway, p.212.
61. Ibid., p.126.
62. Noel, *Through Tibet to Everest*, p.90.

Chapter 5: 'A party of Sahibs are coming'

1. Noel, 'A Journey to Tashirak', p.289.
2. Davis, pp. 79–80.
3. Isserman and Weaver, p.84.
4. Noel, 'A Journey to Tashirak', p.303.
5. Ibid., p.305.
6. Ibid., p.306.
7. Ibid.
8. Ibid., p.307.
9. Davis, p.101.
10. Blakeney, 'The First Steps', p.57.
11. Ibid., pp. 57–8.
12. Ibid., p.58.
13. Ibid., p.57.
14. RGS/EA, Hinks to Kellas, 8 December 1920.
15. Blakeney, 'The First Steps', p.59.
16. Bell, pp. 103–4.
17. Ibid., p.106.
18. Ibid., p.107.
19. Ibid., p.109.
20. Ibid., p.263.
21. Blakeney, 'The First Steps', p.60.
22. Bell, p.115.
23. Blakeney, 'The First Steps', p.63.
24. Bell, p.247.
25. Ibid., pp. 276–7.
26. Ibid., p.275.
27. Blakeney, 'A. R. Hinks and the First Everest Expedition 1921'.
28. Younghusband, *The Light of Experience*, p.57.
29. Bonington, p.94.

30. Blakeney, 'A. R. Hinks and the First Everest Expedition 1921'.
31. Ibid.
32. Young, p.159.
33. RGS/EA letter 3/4/17, Hinks to GLM, 20 March 1921.
34. RGS/EA letter 3/4/62, Hinks to RM, 17 May 1922.
35. Noel, *Through Tibet to Everest*, p.116.
36. Isserman and Weaver, p.85.
37. Ibid.
38. RGS/EA Box 1, Hinks to Kellas, 15 February 1921.
39. Gillman, *The Wildest Dream*, p.19.
40. Robertson, p.42.
41. Holzel and Salkeld, p.39.
42. Gillman, *The Wildest Dream*, p.27.
43. Robertson, p.70.
44. Davis, p.168.
45. Noel, *Through Tibet to Everest*, p.112.
46. Davis, p.178.
47. Gillman, *The Wildest Dream*, p.35.
48. Ibid., p.29.
49. Robertson, pp. 49–50.
50. Davis, p.183.
51. Pye, pp. 67–8.
52. Gillman, *The Wildest Dream*, p.113.
53. Ibid., p.119.
54. Ibid., p.113.
55. Pye, p.73.
56. Gillman, *The Wildest Dream*, p.123.
57. Ibid., p.138.
58. Davis, p.193.
59. Robertson, p.59.
60. Unsworth, *Everest*, p.44.
61. Robertson, p.250.
62. Pye, p.23.
63. Gillman, *The Wildest Dream*, p.48.
64. GLM to RM, 24 May 1921.
65. Robertson, p.63.
66. Unsworth, *Everest*, p.42.
67. Gillman, *The Wildest Dream*, p.166.
68. Ibid., p.171.
69. Pye, p.106.

70. Ibid.
71. J. P. Farrar to H. F. Montagnier, 15 May 1919, Alpine Club Archives.
72. Younghusband, *The Epic of Mount Everest*, p.28.
73. Holzel and Salkeld, p.41.
74. Gillman, *The Wildest Dream*, p.175.
75. J. P. Farrar to H. F. Montagnier, 20 March 1919, Alpine Club Archives.
76. RGS/EA, Box 1, Hinks to Kellas, 17 March 1921.
77. RGS/EA, Box 1, letter 3/4/18, GLM to Hinks, 31 March 1921.
78. Norton, E. F., in *Alpine Journal*, In Memoriam, 34, 1923.
79. Davis, p.135.
80. Isserman and Weaver, p.117.
81. RGS/EA, Box 12, Folder 1, Farrar to Hinks, 29 March 1921.
82. RGS/EA, Box 12, Folder 1, Farrar to Hinks, 9 September 1921.
83. RGS/EA, Box 3, GLM to Hinks, 27 March 1921.
84. Holzel and Salkeld, p.59.
85. Blakeney, 'A. R. Hinks and the First Everest Expedition 1921'.
86. RGS/EA, Box 3, GLM to FY, 31 March 1921.
87. RGS/EA, Mt Everest Committee Minute Book, 1 April 1921.
88. Morris, p.4.
89. Unsworth, *Everest*, p.41.
90. Ibid., p.37.
91. GLM to RM, 17 May 1921.
92. Unsworth, *Everest*, p.43.
93. Ibid.
94. Bonington, p.97.
95. Howard-Bury, *Mount Everest: The Reconnaissance*, p.159.
96. RGS/EA, Box 3, Folder 4, Hinks to RM, 20 January 1922.
97. Davis, p.158.
98. RGS/EA, Hinks to Howard-Bury, 2 April 1921.
99. Pye, p.108.
100. GLM to RM, 17 May 1921.
101. Ibid.
102. Howard-Bury, *Mount Everest: The Reconnaissance*, p.24.

Chapter 6: 'With nothing in between'

1. Isserman and Weaver, p.97.
2. Noel, *Through Tibet to Everest*, p.102.
3. Wheeler, p.12.

4. GLM to RM, 17 May 1921.
5. Davis, pp. 366–7.
6. Howard-Bury, *Mount Everest: The Reconnaissance*, p.281.
7. Davis, p.367.
8. Wheeler, p.14.
9. Howard-Bury, *Mount Everest: The Reconnaissance*, p.29.
10. Temple, pp. 9–10.
11. Freshfield, *Round Kangchenjunga*, p.84.
12. Wheeler, p.16.
13. Hooker, p.98.
14. Howard-Bury, *Mount Everest: The Reconnaissance*, p.35.
15. Ibid., p.32.
16. Bullock, pp. 130–1.
17. GLM to RM, 5 June 1921.
18. Morin, p.30.
19. GLM to RM, 24 May 1921.
20. Howard-Bury, *Mount Everest: The Reconnaissance*, p.35.
21. Hooker, p.116.
22. GLM to RM, 22 May 1921.
23. Younghusband, *The Heart of Nature*, p.21.
24. GLM to RM, 22 May 1921.
25. GLM to RM, 24 May 1921.
26. RGS/EA, Box 13, Folder 1, Younghusband to Howard-Bury, 13 April 1921.
27. GLM to RM, 15 September 1921.
28. Gillman, *The Wildest Dream*, p.193.
29. GLM to RM, 5 June 1921.
30. Unsworth, *Everest*, p.47.
31. Howard-Bury, *Mount Everest: The Reconnaissance*, p.97.
32. Davis, p.218.
33. Bruce, pp. 23–4.
34. Howard-Bury, *Mount Everest: The Reconnaissance*, p.45.
35. Bruce, p.46.
36. Davis, p.135; Bullock, p.135; Noel, *Through Tibet to Everest*, p.83; Bruce, p.47.
37. Howard-Bury, 'The 1921 Mount Everest Expedition', p.200.
38. Bruce, p.46.
39. French, p.336.
40. Howard-Bury, *Mount Everest: The Reconnaissance*, p.26.
41. Ibid., pp. 46–53.

42. GLM to RM, 5 June 1921.
43. Ibid.; Bullock, pp. 132–3.
44. Howard-Bury, *Mount Everest: The Reconnaissance*, p.88.
45. Norton, p.31.
46. Bruce, p.28.
47. Howard-Bury, 'The 1921 Mount Everest Expedition', p.200.
48. Howard-Bury, *Mount Everest: The Reconnaissance*, p.49.
49. Younghusband, *The Epic of Mount Everest*, p.54.
50. Pye, p.109.
51. Ibid., p.110.
52. GLM to RM, 5 June 1921.
53. Howard-Bury, *Mount Everest: The Reconnaissance*, p.54.
54. GLM to RM, 6 June 1921.
55. Unsworth, *Hold the Heights*, p.319.
56. RGS/EA, Box 13, Folder 1, Hinks to Howard-Bury, 26 July 1921.
57. Holzel and Salkeld, p.68.
58. Howard-Bury, *Mount Everest: The Reconnaissance*, p.184.
59. Bullock, p.135.
60. Holzel and Salkeld, p.68.
61. Robertson, p.150.
62. Gillman, *The Wildest Dream*, p.200.
63. Holzel and Salkeld, p.68.
64. Norton, p.261.
65. GLM to RM, 15–22 June 1921.
66. Noel, *Through Tibet to Everest*, p.103.
67. Ibid., p.129.
68. Bruce, pp. 228–9.
69. Davis, p.226.
70. Wheeler, p.18.
71. Bullock, p.135.
72. Younghusband, *The Epic of Mount Everest*, p.49.
73. GLM to RM, 15 June 1921.
74. Howard-Bury, *Mount Everest: The Reconnaissance*, p.186.
75. Macfarlane, p.245.
76. Howard-Bury, *Mount Everest: The Reconnaissance*, p.188.
77. GLM to RM, 15 June 1921.
78. Styles, p.56.
79. Unsworth, *Everest*, p.64.
80. Howard-Bury, *Mount Everest: The Reconnaissance*, p.66.
81. Ibid., p.68.

82. Ibid., pp. 67–8.

83. Davis, p.255.

84. Howard-Bury, 'The 1921 Mount Everest Expedition', p.205.

85. Wheeler, p.30.

86. RSG/EA, GLM to Young, 9 September 1921.

87. Howard-Bury, *Mount Everest: The Reconnaissance*, p.188.

88. RGS/EA, GLM to FY, 31 March 1921.

89. Holzel and Salkeld, p.60.

90. Howard-Bury, in *Alpine Journal*, 'In Memoriam', LXI, 1956, pp. 363–4.

91. Ibid.

92. Howard-Bury, *Mount Everest: The Reconnaissance*, p.189.

93. Ibid., p.74.

94. GLM to RM, 28 June 1921.

95. Howard-Bury, *Mount Everest: The Reconnaissance*, p.191.

96. Bullock, p.139.

97. Ibid.

98. Howard-Bury, *Mount Everest: The Reconnaissance*, pp. 191–2.

99. Ibid.

100. GLM to RM, 27 June 1921.

101. Bullock, pp. 139–40.

Epilogue: 'The col of our desires'

1. RGS/EA, GLM to FY, 13 October 1921.

2. Howard-Bury, *Mount Everest: The Reconnaissance*, p.258.

3. GLM to Young, 11 November 1921.

4. Howard-Bury, *Mount Everest: The Reconnaissance*, p.200.

5. Ibid., p.192.

6. Pye, p.113.

7. Macfarlane, p.246; Unsworth, *Everest*, p.53; Davis, p.274.

8. Howard-Bury, *Mount Everest: The Reconnaissance*, pp. 194–7.

9. Ibid., p.199.

10. Bullock, p.142.

11. RGS/EA, GLM to Young, 9 September 1921.

12. GLM to RM, 6 July 1921.

13. GLM to Farrar, 2 July 1921.

14. Howard-Bury, *Mount Everest: The Reconnaissance*, p.204.

15. Ibid., p.207.

16. GLM to Farrar, 2 July 1921.

17. Howard–Bury, *Mount Everest: The Reconnaissance*, p.204.
18. Bullock, p.142.
19. RGS/EA, Box 3, Folder 4, Hinks to RM, 3 October 1921.
20. Bullock, p.147.
21. Howard–Bury, *Mount Everest: The Reconnaissance*, p.215.
22. Ibid., p.216.
23. Ibid.
24. Ibid., pp. 216–18.
25. GLM to RM, 2 July 1921.
26. GLM to Rupert Thompson, 12 July 1921.
27. Howard–Bury, *Mount Everest: The Reconnaissance*, p.215.
28. Ibid.
29. Isserman and Weaver, p.103.
30. Howard–Bury, *Mount Everest: The Reconnaissance*, p.221.
31. GLM to RM, 21 July 1921.
32. GLM to RM, 28 July 1921.
33. Howard–Bury, *Mount Everest: The Reconnaissance*, p.226.
34. GLM to RM, 7 August 1921.
35. Ullman, p.63.
36. GLM to RM, 14 August 1921.
37. Howard–Bury, *Mount Everest: The Reconnaissance*, p.239.
38. Ibid., p.240.
39. GLM to RM, 16 August 1921.
40. Howard–Bury, *Mount Everest: The Reconnaissance*, p.217.
41. Noel, *Through Tibet to Everest*, p.111.
42. RGS/EA, Box 12, Folder 1, Hinks to Farrar, 17 November 1921.
43. Howard–Bury, *Mount Everest: The Reconnaissance*, p.240.
44. Noel, *Through Tibet to Everest*, p.110.
45. Howard–Bury, *Mount Everest: The Reconnaissance*, p.249.
46. GLM to RM, 22 August 1921.
47. GLM to RM, 15 September 1921.
48. GLM to RM, 15 September 1921.
49. RGS/EA Box 3, Folder 5, GLM to Irving, 15 September 1921.
50. Ibid.
51. GLM to RM, 15 September 1921.
52. Howard–Bury, *Mount Everest: The Reconnaissance*, p.257.
53. GLM to Young, 11 November 1921.
54. Ibid.
55. Ibid.
56. Wheeler, p.25.

57. Howard-Bury, *Mount Everest: The Reconnaissance*, pp. 259–60.
58. Bullock, p.304.
59. Howard-Bury, *Mount Everest: The Reconnaissance*, p.260.
60. Gillman, *Climbing Everest*, p.97.
61. GLM to FY, 11 November 1921.
62. GLM to RM, 29 September 1921.
63. Younghusband, *The Epic of Mount Everest*, p.87.
64. Howard-Bury, *Mount Everest: The Reconnaissance*, p.164.
65. Noel, *Through Tibet to Everest*, p.119.
66. Isserman and Weaver, p.128.

Bibliography

Archives

Alpine Club Archives
Everest Archives of the Royal Geographical Society
George Mallory Collection, Magdalene College, Cambridge

Journals

Aitken, William McKay, 'The 1922 Everest Diary of Dr T. G. Longstaff', *Himalayan Journal*, 39, 1983
——, 'An Enquiry into the Real Name of Mt Everest', *Himalayan Journal*, 59, 2003
Alcock, Helga, 'Three Pioneers: The Schlagintweit Brothers', *Himalayan Journal*, 36, 1980
Alpine Journal, 12 August 1884–May 1886
Alpine Journal, 'In Memoriam', 34, 1923
Alpine Journal, 'In Memoriam', 41, 1956
Blakeney, T. S., 'Whymper and Mummery', *Alpine Journal*, 57, 1950
——, 'A. R. Hinks and the First Everest Expedition 1921', *Geographical Journal*, vol. 136, part 3, September 1970
——, 'The First Steps Towards Mount Everest', *Alpine Journal*, 76, 1971

Bullock, Guy, 'The Everest Expedition, 1921: Diary of G. H. Bullock', *Alpine Journal*, 67, part 1, May 1962

Burrard, S. G., 'Mount Everest: The Story of a Long Controversy', *Nature*, 71, November 1910

Collie, J. N., 'A Short Summary of Mountaineering in the Himalaya with a Note on the Approaches to Everest', *Alpine Journal*, 33, no. 222, March 1921

——, 'The Mount Everest Expedition', *Geographical Journal*, 58, no. 1, July 1921

——, 'The Mount Everest Expedition', *Geographical Journal*, 58, no. 2, August 1921

——, 'The Mount Everest Expedition', *Geographical Journal*, 58, no. 5, November 1921

Crawford, C. G., 'Everest, 1933: Extract from the Everest Diary 1933 of C. G. Crawford', *Alpine Journal*, 46, 1934

Curzon, George, 'Proceedings of the Alpine Club', *Alpine Journal*, 24, 1909

Dangar, F. O., and Blakeney, T. S. (annotators), 'The First Ascent of the Matterhorn: The Narrative of "Young" Peter Taugwalder', *Alpine Journal*, 61, 1957

——, 'The Rise of Modern Mountaineering and the Formation of the Alpine Club, 1854–1865', *Alpine Journal*, 62, 1957

Dickey, Parke, 'Who Discovered Mt Everest?', *EOS*, 66, no. 41, 8 October 1985

Freshfield, D. W., 'Mount Everest v. Chomolungma', *Alpine Journal*, 34, 1922

Gillman, Peter, 'Mallory on the Ben', *Alpine Journal*, 2010–11

Gleanings in Science, 3, Calcutta: Baptist Mission Press, 1831

Goodwin, Steven, 'Everest Revealed?', *Alpine Journal*, 2010–11

Gulatee, B. L., 'Mount Everest: Its Name and Height', *Himalayan Journal*, 17, 1952

——, 'The Height of Mount Everest: A New Determination', *Himalayan Journal*, 19, 1956

Howard-Bury, C. K., 'Some Observations on the Approaches to Mount Everest', *Geographical Journal*, 57, no. 2, February 1921

——, 'The 1921 Mount Everest Expedition', *Alpine Journal*, 224, May 1922

Kellas, Alexander, 'The Mountains of Northern Sikkim and Garhwal', *Alpine Journal*, 40, no. 196, September 1912

——, 'A Fourth Visit to the Sikkim Himalaya, with Ascent of the Kangchenjhau', *Alpine Journal*, 27, no. 200, May 1913

Martyn, John, 'What George Everest Did', *Himalayan Journal*, 33, 1975

Mathews, C. E., 'The Growth of Mountaineering', *Alpine Journal*, 10, 1882

Morshead, Henry, 'Dr Kellas' Expedition to Kamet in 1920', *Geographical Journal*, 57, no. 2, 1921

Mukhopadhyay, Utpal, 'Radhanath Sikdar: First Scientist of Modern India', *Science and Culture*, May–June 2014

Nature, 17 May 1888

Noel, J. B., 'A Journey to Tashirak in Southern Tibet, and the Eastern Approaches to Mount Everest', *Geographical Journal*, 53, no. 5, May 1919

Rodway, George, 'Alexander M. Kellas: Seeking Early Solutions to the Problem of Everest', *Britain-Nepal Society Journal*, 27, 2003

Sorkhabi, Rasoul, 'The Great Game of Mapping the Himalaya', *Himalayan Journal*, 65, 2009

Tanner, H. C. B., and Freshfield, D. W., 'Gaurishankar or Devadhunga vs. Mount Everest', *Alpine Journal*, 12, no. 91 [? 1884–6]

Ward, Michael, 'The Exploration and Mapping of Everest', *Alpine Journal*, 1994

——, 'Northern Approaches: Everest 1918–22', *Alpine Journal*, 1994

——, 'The Height of Mount Everest', *Alpine Journal*, 1995

——, 'The Survey of India and the Pundits: The Secret Exploration of the Himalayas and Central Asia', *Alpine Journal*, 1998

Waugh, Andrew, 'On Mounts Everest and Deodanga', *Proceedings of the Royal Geographical Society of London*, 2, no. 2, 1857–8

West, John B., 'A. M. Kellas: Pioneer Himalayan Physiologist and Mountaineer', *Alpine Journal*, 1989/90

——, 'The G. I. Finch Controversy of 1921–1924', *Alpine Journal*, 2003

Wheeler, E. O., 'The Mount Everest Expedition, 1921', *Canadian Alpine Journal*, 13, 1923

Wollaston, Alexander, 'The Natural History of South-Western Tibet', *Geographical Journal*, 60, 1922

Younghusband, Francis, Letter to the *Morning Post*, 9 November 1920

Books

Allen, Charles, *Duel in the Snows: The True Story of the Younghusband Mission to Lhasa*, London, John Murray, 2004

Bell, Charles, *Portrait of a Dalai Lama: The Life and Times of the Great Thirteenth*, London, Wisdom Publications, 1987

Bonington, Chris, *The Climbers: A History of Mountaineering*, London, BBC Books/Hodder & Stoughton, 1992

Bruce, Charles, *The Assault on Mount Everest, 1922*, Varanasi, Pilgrims Publishing, 2002

Conefrey, Mick, *Everest 1953: The Epic Story of the First Ascent*, London, Oneworld, 2012

Dalrymple, William, *Return of a King: The Battle for Afghanistan*, London, Bloomsbury, 2013

Davis, Wade, *Into the Silence: The Great War, Mallory, and the Conquest of Everest*, New York, Alfred A. Knopf, 2011

De Beer, G., *Early Travellers in the Alps*, London, Sidgwick & Jackson, 1930

Dent, Clinton, *Above the Snowline*, CreateSpace, 2015

Dyhrenfurth, G. O., *To the Third Pole: The History of the High Himalaya*, Milton Keynes, Nielsen Press, 2011

Everest, George, *An Account of the Measurement of an Arc of the Meridian*, London, J. L. Cox, 1830

Fleming, Fergus, *Killing Dragons: The Conquest of the Alps*, New York, Grove Press, 2000

Fleming, Peter, *Bayonets to Lhasa*, Oxford, Oxford University Press, 1985

French, Patrick, *Younghusband: The Last Great Imperial Adventurer*, London, Flamingo, 1995

Freshfield, Douglas, *The Life of Horace Benedict de Saussure*, London, Edward Arnold, 1920

——, *Round Kangchenjunga*, Kathmandu, Ratna Pustak Bhandar, 1979

Gillman, Peter (ed.), *Climbing Everest: The Complete Writings of George Mallory*, London, Gibson Square, 2012

——, and Gillman, Leni, *The Wildest Dream: The Biography of George Mallory*, Seattle, Mountaineer Books, 2000

Goethe, Johann Wolfgang von, *Italian Journey: 1786–1788*, London, Penguin, 1992

Gould, Tony, *Imperial Warriors: Britain and the Gurkhas*, London, Granta, 1999

Hinchcliff, T. W., *Over the Sea and Far Away*, London, Longman's, Green & Co., 1876

Holzel, Tom, and Salkeld, Audrey, *The Mystery of Mallory and Irvine*, Seattle, Mountaineers, 1999

Hooker, Joseph, *Himalayan Journals: Notes of a Naturalist*, New Delhi, Today and Tomorrow's, 1980

Hopkirk, Peter, *Trespassers on the Roof of the World*, London, John Murray, 1982

——, *The Great Game: On Secret Service in High Asia*, London, John Murray, 1990

Howard-Bury, C. K., *Mount Everest: The Reconnaissance, 1921*, London, Forgotten Books, 2016

Isserman, Maurice, and Weaver, Stewart, *Fallen Giants: A History of Himalayan Mountaineering from the Age of Empire to the Age of Extremes*, New Haven, Yale University Press, 2008

James, Lawrence, *Raj: The Making and Unmaking of British India*, London, Little, Brown, 1997

Keay, John, *When Men and Mountains Meet: The Explorers of the Western Himalayas 1820–75*, London, John Murray, 1977

——, *The Great Arc: The Dramatic Tale of How India Was Mapped and Everest Was Named*, London, HarperCollins, 2000

Larson, Edward J., *To the Edges of the Earth*, New York, William Morrow, 2018

Macfarlane, Robert, *Mountains of the Mind: A History of a Fascination*, London, Granta, 2017

Macintyre, Neil, *Attack on Everest*, London, Methuen & Co., 1936

Markham, Clements, *A Memoir of the Indian Surveys*, London, Forgotten Books, 2017

Mason, Kenneth, *Abode of Snow*, Seattle, Mountaineers, 1987

Messner, Reinhold, *The Second Death of George Mallory*, New York, St Martin's Press, 2001

Meyer, Karl E., and Brysac, Shareen Blair, *Tournament of Shadows: The Great Game and the Race for Empire in Central Asia*, New York, Basic Books, 1999

Mitchell, Ian, and Rodway, George, *Prelude to Everest: Alexander Kellas, Himalayan Mountaineer*, Edinburgh, Luath Press, 2011

Morin, Micheline, *Everest: From the First Attempt to the Final Victory*, London, George G. Harrap & Co. Ltd., 1955

Morris, Jan, *Coronation Everest*, London, Faber & Faber, 2003

Murray, W. H., *The Story of Everest*, London, J. M. Dent & Sons, 1954

Noel, J. B. L., *Through Tibet to Everest*, London, Edward Arnold, 1927

Norton, E. F., *The Fight for Everest 1924*, Varanasi, Pilgrims Publishing, 2002

Parker, Philip, *Himalaya: The Exploration and Conquest of the Greatest Mountains on Earth*, London, Conway, 2013

Phillimore, R. H. (comp.), *Historical Records of the Survey of India*, IV: *1830–1843 George Everest*, Dehra Dun, India, Office of the Northern Circle, Survey of India, 1958

Pye, David, *George Leigh Mallory*, Bangkok, Orchid Press, 2002

Rawling, C. G., *The Great Plateau: Being an Account of Exploration in Central Tibet, 1903, and of the Gartok Expedition, 1904–1905*, London, Edward Arnold, 1905

Robertson, David, *George Mallory*, Bangkok, Orchid Press, 1999

Saussure, H. B. de, *Voyages dans les Alpes*, I, Geneva, Barde Manget, 1783

Smith, Ian, *Shadow of the Matterhorn: The Life of Edward Whymper*, Ross-on-Wye, Carreg, 2011

Smythe, F., *Edward Whymper*, London, Hodder & Stoughton, 1940

Stewart, Jules, *Spying for the Raj: The Pundits and the Mapping of the Himalaya*, Stroud, Sutton Publishing, 2006

Styles, Showell, *Mallory of Everest*, New York, Macmillan, 1967

Temple, Richard, *Travels in Nepal and Sikkim*, Kathmandu, Ratna Pustak Bhandar, 1977

Tilman, W. H., *The Seven Mountain-Travel Books*, London, Bâton Wicks, 2003

Twigger, Robert, *White Mountain: A Cultural Adventure Through the Himalayas*, New York, Pegasus, 2017

Ullman, James Ramsey, *Kingdom of Adventure: Everest: A Chronicle of Man's Assault on the Earth's Highest Mountain*, London, Collins, 1948

Unsworth, Walt, *Everest: The Ultimate Book of the Ultimate Mountain*, London, Grafton Books, 1991

——, *Hold the Heights: The Foundations of Mountaineering*, Seattle, Mountaineers, 1994

—— (ed.), *Peaks, Passes and Glaciers: Selections from the Alpine Journal*, London, Penguin, 1982

Verrier, Anthony, *Francis Younghusband and the Great Game*, London, Jonathan Cape, 1991

Ward, Michael, *Everest: A Thousand Years of Exploration*, Glasgow, Ernest Press, 2003

West, John B., *High Life: A History of High-Altitude Physiology and Medicine*, New York, Oxford University Press, 1998

Whymper, Edward, *Scrambles Amongst the Alps*, London, John Murray, 1871

——, *Scrambles Amongst the Alps*, London, Century, 1985

Wibberley, Leonard, *The Epics of Everest*, London, Faber & Faber, 1955

Wilford, John Noble, *The Mapmakers*, New York, Alfred A. Knopf, 1981

Young, Geoffrey, *Mountains with a Difference*, London, Eyre & Spottiswoode, 1951

Younghusband, Francis, *The Heart of Nature*, London, John Murray, 1921

——, *The Light of Experience*, London, Constable & Co., 1927

——, *The Epic of Mount Everest*, Varanasi, Pilgrims Publishing, 2002

——, *Everest: The Challenge*, Varanasi, Pilgrims Publishing, 2009

——, *The Heart of a Continent*, Forgotten Books, 2012

——, *India and Tibet*, Miami, Hardpress, 2012

——, *But in Our Lives*, London, Whitaker Press, 2013

Index

Index